T3-BVR-676

# dBASE III® Plus Advanced Programming

## 2nd Edition

Joseph-David Carrabis

Que™ Corporation
Indianapolis, Indiana

# Dedication

To the man behind the curtain

# Dedication to the 2nd Edition

because he is happy to be there.

*Editors*
Gail S. Burlakoff
Lloyd J. Short

*Technical Editor*
Estel Hines

*Production*
Dan Armstrong
Kelly Currie
Jennifer Matthews
Joe Ramon


Screen reproductions in this book were created by means of the Inset program from The American Programmers Guild, Ltd., Danbury, Connecticut.

# About the Author

## Joseph-David Carrabis

Joseph-David Carrabis has been involved with computers for 16 years. His acquaintance with them began at Lincoln Labs, a government institute at Lexington, Mass. In 1980 he founded JDI, Inc., a business consulting and software design firm specializing in large-scale business systems. His clients, in locations ranging from New England to California and from Texas to Canada, have included several Fortune 500 companies.

Mr. Carrabis also has taught high school computer science and mathematics and has done consultation for the Tuck School of Business, Dartmouth College. He has designed tutorials for Lotus 1-2-3, dBASE II, and WordStar, and has written columns for Que Corporation's *IBM PC Update*.

A man of diverse interests, Mr. Carrabis has studied Old Testament theology and languages, applied mathematics and physics, and gravitational physics, as well as sign language. His first efforts in the computer field were directed toward making computers usable for the handicapped. He has enjoyed being a "designated hugger" for the Special Olympics. He holds a Black Belt in karate and is a member of the Computer Writers' Association and Science Fiction Writers of America.

Carrabis wrote the first edition of *dBASE III Advanced Programming* and is coauthor, with David Ewing, of *Using Javelin*.

# Table of Contents

## 4 Coding in Modules

## 5 Knowing dBASE III Plus's Strengths

## 6 Powerful but Overlooked Commands

# Preface

My hope is that you will read this preface before you buy the book. The information in the preface will help you understand what this book covers better than will anything you can learn in a few minutes of standing in the bookstore, blocking the aisle, and scanning the book while you decide whether to purchase. I'm fully aware, though, that few people read a preface or a foreword, unless it is written by a Stephen King or an Isaac Asimov. Well, this one is written by me, and so it is short.

I'm not writing a book chock-full of code for you to sit and copy. My purpose in writing this book is to help you write logical code in dBASE III Plus.

How will I do this? First, I will define logical code. Then I will show the implications of writing logical code in the dBASE III Plus environment. After that, I'll discuss how the dBASE III Plus interpreter looks at code, and show ways of minimizing execution time and memory consumption. Finally, I will demonstrate some little-known and seldom-used structures that can make dBASE III Plus even more useful than most people think it is.

The book does contain many examples of code. You can use those examples if you wish. More important than the code, however, are the book's explanations and theory about the use of dBASE III Plus. Wading through several pages of text to get to some useful code may seem boring to you. But the several pages of text explain how and why I chose that code and how and why it works. This knowledge is far more important for successful programming than is your mimicking me without knowing why I did what I did.

In the dBASE III Plus code of Chapter 13 and Appendix D, dBASE III Plus programmers will see a stunning similarity with dBASE III code. I upgraded good dBASE III code and edited it into good dBASE III Plus code to prove my point about LIBrary files. Using many of the resources of dBASE II and III, I can maintain a "standard" library of files that are transportable between the two interpreters. Read the Introduction and Part I for more on why I do this.

If you haven't yet purchased dBASE III Plus and are looking through books to see what dBASE III Plus can and can't do, here are some words of advice:

1. dBASE III Plus has a maximum of 128 fields per record. If you need more than 128 fields per record, rethink your application. Something is wrong.

2. dBASE III Plus has a functional file-size limit of approximately five million bytes. The reference section of the user's manual says you have a two-billion-byte maximum on file size, but don't go wild with that information. If you regularly need a database management system capable of handling files larger than two million bytes, you should be prepared to *wait* for it to handle them. If you frequently need to sift through more than five million bytes at a whack, you need a computer bigger than a PC or clone, no matter what DBMS you're using.

3. Some users say dBASE III Plus is slow. I discuss this fact in more detail later, but now I'll point out that most people do a few things expertly, many things well, most things acceptably, many things poorly, and a few things horribly. That goes for everybody. It also goes for DBMS software, dBASE III Plus included. The joy of dBASE III Plus is that it has a great deal of backing from various sectors, is from a company with a long and fruitful history, and is widely used and referenced. These facts are important when you're programming and you need help.

Many readers of the first edition of this book commented that they liked the way I code. Even though they liked the way I code, some readers couldn't understand it. What I thought would be obvious to a casual observer was completely opaque to an informed audience. I hope that this edition is more understandable.

End of preface. Good luck.

# Acknowledgments

Many thanks to Jim, Jake, Chris, Natalie, John, Eric and Peter, of Chips; to Russ and Ben, of Data Spectrum, for letting me borrow books, equipment, and technical manuals during the writing of this book; and to Susan, who makes good coffee.

To Cyrynda—for helping me wake up
To Susan—who was there when I woke up
And to You—please help me stay awake

Thanks to George Tsu-der Chou, for the use of three appendixes from his book, *dBASE III Plus Handbook*, 2nd Edition, published by Que Corporation.

# Trademark Acknowledgments

Que Corporation has made every effort to supply trademark information about company names, products, and services mentioned in this book. Trademarks indicated below were derived from various sources. Que Corporation cannot attest to the accuracy of this information.

Paradox is a trademark of Ansa Corporation.

dBASE, dBASE II, dBASE III, dBASE III Plus, and Framework are registered trademarks of Ashton-Tate Company. dBRUN, Framework II, and RunTime+ are trademarks of Ashton-Tate Company.

UNIX is a trademark of AT&T.

Reflex is a trademark of Borland/Analytica Inc.

db Report Writer is a registered trademark of Concentric Data Systems, Inc. R&R Relational Report Writer is a trademark of Concentric Data Systems, Inc.

DEC is a registered trademark of Digital Equipment Corporation.

CP/M is a registered trademark of Digital Research Inc.

IBM is a registered trademark of International Business Machines Corporation. IBM PC XT is a trademark of International Business Machines Corporation.

Lattice is a registered trademark of Lattice, Inc.

Lotus and 1-2-3 are registered trademarks of Lotus Development Corporation.

Final Word is a registered trademark of Mark of the Unicorn, Inc.

WordStar is a registered trademark of MicroPro International Corporation.

Microsoft, MS-DOS, and Multiplan are registered trademarks of Microsoft Corporation.

Clipper is a trademark of Nantucket, Inc.

Novell is a registered trademark of Novell, Inc.

XyWrite II Plus and XyWrite III are trademarks of XyQuest, Inc.

# Conventions Used in This Book

All declared variables are in uppercase letters.

All undeclared variables are in lowercase letters.

All dBASE III Plus commands and functions are in uppercase.

All expressions and evaluations are in lowercase.

The PLUS symbol in the margin indicates that a paragraph or section discusses commands, operations, or program features that have changed or are new with dBASE III Plus.

I have tried hard to be consistent, but I'm sure some things have slipped through. If something is unclear, make the logical choice. If that fails, experiment.

# Introduction

First, did you read the preface? Do so now if you haven't already.

What is advanced programming? When I started this project, my purpose had little to do with dBASE III® Plus. I was more concerned with the *advanced* part of the title. Advanced programming involves pseudocoding, data design, and system integration. Those and other twenty-six-dollar words are used primarily to impress others at parties. Knowing what the words mean won't help you get the job done, and not knowing exactly what they mean won't stop you from programming at an advanced level. You probably do those things anyway, either in your head or on paper, and knowing their names won't help you write better code.

My intent is neither to bore you nor to frighten you with words that have multiple meanings. I want you to learn to use all that this combination of language and machine—dBASE III Plus and the IBM® PC—has to offer. That knowledge is the sum total of advanced programming.

My purpose in this book is to give you some useful tools for generating better dBASE III Plus code. What types of tools? I'll explain with a personal anecdote. I was incapable of learning math and physics by rote. It simply wasn't enough to watch someone do a grad or a curl or determine orthogonal equations. (BIG WORDS—don't be frightened!) I had to understand why and how those procedures worked before I could use them. That characteristic carries over into my method of programming. I'm not going to show you line after line of code without explaining, step by step, why I chose that code for a specific function. My intention is to get you to think in a specific way, or at least to be aware of some fundamental and powerful concepts.

Back to the first question. What is advanced programming? Experience has shown me that advanced programming has four parts:

1. Writing compact code

2. Writing to minimize execution time and maximize free disk space

3. Writing modular code (I use E. W. Dijkstra as my model)

4. Writing with a firm knowledge of the language

First, consider writing compact code. dBASE III Plus lends itself to the writing of fat code in several ways; the most obvious is the insertion of notes with the NOTE command, asterisk (*), and double ampersand (&&). Those of you who learned programming in a class were taught to incorporate rigorous documentation; get out of that habit.

dBASE III Plus also lends itself to the writing of compact code. Chapters 1 and 2 of this book tell how. One trick for writing compact code has to do with the nature of dBASE III Plus itself; using this trick results in code that minimizes execution time and maximizes free disk space. Suppose that you want to write time-efficient code and have ten active databases (ADBF, BDBF, CDBF, . . . JDBF). You are using JDBF and want to switch to ADBF. Which of the following two lines do you use? What is the actual difference in execution time?

```
SELECT ADBF
SELE A
```

For the answer, read the section called "Using the Four-Letter Word" in Chapter 1.

What does it mean to write modular code? For one thing, it's easier to debug and modify 12 lines than 200. Modular coding also speeds execution, especially if the function of the block of code (or module) isn't required every time dBASE® executes the program.

For example, suppose you are given the task of developing a large accounting program for a company. You are told the different jobs the program must do: Controlling Accounts Receivable, Accounts Payable, General Ledger, General Journal, Payroll, Inventory, Job Costing, and other such. These are all separate jobs that together form the accounting program.

Obviously, you don't do Payroll every day; if your payroll is quite small, it may even be part of the Accounts Payable subsystem. You may do Accounts Receivable as payments come in, so you use this subsystem heavily one day and not at all the next two. You don't want to include all those jobs in your main program. Too many jobs slow execution and make the program unwieldy.

So how do you keep things as simple as possible when you start a project?

At the first meeting with your clients, you are given the skeleton of your program. The clients tell you what they want done. In other words, they give you a *menu* of what they need. In this example, to do modular coding you first design a menu system for the various jobs. Each job becomes a module with its own menu system and tasks.

A menu system is the precursor, backbone, launching point—call it what you will—of a flowchart. Perhaps the most valuable thing you could have learned before opening this book is how to design flowcharts. In particular, I want you to design your charts on the basis of tasks. This book gives examples of task-oriented flowcharting. Also important is the distinction of tasks and jobs, which is covered later in this book.

To keep track of tasks and jobs and to construct a clean flowchart, you must write clear notes. This practice is related to kicking the documentation habit. The accounting system is a good example: Your instinct is to document heavily so that others, looking at your code in the next millennium, can keep track of what you did and follow your program as it does what it does. The documentation further slows the running of the program.

Finally, to do advanced programming you must know your chosen language. What are the strengths and weaknesses of dBASE III Plus?

First, consider the programming aspects of the language. dBASE III Plus doesn't support the typical GOTO statement that is common in many other languages. Nor does dBASE III Plus directly support JMPs or CALLs, as do assemblers. Don't write code that requires these commands. If you're accustomed to using them, learn to code linearly. Your GOTOs, JMPs, and CALLs must be replaced with the dBASE III Plus command structures. This requirement leads us back to modular task-oriented flowcharts.

I have found dBASE III Plus to be more linear in its logic flow than most languages. You can get from A to Z without ever touching B, C, and so on, and sample as many intermediaries as you wish; those are things the language does nicely. But it dislikes spaghetti code. Don't expect dBASE III Plus to go cheerfully from A to C to H to B to C to B to C to Z to D—you get the idea.

You can use dBASE III Plus as a word processor because the program has a built-in text editor; I don't use the program that way. You can use dBASE

III Plus as a spreadsheet program; I use other programs for spreadsheet functions. In a pinch, you can use dBASE III Plus as a database management system. It's very good at that. Many people describe dBASE III Plus as an ADL, or applications development language, and it is that. Knowing that fact will not help you write better code, however.

Now comes a reverse maxim: The fact that dBASE III Plus is an ADL is important to all that comes later in this book and is the key to the power of the language. dBASE III Plus is a language specifically designed for manipulating data.

PLUS

dBASE III Plus is not meant to tweak the brain of the machine or to juggle ports, although the language does have those useful capabilities through the LOAD and CALL commands. The program is not meant to be a number cruncher, although its arithmetic capabilities are extensive. dBASE III Plus is not a general-purpose language, a jack-of-all-trades. dBASE III Plus is a master of one trade: database management. I hope this book will help you use dBASE III Plus as such. That concept again brings us back to forethought and the creation of good task-oriented flowcharts before writing code.

At various points in this book, I use programs in languages other than dBASE III Plus. In truth, most of the other programs I create are written in a variety of dialects and subtongues. Because I can't assume that you have available a variety of languages and compilers, all ancillary programs in this book are in IBM BASIC. If you are reading a book on dBASE III Plus, you must have IBM BASIC available. The BASIC code shows you the flow of the program. You can choose another language and write code from there.

# I
# Advanced Programming Techniques

In Part I, we examine in more depth the four principles of advanced programming presented in the Introduction. You may already be familiar with many of the topics covered. Others may be hazy in your mind. In this part, we lay the foundations for most dBASE III Plus programming techniques. These foundations are used in the turnkey systems that are explained in Part II.

The first consideration is writing compact code. That is not something we programmers do instinctively. Our programs tend to resemble Charles Dickens' novels—they're too long. We should write more like Hemingway; don't use fifty words for what you can say in two.

Writing compact code includes three things: defining the problem, recognizing the solution, and coding for that solution. We code only for the problem at hand, and we don't concern ourselves with multitudes of possibilities.

Then we have to consider how our solution interacts with the language and the machine. Careful thought leads to solutions that are simple and that make efficient use of the machine. Here again we can use Hemingway as a model (or Philip Glass, if you're musically inclined). We must think as minimalists.

We have to learn how dBASE III Plus works in order to learn how to make it work at its best. Getting the most out of dBASE III Plus has two equal parts:

1. *Code only for the job at hand.* Don't concern yourself with I/O, screen or printer graphics and output, or anything else, if your

purpose is to alter data. All other operations can be coded in other modules or subroutines. Accomplishing this goal entails not only writing modular code but also knowing when and how dBASE III Plus looks at subroutines, procedures, and their kin.

2. *Write with a firm knowledge of dBASE III Plus.* I assume that you either are comfortable with dBASE III Plus or are a quick study. If you're neither, some parts of this book may seem opaque to you, especially the sections dealing with dBASE III Plus's strengths. Those sections deal with using dBASE III Plus's undocumented abilities. Some of these abilities include advanced database operations, operations on many active databases (such as linking, cross-referencing, and data chaining), and descriptions and analysis of looping functions.

# 1
# Writing Compact Code

Compact code is the first characteristic of advanced programming, because writing compactly saves both time and space. To write compact code, you must pay attention to three factors: the way you document your code; dBASE III Plus's four-letter words; and the elimination of dead space from your code. This chapter gives you several tricks for writing leaner code.

## Methods of Documentation

Source documentation—the explanations included in working code—is one of the great banes of writing compact programs. Unfortunately, we cannot guarantee our immortality; we must therefore document our programs, both in our source code and externally, so that others can easily modify our code if necessary.

One way to solve the problem is to separate our code and documentation. We can then place the documentation at the end of our code after a RETURN, QUIT, or CANCEL.

This method, however, is usually more trouble than it's worth for the programmer, and more confusing than helpful for the reader. Explanations of our logic given after the fact need to be more carefully worded. That usually means saying in three different ways what really needs to be said only once. ("I know you think you heard what I said, but what you thought you heard is not what I meant to say.")

Also consider the poor readers. They must determine which DO WHILE N2<100 of the 20 listed in the program is the one you're referring to. And if your documentation is inaccurate, the readers are even worse off.

Fortunately, most programmers place explanations where they're needed. Even if we don't document internally, we use the * simply to isolate code segments. Consider the following program.

```
***BLOCKER1.PRG
***WRITTEN BY JOSEPH-DAVID CARRABIS
***PO Box 3861 Nashua, NH 03061
**
***SET UP
**
SET TALK OFF
STORE 0 TO N0,N1,N2
INPUT "What is our starting value -> " TO NUM
NUM2=NUM*NUM
**
***BLOCK 0
**
DO WHILE NUM>1
    ? "BLOCK0"+STR(N0,4,0)
    N0=N0+1
**
***BLOCK 1
**
    DO WHILE NUM<NUM2
        ? "BLOCK1"+STR(N1,4,0)
        NUM=2*NUM
        N1=N1+1
    ENDDO 1
**
***BLOCK 2
**
    IF NUM2<(2*NUM)
        ? "BLOCK2"+STR(N2,4,0)
        NUM=NUM2/NUM
        N2=N2+1
    ENDIF 2
**
ENDDO 0
**
SET TALK ON
```

This program, which juggles the variables NUM and NUM2, demonstrates a fairly typical method of documenting source code. Debugging the program is fairly easy because we always know where the program is, and we can determine where it trashes out by providing a listing of where the program has been, as in figure 1.1.

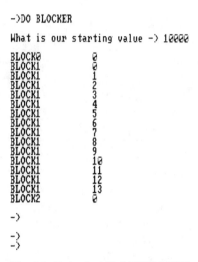

```
->DO BLOCKER

What is our starting value -> 10000

BLOCK0          0
BLOCK1          0
BLOCK1          1
BLOCK1          2
BLOCK1          3
BLOCK1          4
BLOCK1          5
BLOCK1          6
BLOCK1          7
BLOCK1          8
BLOCK1          9
BLOCK1          10
BLOCK1          11
BLOCK1          12
BLOCK1          13
BLOCK2          0

->

->
->
```

Fig. 1.1. Output of BLOCKER1.PRG, showing a simple trace for debugging.

After we've debugged our code and know that it does the job, we can consider making the code compact. Stripping the notes from the code reduces the program from 36 to 19 lines, a savings of about 50 percent. Next, we pull out our debugging lines. That deletion gets us down to 12 lines, the 12 lines that actually do what we want.

The following IBM BASIC program, STRIPPER.BAS, strips out excess lines. The lines I use to debug code are always the same. STRIPPER can be expanded as necessary; it is a useful tool that you would be wise to modify for your own purposes.

```
1 REM        STRIPPER.BAS
10 OPEN "BLOCKER1.PRG" FOR INPUT AS 1
20 OPEN "NEW-01.DB3" FOR OUTPUT AS 2
30 REM  INSERT ADDITIONAL CODE HERE, IF NEEDED
40 N$="***"
50 B$="? ´ BLOCK"
60 Z$="N0"
70 O$="N1"
```

```
80 T$="N2"
90 WHILE NOT EOF(1)
100 LINE INPUT#1,L$
110 IF (INSTR(L$,N$)=0)AND(INSTR(L$,B$)=0)AND(INSTR(L$,Z$)=0)AND
(INSTR(L$,O$)=0)AND(INSTR(L$,T$)=0) GOTO 130
120 GOTO 90
130 PRINT#2,L$
140 LPRINT L$
150 WEND
160 END
```

STRIPPER.BAS works as follows. My debugging and noting follow certain
patterns; hence the variables defined in lines 40 through 80. Extra
variables can be easily inserted in the BASIC program if a particular
application forces me to alter my method. Lines 90 to 150 form a loop
that remains active until the program reaches the end of my dBASE®
source-code file. The code of that loop translates as follows: If none of my
debugging or note-taking methods is used in a line (110), print that line to
a file (130) and to the printer (140); otherwise, get the next line of code
(120). Lines 10 through 30 can be changed to adapt STRIPPER.BAS for
multiple input, to redirect source and target drives, and so on. I print the
stripped program (140) to check the integrity of the source code.

dBASE III Plus gives you one other method of documentation. With
some, but not all, dBASE III Plus commands, you can include notes next
to the command on the same line. This method takes the form

   COMMAND * explanation

COMMAND is a dBASE III Plus command or function, and the * tells
dBASE that the rest of the line can be ignored. dBASE III Plus has a habit
of reading only what the program needs to get a job done. This method
doesn't work, however, with commands that do comparisons or
evaluations. For instance, you cannot use the command

   `CASE NEWKEY=254 *F2 PRESSED`

because dBASE III Plus "assumes" that you are checking to see whether
NEWKEY is equal to the string 254^I*F2 PRESSED. This method of
documentation also uses up more space on the disk, because dBASE III
Plus is interpreted, not compiled. The program doesn't use your notes,
but it acknowledges their presence when writing and reading files.

By this point, you may be tiring of my harangue on compact code. Why
do I repeatedly stress this? Compact code is space- and time-efficient.

Space is a priority both on disk and in memory. Time is a priority to anyone who pays by the hour to have information put into a database and manipulated. Neither dBASE III Plus nor the PC needs or likes copious notes.

# Timesavings

Before describing eye-popping timesavings, I should explain that my dBASE III Plus programs average from 10,000 to 30,000 lines of code. That may cause some readers to think they don't fit in my class of programming. Poobah!

Programs that large are system projects. A system project means I've either designed or selected all the programs the system runs. Usually that means I've coded in dBASE, C, MASM, sometimes LISP and PROLOG, and sometimes BASIC. I've made sure that all of these separate pieces mesh as they should. I've designed error checks, traps, and loops that only a mother could love. Furthermore, I've designed all the Help screens. That alone can be significant.

Two of my vertical-market packages are doing quite well. One contains 1,117 lines of necessary code; the other, 5,386 lines. (Necessary code is what has to be in the program to do what people buy it for.) The former, with Help screens and messages, actually contains 13,225 lines of code. The latter, similarly embellished, is over 26,000 lines.

My point is not to impress, but to inform. You write as much code as I do. You just don't include Help screens and messages. My tricks will benefit you even if you don't code 10,000 to 30,000 lines.

In any case, these are obviously large-scale projects that chew up most of the computer's time and space. Because my system programs are so long, I go out of my way to decrease execution time.

Experience has shown me that the extra effort is worthwhile. Clients and peers have commented on a noticeable decrease in execution time. To have your fireworks appreciated is always nice.

Most programmers—myself included—document their programs externally and internally. So, the first technique worth knowing is as follows. After you have the program totally debugged and everyone is happy with the way it works, make a backup copy. Then take out all the comment lines from the working copy.

Consider program BLOCKER1.PRG. If you key in the program, SET STEP ON, and DO BLOCKER1.PRG, you can see that the PC actually "looks at" each comment line. The PC doesn't do anything with the comment lines, but looking at them slows down the operation.

Now look at BLOCKER2.PRG. It was generated by STRIPPER.BAS, using BLOCKER1.PRG as a source file.

```
SET TALK OFF
INPUT "What is our starting value -> " TO NUM
NUM2=NUM*NUM
DO WHILE NUM>1
    DO WHILE NUM<NUM2
        NUM=2*NUM
    ENDDO 1
    IF NUM2<(2*NUM)
        NUM=NUM2/NUM
    ENDIF 2
ENDDO 0
SET TALK ON
```

What is the actual savings in time? The following simple time-checking program, TIMETEST.PRG, determines average run time. Changes made to both BLOCKER1.PRG and BLOCKER2.PRG are minor and—I hope—obvious.

```
SET TALK OFF
INPUT "How many runs shall we make? -> " TO Q
STORE 0 TO TFSS, TFMM
STORE 1 TO NQ
**
DO WHILE NQ<Q+1
    STORE 1 TO N
**
    STORE TIME() TO T0
***BLOCKER. PRG
**
***SETUP
**
SET TALK OFF
STORE 0 TO N0, N1, N2
NUM=NQ
NUM2=NUM*NUM
**
***BLOCK 0
**
```

```
DO WHILE NUM>1
   ? "BLOCK0"+STR(N0,4,0)
   N0=N0+1
**
***BLOCK 1
**
   DO WHILE NUM<NUM2
      ? "BLOCK1"+STR(N1,4,0)
      NUM=2*NUM
      N1=N1+1
   ENDDO 1
**
***BLOCK 2
**
   IF NUM2<(2*NUM)
      ? "BLOCK2"+STR(N2,4,0)
      NUM=NUM2/NUM
      N2=N2+1
   ENDIF 2
**
ENDDO 0
**
SET TALK ON
   STORE TIME() TO T1
**
   STORE VAL(SUBSTR(T0,7,2)) TO T0SS
   STORE VAL(SUBSTR(T1,7,2)) TO T1SS
   STORE VAL(SUBSTR(T0,4,2)) TO T0MM
   STORE VAL(SUBSTR(T1,4,2)) TO T1MM
**
   IF T1SS<T0SS
      T1SS=T1SS+60
      T1MM=T1MM-1
   ENDIF
**
   TFMM=TFMM+T1MM-T0MM
   TFSS=TFSS+T1SS-T0SS
   NQ=NQ+1
ENDDO
**
TFSS=TFSS/Q
MINUTES=0
**
```

```
DO WHILE TFSS>59
   TFSS=TFSS-60
   MINUTES=MINUTES+1
ENDDO
**
TFMM=(TFMM/Q)+MINUTES
CLEAR
@ 10,0 SAY "AVERAGE TIME ->                        SS"
@ 10,20 SAY TFSS
```

TIMETEST.PRG gives an average run time of 1.35 seconds for
BLOCKER1.PRG on 100 runs. The same program, running
BLOCKER2.PRG, gives an average run time of 0.54 seconds, a 250
percent gain in execution speed. Incidentally, the figure for space savings
is 295 percent. The documented file is 640 bytes long; the stripped file is
217 bytes.

## Using the Four-Letter Word

dBASE III Plus supports the use of shortened commands: SELE for
SELECT, INPU for INPUT, STOR for STORE. What happens if we strip all
our commands to the first four characters when we code? Consider the
following example. In the Introduction you were asked which of the two
commands the computer can read faster:

```
SELECT ADBF
```

```
SELE A
```

Obviously, humans scan the second line quicker than the first. Is this fact
also true for the computer? The average execution times are .01030
seconds for the first line and .00730 seconds for the second. Granted,
both times are minuscule—to us. To the PC with a 4.77 MHz clock,
however, the times represent, respectively, 49,131 and 34,821 cycles.
The difference is a great deal of time to a PC.

PLUS

Now we must further determine why that difference of 14,310 cycles is
so important. All dBASEs, dBASE III Plus included, are basically disk-
intensive systems. You can run dBASE III Plus on a 256K machine,
something no similar DBMS can claim. The only way to run dBASE III
Plus, which has a code kernel of 192K, on a machine with 256K RAM, is
by using the disk as an intermediate storage device. Hitting the disk with
every breath the machine takes is so time-expensive that it's frightening.

Clipping commands to four-letter words can save you time (approximately 14.5 seconds in a one-pass 1,000-line program). That won't quite make up for constantly hitting the disk, but it's a start. As a further note, dBASE III Plus can both sense and be told implicitly how much memory it can play with if you're designing for machines with more than 256K.

## Eliminating Dead Space in a Program File

Clipping my code did not alone buy all my kudos for writing fast programs.

The programs in this book, as you'll see, indent blocks of code. I write somewhat as follows:

```
DO CASE
   CASE condition 1
      condition 1 instructions
   CASE condition 2
      condition 2 instructions
   .

   .

   .
ENDCASE
```

Another format is

```
DO WHILE condition
   instructions
ENDDO
```

and so on.

I write code that way only for other users—for magazine articles and the classes I teach. My own choice is not to indent; in my own programs, I use ** to separate blocks of code.

People tell me, "You must learn to indent properly to make your programs more readable."

"By whom," I ask, "you or the computer?"

Does dBASE III Plus care about indenting? Yes.

Indenting is good if a human is going to try to execute your programs line by line and wants to follow what is going on. But dBASE has a different problem with indented lines. Given the line

```
@ 22,20 GET meadrink
```

dBASE dutifully looks at each of the nine preceding spaces before doing what is asked. Even though you don't see anything in front of @ 22,20, the PC senses nine 20Hs (the hexadecimal value of a blank space). This dead space is detrimental both on disk and during execution. Total the dead space in all your programs and the amount can be staggering. The moral? Don't indent.

# 2
# How To Code Efficiently

What does it mean to code efficiently?

What does it mean to do anything efficiently?

Let's take the latter question first. Given the choice of lifting a loaded sea trunk in a deadlift or using a come-along, I'd choose the come-along. It enables me to do less work and achieve the same result: lifting the sea trunk. Given the choice of a come-along or a three-block pulley, I would take the pulley—again, because I have to do even less work to raise the sea trunk.

I'm making more efficient use of my strength by using the best tools to get the work done. This is the key to efficiency in anything: using minimum effort to achieve maximum results with minimum waste.

Now consider the first question. In programming, any problem has various solutions, any one of which will do the job. But you don't want to write 20K of code when 5K will do the same job. Part of efficiency is learning to notice patterns. Most applications have many similarities. There is usually no need to write new code when something you have written before will do the job.

This chapter will deal primarily with flowchart design and how to make better use of the dBASE programming environment. Primary to this discussion are the concepts of "task" and "job." Tasks (and their structure) are the code that does the work. Jobs are the work to be done by the task.

You want to make coffee, for example. The tasks include measuring and grinding coffee beans, rinsing the pot and setting the filter, getting cold, clear water and heating it to 190°F, pouring a cupful of water over the grounds to set them in the filter, and so on. (Yes, I'm a coffee-aholic, but at least I do it right!) The job is making coffee.

Another part of coding efficiently is recognizing the limits of your environment. Does the PC or dBASE III Plus limit your solutions?

All of these things are nice to know before you start a project. If you've spent much time programming for others, you've learned that clients usually do not comprehend how long the job will take or exactly what they want. You tell them "two months," and they hear "yesterday." As a programmer, you should also be aware that customers are probably going to want more than they anticipated, or want what they asked for to be done differently.

Your clients give you a list of things they want done. They aren't concerned with how the program does the job, but they do want the program to be easy to use and to generate output they can easily understand.

The clients give you the following list of jobs:

1.  Generate a customer mailing list

2.  Report total sales by factory

3.  Report total sales by customer

4.  List all factories

5.  Generate sales commissions

6.  Generate unpaid commissions

7.  List all active customers

8.  List all inactive customers

9.  Keep an updatable customer database

10. Keep an updatable factory database

11. Keep an updatable item-sold database

12. Keep an updatable sales-force database

13. Provide selective backup ability

14. Provide selective retrieval from backup

The problem, then, is to translate the client's wish list into a working program. dBASE III Plus offers several possible solutions. But does it provide a clue as to which solution is better than the others? Yes, it does. Some clues are in the similarities between the things the client wants done. It would appear that the tasks are repetitive, even if the jobs aren't.

As an experiment, let's look at the Bigger Hammer method of programming. A straightforward approach is to create the following code using the DO CASE . . . (OTHERWISE) . . . ENDCASE block.

```
DO CASE
   CASE CHOICE=1
      DO MAILLIST
**
   CASE CHOICE=2
      DO FACTSALE
**
   CASE CHOICE=3
      DO CUSTSALE
**
   CASE CHOICE=4
      DO FACTLIST
**
   CASE CHOICE=5
      DO COMM
**
   CASE CHOICE=6
      DO UNPDCOMM
**
   CASE CHOICE=7
      DO ACCUST
**
   CASE CHOICE=8
      DO INACCUST
**
   CASE CHOICE=9
      DO CUSTOMER
**
   CASE CHOICE=10
      DO FACTORY
**
   CASE CHOICE=11
      DO ITEMSOLD
**
   CASE CHOICE=12
      DO SALESFRCE
**
   CASE CHOICE=13
      DO BACKUP
```

```
**
    CASE CHOICE=14
        DO RETRIEVE
**
    OTHERWISE
        ERROR MESSAGE
ENDCASE
```

# The Flowchart

The preceding code sequence is workable, but heavy and unnecessary.
The code demonstrates thinking in jobs rather than individual tasks. The
distinction between job and task is vital; a flowchart and examples will
make it clear. If we look at what the company has asked for, we can
create a task-oriented flowchart. We also know that dBASE III Plus is a
database manipulator, and we keep that fact in mind as we create the
flowchart shown in figure 2.1.

Ideas should start popping into your head as soon as you have written the
flowchart. (And remember, you haven't even started to code yet!) What
ideas? For example, you have a MAILLIST MODULE. Would your client
like to be able to send mailings to factories or salespeople, as well as to
customers? You have a LISTING MODULE. Perhaps a listing of items sold,
broken down by volume and price, might be useful to your client. Even
more options can spin directly off the tasks (MAIL LIST, SALES,
COMMISSIONS, etc.) listed in the flowchart.

# Jobs and Tasks

I hope that you are beginning to see why I differentiate between jobs and
tasks. A task is necessary to get a job done. Digging a hole is a task. The
job may be planting a tree, digging a well, or putting in a swimming pool.
Each job requires that you dig a hole.

Look at the flowchart. Do you see that the 14 jobs listed in the flowchart
are repetitive? Those 14 jobs can be performed by seven tasks. We can
also place the retrieval and backup jobs in one task, bringing us down to
six tasks to handle 14 jobs. (We all have our own little idiosyncrasies. One
of mine is packing many jobs into a few lines of code.)

By thinking and coding in tasks, you make modifications easier. Working
in tasks also saves you time on future projects because you build up a
library of tasks common to all environments. For instance, every customer

wants easy ways to add, delete, edit, and scan records. One block of code for each can be used for several different databases. For this reason, many of my projects use the same DATABASE ACCESS MODULE (see Chapter 13).

Whether you flowchart in your head or on paper doesn't matter. The purpose of a flowchart is to provide a skeleton to be fleshed out as you go along.

# The Code

Remember also that your primary objective is to get a job done; your code shouldn't be filled with redundancies and superfluous lines. But code does not have to be exact the first time through. Good programmers know that the product they deliver is not always the best it could be. But the program does what was intended, and that capability is the bottom line.

At this point I introduce you to JDI'S Standard Rules of Programming, starting with Number 100:

*If it works, don't fix it.*

Don't worry about perfection.

Remember to think in tasks, and your code will be better. This thought brings us back to the development stage. Our flowchart is good and clean. Now we can begin to code.

## The User Interface

Look at the flowchart again, and notice that it performs two functions: it provides a user interface, and it calls subroutines. Creating the user interface is easy enough. You can use this code:

```
@ 1,0 TO 22,79 DOUBLE
@ 2,30 SAY "M A I N    M E N U"
@ 3,1 TO 3,78 DOUBLE
@ 6,20 SAY [0. EXIT]
@ 7,20 SAY [1. CUSTOMER MAILING LIST]
@ 8,20 SAY [2. FACTORY TOTALS BY MONTH AND YEAR]
@ 9,20 SAY [3. CUSTOMER TOTALS BY MONTH AND YEAR]
@ 10,20 SAY [4. COMMISSION REPORT]
@ 11,20 SAY [5. UNPAID COMMISSION REPORT]
@ 12,20 SAY [6. FACTORY LISTING]
@ 13,20 SAY [7. ACTIVE CUSTOMER LISTING]
```

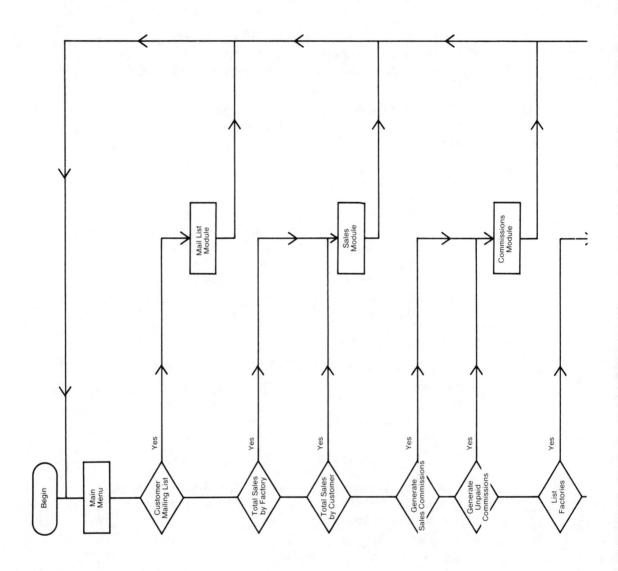

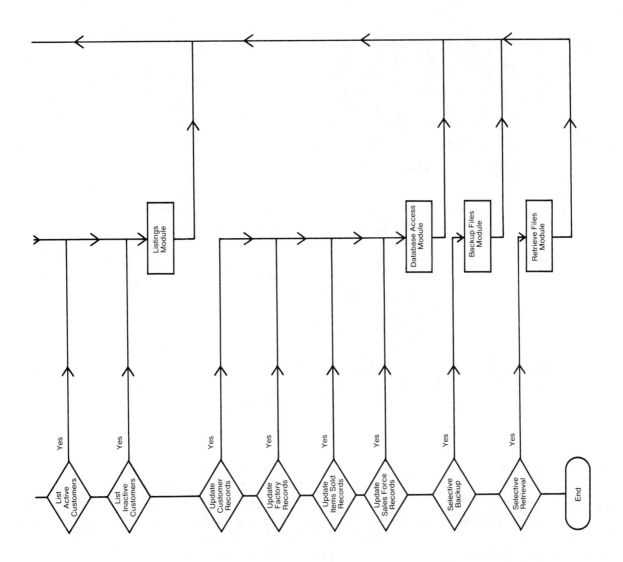

*Fig. 2.1. A task-oriented flowchart.*

```
@ 14,20 SAY [8.  INACTIVE CUSTOMER LISTING]
@ 15,20 SAY [9.  UPDATE CUSTOMERS]
@ 16,20 SAY [10. UPDATE FACTORIES]
@ 17,20 SAY [11. UPDATE ITEMS SOLD]
@ 18,20 SAY [12. UPDATE SALESPEOPLE]
@ 19,20 SAY [13. BACK UP ALL FILES]
@ 20,20 SAY [14. RETRIEVE ALL FILES]
```

to produce this Main Menu screen:

```
┌─────────────────────────────────────────────────────────────┐
│                     M A I N    M E N U                        │
╞═══════════════════════════════════════════════════════════════╡
│                                                               │
│            0.  EXIT                                           │
│            1.  CUSTOMER MAILING LIST                          │
│            2.  FACTORY TOTALS BY MONTH AND YEAR               │
│            3.  CUSTOMER TOTALS BY MONTH AND YEAR              │
│            4.  COMMISSION REPORT                              │
│            5.  UNPAID COMMISSION REPORT                       │
│            6.  FACTORY LISTING                                │
│            7.  ACTIVE CUSTOMER LISTING                        │
│            8.  INACTIVE CUSTOMER LISTING                      │
│            9.  UPDATE CUSTOMERS                               │
│           10.  UPDATE FACTORIES                               │
│           11.  UPDATE ITEMS SOLD                             │
│           12.  UPDATE SALESPEOPLE                            │
│           13.  BACK UP ALL FILES                            │
│           14.  RETRIEVE ALL FILES                           │
└─────────────────────────────────────────────────────────────┘
```

The first thing to notice is that I've rearranged the list. Now similar tasks are next to each other on the menu. This arrangement is helpful when I begin writing the code to call the different subroutines.

Writing the user interface is (or should be) one of the least significant jobs. All you want to do is put some fairly basic options on the screen. Draw the screen and get on to the next part of the application. A useful trick is to write the prototype interface as a TEXT . . . ENDTEXT block. This trick allows you to set up the screen quickly, without worrying about using @ SAYs to position things.

**PLUS**

Another reason not to use @ SAY has to do with what I call input aesthetics. You can more easily enter the contents of the screen exactly as you want it to appear by using TEXT . . . ENDTEXT than by using @ SAYs. In this case, however, I also break one of my own rules, because the @ SAY command executes far faster than the TEXT . . . ENDTEXT. You can use this method and still end up with fast-running code by running the TEXT . . . ENDTEXT block through the MODI SCRE command or a similar utility. Such utilities allow the programmer to print a screen and then transform it into a rack of @ SAYs.

## Subroutines

Let's move on to the second function shown in the flowchart, which is equally easy to code. We're going to call subroutines that perform each task. dBASE III Plus offers two methods of enabling the user to select one of several options: DO CASE . . . (OTHERWISE) . . . ENDCASE and IF . . . (ELSE) . . . ENDIF.

The following code segments illustrate three ways these options may be used.

1. DO CASE . . . (OTHERWISE) . . . ENDCASE

```
DO CASE
    CASE CHOICE=0
        RETURN
**
    CASE CHOICE=1
        DO MAILLIST
**
    CASE CHOICE<4
        DO TOTALS
**
    CASE CHOICE<6
        DO COMMRPRT
**
    CASE CHOICE<9
        DO LISTINGS
**
    CASE CHOICE<13
        DO MAIN
**
    CASE CHOICE=13
        DO BACKUP
**
    CASE CHOICE=14
        DO RETRIEVE
**
    OTHERWISE
        ERROR MESSAGE
ENDCASE
```

2. IF . . . (ELSE) . . . ENDIF #1

```
IF CHOICE=0
   RETURN
ELSE
**
   IF CHOICE=1
      DO MAILLIST
      LOOP
   ELSE
**
      IF CHOICE<4
         DO TOTALS
         LOOP
      ELSE
**
         IF CHOICE<6
            DO COMMRPRT
            LOOP
         ELSE
**
            IF CHOICE<9
               DO LISTINGS
               LOOP
            ELSE
**
               IF CHOICE<13
                  DO MAIN
                  LOOP
               ELSE
**
                  IF CHOICE=13
                     DO BACKUP
                     LOOP
                  ELSE
**
                     IF CHOICE=14
                        DO RETRIEVE
                     ELSE
                        ERROR MESSAGE
                     ENDIF14
**
                  ENDIF13
```

```
**
              ENDIF<13
**
            ENDIF<9
**
        ENDIF<6
**
      ENDIF<4
**
    ENDIF1
**
ENDIF0
```

A better alternative to the preceding code is to use the IF . . . (ELSE) . . . ENDIF structure as follows:

3. IF . . . (ELSE) . . . ENDIF #2

```
IF CHOICE=0
    RETURN
ENDIF
**
IF CHOICE=1
    DO MAILLIST
    LOOP
ENDIF
**
IF CHOICE<4
    DO TOTALS
    LOOP
ENDIF
**
IF CHOICE<6
    DO COMMRPRT
    LOOP
ENDIF
**
IF CHOICE<9
    DO LISTINGS
    LOOP
ENDIF
**
```

```
IF CHOICE<13
   DO MAIN
   LOOP
ENDIF
**
IF CHOICE=13
   DO BACKUP
   LOOP
ENDIF
**
IF CHOICE=14
   DO RETRIEVE
   LOOP
ENDIF
**
ERROR MESSAGE
```

Counting the lines of the code segments, we note that the DO CASE . . . (OTHERWISE) . . . ENDCASE has 20 lines. IF . . . (ELSE) . . . ENDIF #2 has 32 lines, and IF . . . (ELSE) . . . ENDIF #1 has 39 lines. The obvious choice, therefore, is the DO CASE . . . (OTHERWISE) . . . ENDCASE.

The fact that we code in tasks facilitates the use of CASEs. When dBASE III Plus encounters CASEs, the program finds the first CASE that meets the condition, executes the commands of that CASE, and exits from the DO CASE . . . (OTHERWISE) . . . ENDCASE command. Once a CASE has been selected, all other CASEs are ignored. This method is an efficient means for assigning different tasks.

We can hasten the return to the top of the DO WHILE . . . ENDDO block by including LOOPs at the end of each CASE. I would do this if there were more than thirty CASEs. (Because there aren't that many CASEs in this example, the time savings is truly insignificant.) Note, however, that each of my CASEs has a single line. If each CASE had its own code block (half a K of code or more per block), I would include the LOOP command at the end of each CASE.

Because we place the most frequently used jobs on the top of the pile, much of the code is ignored. That same method is used with the IF . . . (ELSE) . . . ENDIF command when we introduce LOOP. dBASE stops any further looking and brings us back to the top of the flowchart.

## Linking the Functions

We've spoken of the two necessary functions of our flowchart: creating a user interface and calling subroutines. We haven't talked about how these two functions are linked. We link them with a DO WHILE . . . ENDDO command.

If we follow the steps outlined thus far, the finished product is as follows:

```
DO WHIL .T.
   CHOICE = Ø
   CLEA
   @ 1,Ø TO 22,79 DOUBLE
   @ 2,30 SAY "M A I N    M E N U"
   @ 3,1 TO 3,78 DOUBLE
   @ 6,20 SAY [Ø. EXIT]
   @ 7,20 SAY [1. CUSTOMER MAILING LIST]
   @ 8,20 SAY [2. FACTORY TOTALS BY MONTH AND YEAR]
   @ 9,20 SAY [3. CUSTOMER TOTALS BY MONTH AND YEAR]
   @ 10,20 SAY [4. COMMISSION REPORT]
   @ 11,20 SAY [5. UNPAID COMMISSION REPORT]
   @ 12,20 SAY [6. FACTORY LISTING]
   @ 13,20 SAY [7. ACTIVE CUSTOMER LISTING]
   @ 14,20 SAY [8. INACTIVE CUSTOMER LISTING]
   @ 15,20 SAY [9. UPDATE CUSTOMERS]
   @ 16,20 SAY [10. UPDATE FACTORIES]
   @ 17,20 SAY [11. UPDATE ITEMS SOLD]
   @ 18,20 SAY [12. UPDATE SALESPEOPLE]
   @ 19,20 SAY [13. BACK UP ALL FILES]
   @ 20,20 SAY [14. RETRIEVE ALL FILES]
   @ 22,29 SAY [ Your Choice ->    <- ]
   @ 22,44 GET CHOICE PICT "99"
   READ
**
   DO CASE
      CASE CHOICE=Ø
         RETURN
**
      CASE CHOICE=1
         DO MAILLIST
**
      CASE CHOICE<4
         DO TOTALS
```

```
**
      CASE CHOICE<6
          DO COMMRPRT
**
      CASE CHOICE<9
          DO LISTINGS
**
      CASE CHOICE<13
          DO MAIN
**
      CASE CHOICE=13
          DO BACKUP
**
      CASE CHOICE=14
          DO RETRIEVE
**
      OTHERWISE
          WAIT "Valid Choices are 0-14. Press any key to continue. "
    ENDCASE
**
ENDDO
```

I've omitted the code used to select specific databases for each job. That code is the same no matter what method you choose, unless you make each subroutine separately access the necessary data and related files.

Some users may wonder why I don't use a RANGE qualifier in this code's @ GET command. Using RANGE would be more efficient (in terms of code) than including the OTHERWISE option.

But will users know what's going on if dBASE III Plus doesn't let them off the menu? I think not. This is a case (no pun intended) in which we need to include extra code to keep the customer satisfied.

You may have noticed also that I can't count lines of code. No, actually, I just don't count lines that are preceded by the *. Those lines come out after the program is debugged and running smoothly, anyway. It is important to remember that all source documentation, even if it's only some asterisks separating blocks of code, will be removed once the program is working as the client intends.

Last, a minor point. I initialize CHOICE to the value needed to exit from the program—one more bailout for those too fearful to press anything but Return.

Before we move on to the next section, consider why I have emphasized a modular, task-oriented approach to programming. My intent is to get you thinking in small, easily coded sections instead of seeing a whole job before you and growing faint.

One last word on modular programming. As I said, I tend to pack as much as I can into as little code as possible. That is one side of the scale, but the scale has to balance. The other side is to keep your code and logic as simple as possible. Don't follow the old BASIC logic of

```
FOR I=1 TO 10: STEP1: STEP2: STEP3:...: STEP99:NEXT
```

Debugging that can be nauseating.

# Input/Output, dBASE III Plus, and the PC

We need to bear in mind two things regarding input/output and the PC: one has to do with the particular input/output methods of the PC; the other concerns sequential and random access of disks.

dBASE III Plus is a disk-intensive language designed to run on a computer with a minimum of 256K of memory. The original dBASE was designed to run on a 64K machine. The only way to accomplish this feat was to have dBASE go to the disk for code and data, because there was no room for them in the machine's memory.

dBASE III Plus retains that same method. A minimum of 256K of memory is necessary just so there will be room for all the background tasks needed to make the program run. Once those tasks are in memory, dBASE III Plus reads in as much of your code as the computer has room for. The obvious moral is to get a PC with as much memory as you can afford.

Unfortunately, dBASE III Plus doesn't treat data the same way. Data remains on the disk and is accessed as needed. One way around this limitation is to change the CONFIG.SYS file. Another way is to buy or write RAM-disk or V-disk software. And still another way is to set up part of the computer's memory as a disk cache.

There are some features of dBASE III Plus that make memory management a pleasure. These features come in two flavors: masking files and CONFIG.DB commands.

*Masking files* are files that act as filters on the system. Two files in particular perform this function—the VUE and CAT files.

PLUS

PLUS

The VUE file limits the active environment for any work session. Programmers not familiar with the VUE file should read the dBASE III Plus documentation. Basically, VUE files contain information normally reserved to the SET RELATION TO command. The advantage of a VUE file is the ability to SET RELATIONs, SET FORMATs, SET INDEXes, SET (QRY FILE) FILTERs, and so on. The VUE file SETs these things internally; the user doesn't have to type them in whenever a particular collection of files, filters, or formats is needed. These VUE files are generated in two ways.

PLUS

One method is to use ASSIST mode or the CREATE VIEW command. These approaches are interchangeable; ASSIST mode drops you into the CREATE VIEW command screens. This is a useful method for developers who know exactly how things will be linked in a full implementation. Developers don't always know such things, however, so I offer the second method.

The second method is to use the

```
CREATE VIEW FROM ENVIRONMENT
```

command, which allows the developer to generate a VUE file based on the current SETtings in dBASE III Plus. This second method is used more frequently during development than is the first. The reason is simple. As they begin a project, few people know exactly what they want. Thanks to this command, you can sit in the customer's office for a few hours when you deliver the application, ask what you've done right and what you've done wrong, and, based on the answers, link files.

PLUS

The VUE file configures the environment; the CAT file limits it. Don't confuse CAT files, which act as file filters to the dBASE III Plus system, with any aspect of the SET FILTER TO command. The CAT file is a file filter; dBASE III Plus acts as if only those files listed in the CAT file exist in the system. Your disk may have hundreds of DBFs, NDXes, FMTs, QRYs, and so on. By SETting a CATALOG TO a particular file, you tell dBASE III Plus to work only with the files listed in the current CATALOG.

Both file types (CAT and VUE) aid memory management. They let dBASE III Plus concentrate on handling the application that is running, instead of searching on disk for extraneous information. This doesn't mean that dBASE III Plus won't go to disk to get information from the files listed in the CAT and VUE files. The disk searches will continue, but they will be specific, and unique links (rather than randomized search patterns) will be formed.

dBASE III Plus also has some new CONFIG.DB commands that aid memory management. BUCKET, GETS, MAXMEM, MVARSIZ,

HISTORY, and TYPEAHEAD, in particular, all affect the way dBASE III
Plus works with available memory. To understand this better, let's
consider what each command does.

BUCKET is used to reserve memory space for PICTURE, PICTURE
FUNCTION, and RANGE qualifiers to @ GET commands. Because these
three qualifiers do data checks and comparisons that are all memory
resident, memory must be reserved for these operations or dBASE III Plus
will allocate memory for each operation whenever one comes up during
execution. What happens when dBASE III Plus hits one of these qualifiers
and there's no memory to play with? Pixies run rampant with teeny-
weeny sabers in their hands, slashing and dashing all your work.

PLUS

GETS tells dBASE III Plus how much memory to reserve for @ GET
inputs. This is important if your system has large FMT files or similar GET
files. When dBASE III Plus READs more GETs than it has room for, you
lose information. (The laws of life dictate that you lose the most important
information first.) The GET buffer works FIFO. If the buffer is set to hold
50 GETs and you enter 51, you lose the first GET entered.

PLUS

MAXMEM tells dBASE III Plus how much memory to reserve for itself
when you RUN or ! an external application. This command has special
meaning for programmers who use CALL and LOAD commands. You
must make sure that dBASE III Plus MAXMEMs enough memory to
include the LOADed BIN files. Not doing so can spell catastrophe. dBASE
III Plus CALLs LOADed BIN files by memory address. Accessing an
external application that uses the addresses a BIN file was LOADed into is
lethal.

PLUS

MVARSIZ is discussed in Chapter 5. Its basic purpose is to reserve
memory for variable precision. Your application's needs will determine
how much precision your variables need.

PLUS

Of the commands mentioned in this discussion, HISTORY and
TYPEAHEAD are unique because you can control their respective buffers
also with SET commands. The HISTORY buffer tells dBASE III Plus how
many commands to store in the HISTORY buffer. This feature is useful
during the debugging process but is not necessarily useful in a finished file.
Note, however, that some versions of dBASE III Plus can't handle the
command

PLUS

HISTORY = 0

especially when you RUN/! an external file. The safest bet, if you're not
compiling the dBASE code, is to place

HISTORY = 1

in the CONFIG.DB file. No HISTORY command tells dBASE III Plus to set up its own default (20 lines, in my release). TYPEAHEAD is for speed typists and other key pounders. It allows typists to keep typing while dBASE III Plus is busy with some operation that directs its attention away from the keyboard. (Note that the TYPEAHEAD buffer is affected by ON ESCA and ON KEY commands.) There may be times when you don't want the typist to type ahead of what dBASE III Plus is doing. In such cases, you can enter

SET TYPEAHEAD TO 0

in your application, and then reset it later.

I mention all these commands because they affect dBASE III Plus's I/O capabilities. TYPEAHEAD, GETS, and BUCKET obviously affect input. Realize, however, that these and the other listed CONFIG.DB commands tell dBASE III Plus to create its own buffers in addition to the buffers DOS was told to set up in the CONFIG.SYS file. You will be using memory, and limiting parts of your system.

Scales have to balance. Used properly, these commands can speed up a system because they configure memory efficiently for a given application. I strongly suggest that you develop your application first and then fiddle with memory configurations, rather than vice versa.

The CAT and VUE files also aid I/O and PC memory usage because they tell dBASE III Plus what's coming down the road. Both CAT and VUE files say, "We're going to use these files in these ways. Get ready." Good. dBASE III Plus and DOS know which system parameters you've established in your CONFIG.SYS and CONFIG.DB files. Now they can determine how to make the best use of those parameters.

## Changing the CONFIG.SYS File To Manage I/O

Changing the CONFIG.SYS file does not physically alter the way dBASE III Plus gets data from a disk. What changes is the number of times dBASE III Plus has to look for data on the disk. This change has to do with buffers and the way the PC uses them.

Another reason for considering modification of the CONFIG.SYS file has to do with programming in tasks. I have been asking you to code in tasks. If you open enough files, however, and ask dBASE III Plus to perform enough tasks, you run into a wall: the number of files you can open at one time is limited.

## Handling Files and Buffers

You can increase the number of files and buffers open at one time by altering the CONFIG.SYS file. (dBASE II® programmers, who are accustomed to SELECTing either PRIMARY or SECONDARY, often have some difficulty in getting used to dBASE III Plus's ability to manage ten active databases.) With 256K of memory, you have no real reason to alter the CONFIG.SYS file; altering your programs to open fewer files is a better choice.

At this point, it is worthwhile to see how Ashton-Tate® configures its 256K systems. SYSTEM DISK #1 contains four different files: CONFI256.DB, CONFI256.SYS, CONFIG.DB, and CONFIG.SYS. Let's start at the bottom of the ladder and look at the SYS files.

| *CONFI256.SYS file* | *CONFIG.SYS file* |
|---|---|
| FILES = 20 | FILES = 20 |
| BUFFERS = 4 | BUFFERS = 15 |

Notice that both SYS files contain the line

```
FILES = 20
```

As stated earlier, being able to open at least 20 files is necessary with dBASE III® and III Plus, so you would expect that command no matter what system you're working on. The next command, however, is the key to memory work.

The CONFI256.SYS file allows only four buffers to be opened at a given time. Furthermore, these four buffers aren't very big. You don't have much room for work—the penalty of a 256K system. You'll find yourself going to disk more often than you or the PC would like—a necessity on such a system. You really can't increase the buffer count much beyond four without adversely affecting how much of its own kernel dBASE III Plus can load.

The other Ashton-Tate CONFIG.SYS file tells the PC to prepare for 15 buffers. Fifteen buffers is good for systems that range from 320 to 512K. For the higher end of 512 and beyond, I strongly recommend 24 buffers or more. Moreover, you should increase the number of files. With more memory available, you can rewrite the CONFIG.SYS file as follows:

```
FILES = 30
BUFFERS = 24
```

(Include whatever lines were previously in the file.)

| PLUS |

That brings us to the CONFIG.DB files. How does Ashton-Tate configure dBASE III Plus for a 256K machine?

*CONFI256.DB*

```
COMMAND = ASSIST
STATUS = ON
BUCKET = 1
GETS = 35
MVARSIZ = 3
HISTORY = 10
TYPEAHEAD = 10
```

*CONFIG.DB*

```
STATUS = ON
COMMAND = ASSIST
```

The big news is that Ashton-Tate is concerned with overriding III Plus's memory defaults in a low-memory environment. The CONFIG.DB file only turns on a STATUS line and gets us started in ASSIST mode; the CONFI256.DB file, on the other hand, is set up to minimize dBASE III Plus's memory use. But notice how limiting the memory use is!

You can hold in memory only one PICTURE, PICTURE FUNCTION, or RANGE qualifier at a time. Not much room to play in. You're further limited to 35 GETS in the input buffer, and the memory variable limit is 3,000 bytes. Whoosh! Try working in that environment, and you'll find yourself tripping over your own data fields. HISTORY and TYPEAHEAD are equally clipped, but can even be set to 0—with the provisions I mentioned earlier—to increase space for other memory-management functions.

Why do I harangue on memory management, CONFIG.SYS, and CONFIG.DB files?

The problem with limited memory and many active files and buffers is that both files and buffers take up room in memory whether they are used or not. This limitation pertains to more than just dBASE III Plus files. Every time a file, any file, is opened, dBASE III Plus loses some room in the memory of the machine.

For example, the line

```
FILES = 20
```

tells DOS to allow twenty open files; DOS passes the message along to dBASE. Those twenty files get eaten quickly, however. You start with DOS—there go two files. Next is DBASE.COM—three down. You'd like to know what you're doing, so you have DBASE.OVL working—four down. Need some help? Add HELP.DBS—five away. This scenario is simple, but you get the picture. Add a few databases, their index files, a dBASE program file or two (each of which calls in a subroutine), a format file, perhaps a memo file, maybe old files from which you're creating a new database, and so on. Available files get chewed up pretty fast.

Programs that open too many files without any place to put them, because of limited memory or an incorrect CONFIG.SYS file, result in the message

```
TOO MANY FILES OPEN
```

Far more aggravating is getting no message or warning whatsoever and seeing dBASE slow to a crawl because of an overtaxed memory.

With a low-memory system, you'd rather have buffers open than files. With buffers, the PC (and therefore dBASE III Plus) can keep track of the information around the last-requested information. Sound cryptic? This concept has to do with contiguous INDEXed files and is discussed in more detail later in this book (see "Operations with Index Files" in Chapter 5).

A nice way to think of files and buffers is to think of files as Indian clubs and buffers as drinking glasses. The PC juggles Indian clubs and drinks out of glasses. When your CONFIG.SYS file supports only ten open files and you throw in an eleventh Indian club, everything falls to the ground. When you have only ten glasses in front of you and you want to taste an eleventh drink, you have to empty a glass before you can refill it.

A somewhat more worthy explanation is that the PC keeps track of information internally as much as possible. This aspect of the PC's design makes things happen faster because the machine doesn't have to read and write to the disk as often. Of course, a good chunk of the computer's memory is used for housekeeping. When you are opening and closing data files, command files, text files, and format files, you are using up memory to keep track of where things are on the disks. The maximum number of files you can have active with dBASE III Plus is 20. This number is cut in half when you use just database files. But it's a bear to have all those files open and subsequent readings and writings to disk for each file.

The problem is one of knowing and working within the PC's limits. You want to design your system so that memory is used as much as possible. Each disk access slows down the program; but when much of the memory is used for housekeeping, you run the risk, on a 256K machine, of forcing DOS to throw the interpreter, HELP, and other necessary files back out to the disk. The trade-off is between memory management and program execution speed. This is a delicate problem that you can often avoid when you know something about DOS.

The problem is remedied by using buffers. But buffers exist only in the memory of the machine, never on the disk. Buffers make the PC work faster, but they chew up memory. The moral? Decrease the number of buffers if you need more files open. The less RAM you have, the smaller the buffers must be and the slower the machine will run. As a result, 20 to 24 is a nice range for the number of buffers for most applications. I use a 512K PC and set the buffers at 40. Using more than 40 buffers can adversely affect the performance of other programs.

For readers really interested in witnessing the handling of buffers and files firsthand, I offer the following experiment.

Start up dBASE III Plus. After the disk check has frustrated you, and the program is finally running, type

```
SET ALTER TO TEST
SET ALTER ON
```

Now USE a database, preferably a small one (fewer than 20 fields). Type

```
DISP STAT
```

to make sure that ALTERNATE is ON and the alternate file is TEST.TXT, as shown in figure 2.2.

Now type

```
DISP STRUC
```

You should now have in your ALTERNATE file facsimiles of the DISP STAT screen and the DISP STRUC screen for the database in USE. Now type

```
SET ALTER OFF
TYPE TEST. TXT
```

More than likely, you get a message that the file is open, an error message at the DOS level, or some such nonsense. You might get no response, other than to be dropped back at the dBASE prompt. But you have the ALTERNATE OFF, and the file is properly named. Don't fret. Type

```
QUIT
```

and wait until dBASE III Plus says good-bye and you're back at the DOS prompt. Now type

```
TYPE TEST. TXT
```

Voilà! End of experiment.

```
-> DISP STAT

Currently Selected Database:
Select area:  1, Database in Use: D:STUDENTS.dbf    Alias: STUDENTS

Alternate file: A:TEST.txt
File search path:
Default disk drive: D:
Print destination:  PRN:
Margin =      0
Current work area =    1   Delimiters are ':' and ':'

Press any key to continue...

ALTERNATE  - ON     DELETED     - OFF    FIXED      - OFF    SAFETY     - OFF
BELL       - OFF    DELIMITERS  - ON     HEADING    - ON     SCOREBOARD - OFF
CARRY      - OFF    DEVICE      - SCRN   HELP       - OFF    STATUS     - OFF
CATALOG    - OFF    DOHISTORY   - OFF    HISTORY    - ON     STEP       - OFF
CENTURY    - OFF    ECHO        - OFF    INTENSITY  - ON     TALK       - OFF
CONFIRM    - OFF    ESCAPE      - ON     MENU       - OFF    TITLE      - ON
CONSOLE    - ON     EXACT       - OFF    PRINT      - OFF    UNIQUE     - OFF
DEBUG      - OFF    FIELDS      - OFF

Programmable function keys:
F2  - assist;
F3  - list;
F4  - dir;
F5  - display structure;
F6  - display status;
F7  - SET ALTER TO A:ALTER;SET ALTER ON;
F8  - CLOSE ALTER;
F9  - CLEAR;
F10 - EJECT;

-> DISP STRUC
Structure for database: D:STUDENTS.dbf
Number of data records:      51
Date of last update   : 09/12/86
Field  Field Name  Type        Width    Dec
    1  SSNUMBER    Character     11
    2  CLASS       Character      6
    3  FIRSTNAME   Character     15
    4  LASTNAME    Character     15
    5  DAY         Date           8
    6  CLASSGRADE  Character      1
    7  WASHOMEWRK  Logical        1
    8  HOMEWORK    Numeric        3
** Total **                     61

-> SET ALTER OFF
```

Fig. 2.2. Contents of the ALTERNATE file.

This is a prime example of how DOS handles both files and buffers. Inside dBASE, with SET ALTER ON, all the screen information is sent first to a buffer. Every once in a while the buffer fills with information and flushes itself to the ALTERNATE file (TEST.TXT in the experiment). The buffer is now empty and ready for the next set of screens.

In our experiment, however, we don't give the buffer a chance to flush itself when we are in dBASE. QUITting dBASE forced dBASE to close all open files, one of which was the ALTERNATE file. Further, DOS was forced to purge all buffers. This flushing is standard operating procedure for DOS when it exits a program. The result is that DOS first flushes the buffers, and then dBASE closes the files. Thus the difference between a buffer and a file is dramatically demonstrated.

The magic has to do with the fact that dBASE III Plus (usually) stores the ALTERNATE file text in a buffer until the buffer is full. Once the buffer is full, dBASE III Plus writes that information to the disk file. By QUITting to the system, you can force dBASE to write the information to the disk.

Using the same procedure to experiment with different size buffers is also worthwhile. Putting

    BUFFERS = 80

in your CONFIG.SYS file and rebooting the machine gives you much smaller buffers than using 20 or even 40 buffers. The smaller buffers cause dBASE III Plus to write the information to the ALTERNATE file more often than do fewer, hence larger, buffers.

So much for getting information from buffers to the disk. Now we consider the reverse process.

## Retrieving Data from the Disk

The diagram in figure 2.3 is meant to be an example, and is not a realistic representation of the way data is actually stored or retrieved. Imagine this illustration as part of a disk file containing data.

REQUESTED
DATA

| BLOCK 1 | BLOCK 2 | BLOCK 3 | BLOCK 4 | BLOCK 5 |

*Fig. 2.3. Blocks of data in a disk file.*

We are interested in accessing data block 3. When we are using the buffers created by the CONFIG.SYS file and we request block 3, we also pull into that buffer blocks 1, 2, 4, and 5. Why? Because sometime during the development of the PC and DOS systems, someone decided that keeping information in buffers would be good. The point is not that buffers are new to the PC; all computers, from large mainframes to lowly 8-bit machines, use them. The point is that the information usually kept in those buffers is close (in the disk file) to the last information requested.

The strength of the PC is that the algorithms for managing data in buffers are fairly sophisticated. The PC often employs a "most-used" referencing algorithm that keeps in memory the data accessed most often.

Buffering information that is close to the last information requested makes sense if you're working with word-processing files or programs too large to fit into machine memory. Usually these applications get information in a linear fashion. (We look at the last paragraph, this paragraph, and then the next paragraph, or we look at program line 2000, 2010, 2020, 2030 . . . .) But we don't always request information from a database in that order.

If you constantly reference block 3, you have no problem. That information is kept in a buffer close to the top of a stack of buffers. But now imagine that you request information in block 10. DOS pushes down the block 3 information and places the block 10 information on top of the stack. Now you look at block 90. The stack, reading from the top down, becomes

```
┌──────────┐
│          │
│    90    │
│          │
└──────────┘

┌──────────┐
│          │
│    10    │
│          │
└──────────┘

┌──────────┐
│          │
│    03    │
│          │
└──────────┘
```

Now you want 3's information again and the stack shifts (it doesn't "pop") the block 3 information to the top:

```
┌──────────┐
│          │
│    03    │
│          │
└──────────┘

┌──────────┐
│          │
│    90    │
│          │
└──────────┘

┌──────────┐
│          │
│    10    │
│          │
└──────────┘
```

Suppose that all 20 buffers get filled up. You're most often referencing data blocks 3, 90, 10, and 7, in that order, with block 82 referenced least often. The buffer stack looks like the following diagram:

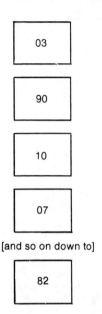

[and so on down to]

You now reference a new data block, 32, which has never been referenced before. Block 82's information gets popped off the bottom because 82 is the least used. The most-used buffers stay in the buffer stack, with the most used closest to the top.

Keep this concept in mind when you are opening work areas and designing databases in dBASE III Plus applications. The best uses of this concept can be seen in the sections on database templates and various types of data files.

## Ram Disks, Virtual Disks, Caches, and dBASE Files

Other ways to solve the I/O problem involve using the computer's memory to eliminate disk accesses. One way is to use Ram-disk or V-disk software to create a high-speed drive, and then copy everything needed to that drive. This practice has more advantages than the obvious ones. Another way is to set up a disk cache for more efficient retrieval of your code from the disk.

As mentioned earlier, the dBASE programs are disk-based. Worse, they are interpreted at each run. This aspect of dBASE's design makes the computer run as fast as molasses flowing uphill in January. The smart use of RAM disks or virtual disks, then, is not necessarily to use them for database files or their kin. Instead, it may be wiser to load your program and related files (rather than huge databases) onto electronic disks, especially if your program is read more often than the database information. The data is stored and manipulated in buffers, but the code to execute the manipulations (a long DO WHILE . . . ENDDO, for example) is pulled from the disk each time that code is needed.

A disk cache can provide similar benefits, except that a cache can speed up access not just to your programs but also to your databases. A cache works like the disk buffers described in the last section: When information is requested from the disk, copies of that information—along with other information—are kept in the cache. Information in a cache, like information on a RAM disk, can be retrieved much more quickly than information on a physical disk.

One nice thing about a disk cache is that it works automatically. To use a RAM disk or virtual disk, you have to copy your program files to the electronic disk. That isn't necessary with a cache, because algorithms similar to those used in DOS's management of buffers are used to manage the cache.

A combination of the two techniques—using the computer's memory to eliminate physical disk accesses and using only the necessary parts of a database—is an excellent method for keeping your applications clicking along at a good pace.

## Physical Records

Place 100 folders containing information into a box. Pick up the folders one at a time. They are physical records. Now pretend that the information in those 100 folders is in a dBASE III Plus database file in the same sequence as in the folders. The records in the database file are still physical records. We call them *physical* because they are not *logical*, which is a word we reserve for discussions of random access.

The only thing worth remembering about all this is that physical records are the actual records in the database. That's it, nothing more. The following is an example of a check register file. It is physical in that the checks are listed as they were written.

| RECNO( ) | PAIDTO | AMOUNT |
|----------|--------|--------|
| 232 | SEARS | $   59.95 |
| 233 | MOBIL | $   22.75 |
| 234 | CASH  | $1000.00 |
| 235 | MOBIL | $   30.00 |
| 236 | CASH  | $    5.00 |
| 237 | SEARS | $   20.00 |

## Sequential Access

When we access data one record after another—first, second, and so on to the last—we are sequentially accessing the data. That we don't do anything with the majority of the records makes no difference; all that matters is that we look at them one after the other.

Sequential access is another great time-eater in dBASE III Plus programming. One reason is that sequential processing always uses disks; it doesn't involve buffers at all. When you use LOCATE, or use a command with a FOR qualifier, for instance, get ready for a long wait, because you are using sequential access.

One way to speed up LOCATEing records involves forethought—something I've said never goes well with programming.

No matter what anyone says, data access is not random. No matter what kind of data is stored in the database, the access of the data follows a bell curve. It may not follow a bell curve for the most significant INDEXed fields, but it definitely follows the curve on one if not several other fields. Examples of this are given in the sections on "Primary and Secondary Keys" (this chapter) and "Index Files and Bell Curves" (Chapter 5). At times, sequential access is the only way to go, but sequential access is best reserved for management rather than manipulation.

Management rather than manipulation? The difference concerns the size of the working database. We manage large DBF files. In other words, we have no intention of making any changes directly to the files. What we do is look for information we need, bring that data to a smaller database file, and manipulate the data there. Database management, for the purposes of this book, can be likened to file management. Database manipulation is what I do when I alter records in a file.

Unless we are careful in writing our files to disk, they are written in a hodgepodge sequential manner. And that aspect of file structure is the reason for separating files logically. Records are appended to a file as they are entered, with no order whatsoever. Consider the following data set:

| City | State |
|------|-------|
| Portsmouth | NH |
| Hanover | NH |
| Manchester | MA |
| Manchester | NH |
| Boston | MA |
| New Boston | NH |
| New Bedford | MA |
| Bedford | NH |

This data set is appended, one record at a time, to a file containing the names of several other cities in New England.

| City | State |
|------|-------|
| Norwich | VT |
| Lebanon | NH |
| Burlington | VT |
| Keene | NH |
| Colebrook | NH |
| St. Johnsbury | VT |
| Brattleboro | VT |

Readers who are familiar with New England will perceive some order in my listing, but that order results entirely from associations in my own mind; I listed the cities as I thought of them.

If the names of the cities are entered in the order in which they are listed, they go sequentially into the database:

| City | State |
|------|-------|
| Portsmouth | NH |
| Hanover | NH |
| Manchester | MA |
| Manchester | NH |
| Boston | MA |
| New Boston | NH |
| New Bedford | MA |
| Bedford | NH |
| Norwich | VT |
| Lebanon | NH |
| Burlington | VT |
| Keene | NH |
| Colebrook | NH |
| St. Johnsbury | VT |
| Brattleboro | VT |

This data set has no order; we were not careful in entering the data. Because we have little control on how data is sent to disk, we are not careful in writing our files to disk. The data is stored on disk as it was entered. The result is a data mess. And that is exactly how the data will be read back out: as a disorderly mess.

## Logical Records

The term *logical* record implies that we, the humans who use the computer, have chosen some method of ordering physical records. We have chosen an INDEXing method.

For example, the check-register data in the previous section consists of physical records. We make their order logical by grouping the records according to PAIDTO.

| RECNO( ) | PAIDTO | AMOUNT |
|----------|--------|--------|
| 234 | CASH | $1000.00 |
| 236 | CASH | $   5.00 |
| 233 | MOBIL | $  22.75 |
| 235 | MOBIL | $  30.00 |
| 232 | SEARS | $  59.95 |
| 237 | SEARS | $  20.00 |

We can be even fancier and order the list by PAIDTO and then by AMOUNT, in increasing order.

| RECNO( ) | PAIDTO | AMOUNT |
|----------|--------|--------|
| 236 | CASH | $   5.00 |
| 234 | CASH | $1000.00 |
| 233 | MOBIL | $  22.75 |
| 235 | MOBIL | $  30.00 |
| 237 | SEARS | $  20.00 |
| 232 | SEARS | $  59.95 |

We've taken items entered "at random" and arranged them according to some predetermined "logical" method.

## Random Access

Now the question is, "What does *random* mean?" In this connection, it means "highly ordered." No, I haven't been in the wine cellar too long.

Random means taking things, one here, one there, one somewhere else. Consider the following sequence of random numbers:

01,   21,   30,   62,   67,   68,   70,   79,   80

Say that these numbers represent record numbers in a database of 100 records. Further, say that they represent the only records in our database that share some common bond. We INDEX on this common bond and behold! Our random sequence becomes highly ordered. We still pick one here, one there, one somewhere else. But now we're exact in what we pick from here, there, and elsewhere. So our random access is not so random. The order is definitely not sequential, however.

A truly random access occurs when we use LOCATE or a FOR condition. The records are read sequentially (in their physical order). The condition we're interested in occurs at random in the database.

## Primary and Secondary Keys

The mechanism that orders our random access relies upon primary and secondary keys. A primary key is what the computer uses to keep track of where information is in a database. dBASE III Plus uses record numbers—the RECNO( ) function—as the primary key for finding information.

This is all well and good for dBASE III Plus, but not for us mortals. The secondary key is what we mortals can understand; it points to the primary key, which the computer can understand.

For instance, our checkbooks contain dates, check numbers, debit and credit information, balances, and descriptions (interest, activity charge, phone bill). When Sears says we didn't pay our bill, we look through our descriptions for references such as "SEARS." The references appear at random, and we order them with the index key

```
description="SEARS"
```

Once we've found all our "SEARS" descriptions, we note check numbers and amounts to inform Sears of the error. This example illustrates the use of primary (check number) and secondary (description="SEARS") keys.

More practical examples of the use of primary and secondary keys can be seen in the programs UPDATER.PRG (Chapter 5) and NEWUPDTR.PRG (Chapter 7). UPDATER.PRG uses sequential access; NEWUPDTR.PRG uses random access. Note that UPDATER.PRG uses a sequential (unINDEXed) file and examines each record FOR a condition. NEWUPDTR.PRG starts with a logically ordered file, FINDs the first record that meets our condition, and then takes only those records that meet our condition. All records that match our condition are next to each other in a logically ordered file.

# 3
# Subroutines and dBASE III Plus PROCEDURE Files

A *subroutine* is a group of commands that the main program uses to perform a specific task. More precisely, a subroutine is a group of commands not needed every time the main program is executed; it is used only if certain conditions are met in the main body of the program. Menu systems are almost always subroutines of a central program. A good example of the use of subroutines is the front-end system designed in Chapter 2, the Main Menu. This system employs a central program that uses other modules to do tasks as needed.

The question arises whether some subroutines should be kept in the main body of the program. Well, yes; some subroutines are used so often that they should be in the main body of the program. But I also say to use modular coding, which produces many little files. Using small files can mean eating up a great deal of disk space, and most certainly means more wear and tear for the disk and drive than is healthy for your computer system.

## Creating PROCEDURE Files

Fortunately, dBASE III Plus has a way to solve this dilemma. The solution is dBASE III Plus's PROCEDURE file. Before I talk about forming PROCEDURE files, I will describe how they work.

Assume that you have a program called BLACKBOX. Inside BLACKBOX is something called THRDSIDE, which determines the third side of a right triangle. When you give the program the measurements of two sides, it tells you the third. You don't care how THRDSIDE works; all you care about is the fact that when you supply the dimensions of two sides, THRDSIDE gives you the third. If THRDSIDE is a subroutine, THRDSIDE is outside of BLACKBOX. If THRDSIDE is part of a PROCEDURE file, the routine never leaves BLACKBOX.

Following are three ways to activate THRDSIDE:

| *English* | *dBASE III Plus Subroutine* | *dBASE III Plus PROCEDURE* |
|---|---|---|
| "Hey, THRDSIDE, | PUBLIC SIDE3 | SET PROC TO BLACKBOX |
| one side is 10 units; | SIDE1=10 | SIDE1=10 |
| the other is 20 units. | SIDE2=20 | SIDE2=20 |
| What's the third side?" | SIDE3=0 | SIDE3=0 |
| | DO THRDSIDE | DO THRDSIDE WITH; |
| | | SIDE1, SIDE2, SIDE3 |

At this point THRDSIDE does some juggling, comes up with an answer, and sends the answer back to you as SIDE3. Slick!

Notice that the dBASE III Plus procedure code looks very much like a simple subroutine call. Why do we use procedures rather than subroutines?

Suppose that you are interested in several geometric oddities. You have a clutter of subroutines: THRDSIDE, ANGLE, CIRCLE, DIAMETER, RADIUS, ULNA, and so on. One program, GEOMETRY, uses these subroutines frequently. None of the subroutines is particularly large, so you string them together in a PROCEDURE file. The following code consists of the GEOMETRY.PRG file, which uses the subroutines, and the PROCEDURE file, which does the actual work.

```
***GEOMETRY.PRG FILE
***BY JOSEPH-DAVID CARRABIS
**
SET TALK OFF
SET PROCEDURE TO ODDITIES * ODDITIES.PRG IS A FILE CONTAINING OUR SUBROUTINES
CLEAR
@  1, 19  SAY "PRESS A FUNCTION KEY TO ANSWER A QUESTION"
@  5, 17  SAY "F1 -> EXIT"
@  6, 17  SAY "F2 -> CIRCLE RADIUS          (NEEDS AREA)"
@  7, 17  SAY "F3 -> CIRCLE DIAMETER        (NEEDS PERIMETER)"
@  8, 17  SAY "F4 -> CIRCLE PERIMETER       (NEEDS RADIUS)"
@  9, 17  SAY "F5 -> RT TRIANGLE HYPOTENUSE (NEEDS TWO SIDES)"
@ 10, 17  SAY "F6 -> RT TRIANGLE PERIMETER  (NEEDS TWO SIDES)"
```

```
@ 11, 17  SAY "F7 -> BOX AREA              (NEEDS TWO SIDES)"
@ 12, 17  SAY "F8 -> BOX PERIMETER         (NEEDS TWO SIDES)"
@ 13, 17  SAY "F9 -> IS BOX A QUADRILATERAL?  (NEEDS ONE ANGLE)"
@ 14, 17  SAY "F10 -> I HATED GEOMETRY CLASS!  (NEEDS HELP)"
@  0,  0  TO 17, 79    DOUBLE
@  2,  1  TO  2, 78    DOUBLE
**
DO WHILE .T.
   WAIT ' ' TO KEY
   @ 18, 0 CLEAR
   KEYVALUE=ASC(KEY)
**
   DO CASE
      CASE KEYVALUE<246
         CLOS PROC
         CANCEL
**
      CASE KEYVALUE=254
         INPU "CIRCLE AREA?" TO VALUE
         DO RADIUS WITH VALUE
**
      CASE KEYVALUE=253
         INPU "CIRCLE PERIMETER?" TO VALUE
         DO DIAMETER WITH VALUE
**
      CASE KEYVALUE=252
         INPU "CIRCLE RADIUS?" TO VALUE
         DO CPERIM WITH VALUE
**
      CASE KEYVALUE=251

         STORE 0 TO VALUE1, VALUE2, VALUE3
         DO THRDSIDE WITH VALUE1, VALUE2, VALUE3
         DO CLEARER WITH VALUE3
**
      CASE KEYVALUE=250
         STORE 0 TO VALUE1, VALUE2, VALUE3
         DO TPERIM WITH VALUE1, VALUE2, VALUE3
**
      CASE KEYVALUE=249
         DO BOXAREA
```

```
**
      CASE KEYVALUE=248
          DO BPERIM
**
      CASE KEYVALUE=247
          DO QUAD
**
      OTHERWISE
          ? "YEAH, BUT YOU REMEMBERED WHAT SHE TAUGHT YOU!"
    ENDCASE
**
ENDDO
CLOS PROC
**
***END OF GEOMETRY.PRG

***ODDITIES.PRG PROCEDURE FILE
***BY JOSEPH-DAVID CARRABIS, AND SO ON AND SO FORTH
**
PROCEDURE CLEARER * TO DISPLAY THE ANSWER AND CLEAR THE SCREEN
PARAMETER ANSWER
@ 18,0 CLEAR
WAIT "THE ANSWER IS "+STR(ANSWER,10,5) + ". PRESS ANY KEY TO CONTINUE. "
@ 18,0 CLEAR
**
PROCEDURE RADIUS * RADIUS = PI*SQR(R)
PARAMETER AREA
RADIUS=SQRT(AREA/3.141)
DO CLEARER WITH RADIUS
**
PROCEDURE DIAMETER * DIAMETER=2R=PERIMETER/PI
PARAMETER PERIMETER
DIAMETER=PERIMETER/3.141
DO CLEARER WITH DIAMETER
**
PROCEDURE CPERIM * CIRCLE PERIMETER=2RPI
PARAMETER RADIUS
PERIMETER=RADIUS*6.282
DO CLEARER WITH PERIMETER
**
```

```
PROCEDURE THRDSIDE * HYPOTENUSE=SQRT(SUM OF SQUARES OF SIDES)
PARAMETER SIDE1,SIDE2,SIDE3
INPU "WHAT IS SIDE 1? " TO SIDE1
INPU "WHAT IS SIDE 2? " TO SIDE2
SIDE3=SQRT(SIDE1*SIDE1+SIDE2*SIDE2)
**
PROCEDURE TPERIM *
PARAMETER SIDE1,SIDE2,SIDE3
DO THRDSIDE WITH SIDE1,SIDE2,SIDE3
PERIMETER=SIDE1+SIDE2+SIDE3
DO CLEARER WITH PERIMETER
**
PROCEDURE BOXAREA * AREA=SIDE1*SIDE2
INPU "WHAT IS SIDE 1? " TO SIDE1
INPU "WHAT IS SIDE 2? " TO SIDE2
AREA=SIDE1*SIDE2
DO CLEARER WITH AREA
**
PROCEDURE BPERIM * PERIMETER=2*(SIDE1+SIDE2)
INPU "WHAT IS SIDE 1? " TO SIDE1
INPU "WHAT IS SIDE 2? " TO SIDE2
PERIMETER=2*(SIDE1+SIDE2)
DO CLEARER WITH PERIMETER
**
PROCEDURE QUAD * IF ANGLE<>90 DEGREES -> BOX IS NOT QUADRILATERAL
INPU "WHAT IS THE ANGLE (IN DEGREES)? " TO ANGLE
IF ANGLE<>90
    ? "NO, IT IS NOT. "
ELSE
    ? "YES, IT IS. "
ENDIF
WAIT
@ 19,0 CLEAR
RETURN
**
***END OF PROCEDURE FILE
```

You need to know why I choose to lump all these oddities into one PROCEDURE file, and how using the PROCEDURE file helps dBASE III Plus. First, all the oddities are small. Creating several subroutines would only tie up disk space and slow down the system with endless I/O.

Second, this one large PROCEDURE file can be loaded into memory as one block of code and accessed from there. One disk access now handles the I/O for several subroutines.

## Standards for Creating a PROCEDURE File

The requirements for setting up a PROCEDURE file are

1. All the subroutines should be short (3 to 50 lines of code).

2. The entire PROCEDURE file should comfortably fit in memory. (Determine the sizes of DOS and necessary dBASE III Plus files; find out what is left over for your working files; and you'll have the size your PROCEDURE file should be. If you don't have a great deal of memory to play with, use subroutines. You'll be going to the disk no matter what.)

3. All the subroutines in the PROCEDURE file should be used frequently by the calling program during a session—either because a standard work session is long or because the files call each other.

4. You must have more than one subroutine. If not, include the one subroutine in the main body or leave the subroutine as a separately called program. It would be easier to code, anyway.

5. The maximum number of subroutines in a PROCEDURE file is 32.

The ODDITIES.PRG PROCEDURE file is set up following standard programming logic. The most frequently used subroutine, CLEARER, is at the top of the list. Repetitive questions (regarding triangles and boxes) are kept in the subroutines. We have no reason to weigh down the main body of the program with questions that might never be asked (if we were interested only in circles, for example). The other subroutines follow in the order they appear on the calling menu.

## Other Features of PROCEDURE Files

The preceding file is also an example of some other interesting features of PROCEDURE files. Notice that I don't always pass PARAMETERs to the subroutines. A PROCEDURE-based subroutine doesn't always need to be handed a baton to be able to run its leg of the race. This flexibility is useful, but it demands a warning note:

> If a PROCEDURE-based subroutine is called at several different locations or by several different programs, the calling commands must all agree in the number of PARAMETERs being passed.

You cannot use the command

    DO RADIUS

because PROCEDURE RADIUS wants to get

    PARAMETER AREA

from the calling program. Likewise, if EXAMPLE is a PROCEDURE-based subroutine with the first line

    PARAMETER ONE, TWO, THREE

the subroutine can't be called with any of the following:

    DO EXAMPLE WITH 5
    DO EXAMPLE WITH DUCK, SOUP
    DO EXAMPLE WITH THE, ALLAN, BRADY, SHOW

The reason for this restriction is that none of these calls to EXAMPLE passes the correct number of PARAMETERS. A call that works is

    DO EXAMPLE WITH CALVIN, KLEIN, JEANS

If dBASE can't find subroutines in the declared PROCEDURE file, it looks elsewhere. The first search is made of the immediate directory, the next is of the default drive (as in SET DEFA TO), and the last is of the default path (as in SET PATH TO). These subroutines can be passed values exactly like their PROCEDURE-file cousins; you must have a PARAMETER command as the first executable command in the subroutine.

Those who have programmed with dBASE III Plus may know that the preceding statement isn't exactly true. You should have a PARAMETER command as the first executable command of your subroutine, but it isn't necessary. Why is that?

The PARAMETER command tells the called routine that something from the calling routine is going to be used in a special way. Specifically, a value from the calling routine is going to be used in the called routine; a specific variable's value will be used. This implies that a variable in the called routine will carry the value from the calling routine's variable. True.

And there's the catch. dBASE III Plus doesn't care when the called routine's PARAMETER command initializes the carrier variable with the carried value. You can even neglect to use the carrier variable, with no ill effects. This characteristic becomes quite useful in a situation in which a single variable will be used in a routine, first to perform some calculations and then to carry the calling routine's variable value. Such situations often occur in tax preparation and medical record keeping. For example

```
** CALLED ROUTINE
**
CARRIER = 0
**
** PERFORM SOME FUNCTIONS WITH CARRIER
**
PARAMETER CARRIER
**
** PERFORM SOME FUNCTIONS WITH CARRIED VALUE
**
** EOF
```

Note that the value returned to the calling routine is the last value assigned to CARRIER. All operations prior to the PARAMETER command don't affect the carried value. The benefits are seen when variable memory space is at a premium.

Another point worth noting is that subroutines in PROCEDURE files can DO other subroutines in the same PROCEDURE file. Notice, for example, that CLEARER is accessed by most of the other subroutines in ODDITIES.

CLEARER is also the first subroutine in the file. This fact brings us to an interesting point. With many of the higher-level languages, programmers can define subroutines as procedures at the beginning of the main body of code. dBASE III Plus is an exception to this rule in a certain sense: In dBASE III Plus you cannot place PROCEDUREs directly before the working code in the main program. Doing so causes dBASE to exit the program as soon as it reaches the first PROCEDURE name in the list. Because dBASE III Plus is interpreted one line at a time, placing PROCEDURES at the end of the main body of code is also out of the question.

You can, however, design your PROCEDURE files to be recursive to themselves if the called PROCEDUREs are placed before the calling PROCEDUREs in the file. Proper design of these files can get you some highly memory-intensive programs that access the disk only at the start and end of a work session.

All the PROCEDURE files I've designed originated as a group of related subroutines. The Main Menu system developed earlier in this book shows a group of jobs performed by similar tasks. Each task is a subroutine that performs a specific function. Once the separate subroutines are debugged and functional, I revise the menu and code to create the following:

```
SET PROC TO FROMFRST
DO WHILE . T.
CHOICE=0
CLEAR
DO WHIL . T.
   CHOICE = 0
   CLEA
   @ 1,0 TO 22,79 DOUBLE
   @ 2,30 SAY "M A I N    M E N U"
   @ 3,1 TO 3,78 DOUBLE
   @ 6,20 SAY [0.  EXIT]
   @ 7,20 SAY [1.  CUSTOMER MAILING LIST]
   @ 8,20 SAY [2.  FACTORY TOTALS BY MONTH AND YEAR]
   @ 9,20 SAY [3.  CUSTOMER TOTALS BY MONTH AND YEAR]
   @ 10,20 SAY [4.  COMMISSION REPORT]
   @ 11,20 SAY [5.  UNPAID COMMISSION REPORT]
   @ 12,20 SAY [6.  FACTORY LISTING]
   @ 13,20 SAY [7.  ACTIVE CUSTOMER LISTING]
   @ 14,20 SAY [8.  INACTIVE CUSTOMER LISTING]
   @ 15,20 SAY [9.  UPDATE CUSTOMERS]
   @ 16,20 SAY [10. UPDATE FACTORIES]
   @ 17,20 SAY [11. UPDATE ITEMS SOLD]
   @ 18,20 SAY [12. UPDATE SALESPEOPLE]
   @ 19,20 SAY [13. BACK UP ALL FILES]
   @ 20,20 SAY [14. RETRIEVE ALL FILES]
   @ 22,29 SAY [ Your Choice ->    <- ]
   @ 22,44 GET CHOICE PICT "99"
   READ
*
   DO CASE
      CASE CHOICE=0
         RETURN
*
      CASE CHOICE=1
         DO MAILLIST WITH CUSTOMERS
*
```

```
        CASE CHOICE=2
           DO TOTALS WITH FACTORY
*
        CASE CHOICE=3
           DO TOTALS WITH CUSTOMER
*
        CASE CHOICE<6
           DO COMMRPRT
*
        CASE CHOICE=6

           DO LISTINGS WITH FACTORY
*
        CASE CHOICE<9
           DO LISTINGS WITH CUSTOMER
*
        CASE CHOICE=9
           DO MAIN WITH CUSTOMER
*
        CASE CHOICE=10
           DO MAIN WITH FACTORY
*
        CASE CHOICE=11
           DO MAIN WITH ITEMSOLD
*
        CASE CHOICE=12
           DO MAIN WITH SALESTAF
*
        CASE CHOICE=13
           RUN BACKUP
*
        CASE CHOICE=14
           RUN RESTORE
*
        OTHERWISE
           WAIT "Valid Choices are 0-14. Press any key to continue. "
     ENDCASE
*
ENDDO
```

The PROCEDURE file, FROMFRST.PRG, looks like this:

```
***PROCEDURE FILE FROMFRST.PRG
***BY JOSEPH-DAVID CARRABIS ETC.
**
PROCEDURE MAIN
PARAMETER FILENAME
USE &FILENAME INDE &FILENAME

    [code for MAIN subroutine]

**
PROCEDURE LISTINGS
PARAMETER FILENAME
USE &FILENAME INDE &FILENAME

    [code for LISTINGS subroutine]

**
PROCEDURE TOTALS
PARAMETER FILENAME
USE &FILENAME INDE &FILENAME

    [code for TOTALS subroutine]

**
PROCEDURE MAILLIST
PARAMETER FILENAME
USE &FILENAME INDE &FILENAME

    [code for MAILLIST subroutine]

**
***END OF FROMFRST PROCEDURE FILE
```

Again notice that I followed the logic of tasks, and I gave the problem some forethought. Extra menu selections can be added without changing the PROCEDURE file. BACKUP.PRG and RESTORE.PRG files are not included in the PROCEDURE file because they do not follow one of the rules dictating the inclusion of a subroutine in such a file—that is, they are not called frequently during a session.

## The RUN/! Command

The philosophy presented in the preceding section has been to put complete and repeatedly called dBASE III Plus subroutines in a PROCEDURE file. And, in this sentence, I added an implication not mentioned earlier.

The implication is in the phrase "repeatedly called dBASE III Plus." Subroutines that are called repeatedly should be placed in PROCEDURE files.

But what about modules that are called only once in a while and are not coded in dBASE III Plus? How can we utilize a COM or EXE file that is needed only at startup, perhaps to change the access codes of some files?

dBASE III Plus has a powerful command that many programmers fail to use: the RUN, or !, command. Many experienced dBASE II programmers have suffered because they overlooked that command. But those dBASE II programmers who used

```
QUIT TO "COMFILE1", "COMFILE2", . . .
```

will definitely use

```
RUN  COMFILE1
RUN  COMFILE2
     .
     .
     .
```

The only problem is that to RUN anything requires more than 256K of main memory. Many utilities, including DOS, can be run if you are using 320K. The advantages are immediately obvious once you realize that instead of coding

```
COPY FILE filename.ext TO DN:filename.ext
```

you only have to code

```
RUN COPY filename.ext DN:
```

(DN: designates Drive Name in these examples.)

The power of RUN is that we can access subroutines that are not dBASE III Plus subroutines just as if they were part of the dBASE III Plus system. What might we use such subroutines for?

Typically, I use subroutines that are not dBASE III Plus for data and program encryption and decryption, for running DOS BACKUP and RESTORE programs, for word processors, for spreadsheets, and so on.

I did not include CHOICES 13 and 14 of my MAINMENU in my FROMFRST PROCEDURE file. Such mass backup and restore functions are already handled well by DOS programs. We don't need to recode them, because no one expects us to reinvent the wheel. (Advanced programmers never work harder than they have to.) Hence, the end of the Main Menu can take one of two forms, depending on whether I have a hard disk system or dual floppies.

HARD DISK SYSTEM METHOD

```
CASE CHOICE=13
RUN BACKUP * YOU CAN ALSO INCLUDE APPROPRIATE SWITCHES
CASE CHOICE=14
RUN RESTORE * YOU CAN ALSO INCLUDE APPROPRIATE SWITCHES
ENDCASE
```

DUAL FLOPPY DISK METHOD

```
CASE CHOICE<=14
CLEAR
RUN DISKCOPY A: B:
ENDCASE
```

The point is simple enough: the more you use a piece of code, the more accessible it is to the main program (see fig. 3.1).

In all likelihood, the only COM or EXE files you use in your application are either utilities you've written or non-dBASE applications (word processor, telecommunications, spreadsheet). These applications will not be called often during a work session, so you need only to RUN them.

Next in ease of access are modules that can be coded in dBASE III Plus, but are not called often—for example, a module that checks each database for deleted or altered records, and then makes backup databases and packs the working databases. These functions can be written in dBASE III Plus syntax, but are used only once (if at all) during a work session. These modules are summoned from the main body by a DO.

PLUS

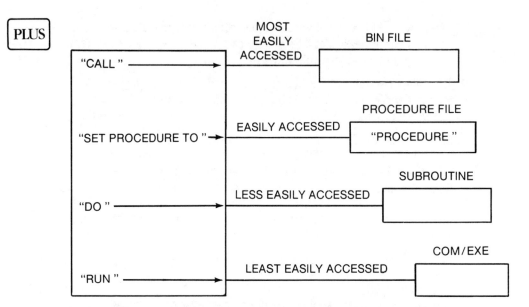

Fig. 3.1. Accessibility of code from the main program.

Modules that are not necessary for the function of the main program as a whole but are necessary to specific elements of the main program are placed in PROCEDURE files. Such a PROCEDURE File might contain modules that call up HELP files or redefine function keys. These modules are not important for the working of the main program, but are necessary for you to be able to work with the main program.

PLUS
## The CALL Command and Specialized Subroutines

Unlike previous releases of dBASE III, dBASE III Plus has no PEEK and POKE commands. Normally, this would be a pity. But Ashton-Tate has made up for the lack of POKE and PEEK by implementing two commands that were left out of dBASE III. These two commands—CALL and LOAD—will bring back memories of the heyday of dBASE II.

PLUS
LOAD is used to get a BIN file from disk and place it in memory. You don't have to tell dBASE III Plus where you'll place it in memory. All that's necessary is to give the BIN file a name not used by any other BIN file already LOADed in memory. Each BIN file is CALLed by name, not by location. This more than makes up for the loss of POKE and PEEK.

POKE and PEEK also allowed for machine-based juggling of memory (not to be confused with dBASE III Plus juggling of memory). Getting 200 bytes of BIN file into machine memory, however, required several separate POKE commands of the form

```
POKE starting address, byte1, byte2, byte3, . . .
```

Now all you have to do is place the 200 bytes into a BIN file and use the one command

```
LOAD filename
```

to achieve the same result. Before, you had to CALL the starting address; now you just CALL the name of the file. Much nicer.

In processing speed, CALLed BIN files are one level above PROCEDURE files. Both BIN and PROCEDURE files are memory-resident files. The difference is that the BIN file is in machine code to begin with. No interpreting is necessary.

The fact that CALLed BIN files are in machine code makes them useful to the system developer. I offer the following example to illustrate my point.

Many of the projects I take on are turnkey systems. The code I write is read either before or after the system runs its memory check (depending on whether or not I alter DOS), and continues being read and worked with until the client shuts the machine off. All well and good. I make it a point to have my clients purchase hard disk machines.

For obvious reasons, I like to make sure that the hard disk system doesn't die. One of the things I do is create a BIN file that parks the hard disk heads off the hard disk medium. This file isn't difficult to write. In most cases, I don't write the file at all. I get the file that comes with the system, usually on the DOS disk under the names DIAGNSTC.COM, PARK.COM, HDPARK.COM, SERVICES.COM, and others. Each of these files serves (or has a part that serves) to position the read/write heads off the disk medium, out of harm's way. The files are different only in the disk manufacturer's specifications. You can use any debugging editor to find the code that actually does the parking, and move that code to a separate BIN file. Then, with a CALL command, you can incorporate the code into your dBASE III Plus code.

# 4

# Coding in Modules

What does it mean to code in modules, and who is Dijkstra, anyway?

Starting with E. W. Dijkstra. He "invented" structured programming, a technique I hammer into my students and strive to practice in my own work. So much for Dijkstra; let's talk about structured programming.

## Doing Structured Programming

Structured programming is also called top-down programming. Use either term; both terms mean that you code in tasks. If the fact that I'm talking about tasks is a surprise to you, well, you probably did as well in college as I did.

My flowcharts begin pretty much like anything else—they're nebulous. They don't stay that way for long, however. As soon as I have a good idea of what has to be done, I write the flowchart. It shows me what tasks need to be done.

### Organizing the Program

Now comes the real work. Now comes top-down programming.

We take each task separately. The Main Menu of the program presented in Chapter 2 shows seven tasks needed to do 14 jobs. Let's look at the database access module; forget the other modules for now. We are going to concentrate on one task: database access.

Ask yourself this question: Given a database, what operations would you do on it? You may have answers like

Edit specific records
Find specific records by a key
Locate anything
Move forward and backward
Replace selected fields in selected common records
Display data
Report data
Delete records
Pack the database

You may think of other options, but these seem enough to me. Let's code what we have thus far but not worry about writing perfect dBASE III Plus code. We can make the code perfect after we have the idea in a logical form.

```
GET RESPONSE
     IF RESPONSE=EDIT
        GOTO RECORD TO EDIT
        EDIT
     IF RESPONSE=FIND
        GET KEY
        FIND KEY
        SHOW RECORD CONTAINING KEY
     IF RESPONSE=LOCATE
        GET FIELDNAME AND VALUE
        LOCATE FIELDNAME FOR VALUE
        WHILE NOT EOF
             LOCATE AGAIN? -> YES => CONTINUE
                          -> NO  => EXIT WHILE
        END WHILE
     IF RESPONSE=MOVE
        FORWARD OR BACK?
           SKIP AS INDICATED
     IF RESPONSE=REPLACE
        ALL OR NEXT N?
        GET FIELDNAME AND VALUE
        REPLACE [NEXT N] FIELDNAME WITH VALUE
     IF RESPONSE=DISPLAY
        DISPLAY WHAT?
        DISPLAY
     IF RESPONSE=REPORT
        REPORT TO PRINTER OR SCREEN?
        CONDITION?
           REPORT [FOR CONDITION] TO [PRINTER OR SCREEN]
```

```
IF RESPONSE=DELETE
   DELETE WHAT
   FOR, WHILE, NEXT N?
   IF FOR/WHILE GET CONDITION
      DELETE [NEXT N] [FOR/WHILE [CONDITION]]
IF RESPONSE=PACK
   PACK
```

One item is missing from our logical form; we haven't mentioned our database. We move through the database and manipulate it, but we don't declare it. Very well, the top of our logical form can include the lines

```
USE DATABASE
PUT INFORMATION ON SCREEN
```

## Writing the dBASE III Plus Code

The logical form of the code is complete. Now we take this logical form and transform it into a dBASE III Plus structure.

```
**DBACCESS.PRG
**
LOGICAL=.T.
USE &DATABASE INDE &DATABASE
GOTO TOP
CLEAR
DO &FRAMER
**
DO WHILE .T.
   VALUE=SPACE(40)
   DO &GETTER
   CLEAR GETS
   @ 20,0 CLEAR
   WAIT "Your choice (any other key to exit) -> " TO RESPONSE
   RESPONSE=ASC(RESPONSE)
**
   DO CASE
      CASE RESPONSE<240
         RETURN
      CASE RESPONSE=254
         @ 20,0 CLEAR
         @ 21,0 SAY "How far (use '-n' to go backward) -> " GET VALUE
         READ
         SKIP VAL(VALUE)
```

```
            CASE RESPONSE=253
               @ 20,0 CLEAR
               @ 21,0 SAY "&KEYFIELD = " GET VALUE
               READ
               FIND &VALUE
            CASE RESPONSE=252
               @ 20,0 CLEAR
               @ 21,0 SAY "Locate expression -> " GET VALUE
               READ
               SET ORDE TO
               LOCATE FOR &VALUE
               **
               DO WHILE .NOT. EOF()
                  DO &GETTER
                  CLEAR GETS
                  RECNUM=RECNO()
                  @ 23,0 SAY "Continue (Y/N)? " GET LOGICAL
                  READ
                **
                  IF LOGICAL
                     CONTINUE
                  ELSE
                     EXIT
                  ENDIF
               **
               ENDDO
               **
               SET ORDE TO 1
               GOTO RECNUM
            CASE RESPONSE=251
               DO &GETTER
               READ
            CASE RESPONSE=250
               @ 20,0 CLEAR
               ACCEPT "What field? " TO FIELDTYPE
               ACCEPT "Change it to? " TO NEWDATA
   @ 23,0 SAY "(A)ll, (F)or condition, or number of records to replace -> ";
               GET VALUE
               READ
               **
```

PLUS

PLUS

```
       DO CASE
          CASE UPPER(VALUE)="A"
             REPLACE ALL &FIELDTYPE WITH "&NEWDATA"
          CASE UPPER(VALUE)="F"
             ACCE "Condition -> " TO CONDITION
             REPLACE ALL &FIELDTYPE WITH "&NEWDATA" FOR &CONDITION
          CASE ASC(VALUE)<58
             REPLACE NEXT VAL(VALUE) &FIELDTYPE WITH "&NEWDATA"
       ENDCASE
    **
    CASE RESPONSE=249
       @ 20,0 CLEAR
       ACCE "What fields (separate fields with ',')? " TO FIELDTYPE
@ 22,0 SAY "(A)ll, (F)or condition, or number of records to display -> ";
       GET VALUE
       READ
       **
       DO CASE
          CASE UPPER(VALUE)="A"
             DISPLAY ALL &FIELDTYPE
          CASE UPPER(VALUE)="F"
             ACCE "Condition -> " TO CONDITION
             DISPLAY ALL &FIELDTYPE FOR &CONDITION
          CASE ASC(VALUE)<58
             DISPLAY NEXT VAL(VALUE) &FIELDTYPE
       ENDCASE
       **
       WAIT
       CLEAR
       DO &FRAMER
    CASE RESPONSE=248
       @ 20,0 CLEAR
@ 21,0 SAY "(A)ll, (F)or condition, or number of records to report -> ";
       GET VALUE
       READ
       ACCE "P(rinter) or S(creen)? (P/S) -> " TO PORS
       ACCE "Report name (8 char max)? -> " TO FORMTYPE
       **
       IF UPPE(VALUE) = 'F'
          ACCE "Condition -> " TO CONDITION
          CONDITION = "FOR " + CONDITION
```

```
        ELSE
           CONDITION = " "
        ENDI
        **
        IF UPPE(VALUE) = 'P'
           TOPRINT = "TO PRINT"
           SET CONS OFF
        ELSE
           TOPRINT = "PLAIN"
        ENDI
        **
        DO CASE
           CASE UPPE(VALUE) = 'A'
              REPO FORM &FORMTYPE &TOPRINT
           CASE UPPE(VALUE) = 'F'
              REPO FORM &FORMTYPE &CONDITION &TOPRINT
           CASE UPPE(VALUE) < 58
              REPO FORM &FILETYPE NEXT VAL(VALUE) &TOPRINT
        ENDC
        **
        SET CONS ON
        WAIT
        CLEA
        DO &FRAMER
     CASE RESPONSE=247
        @ 20,0 CLEAR
@ 21,0 SAY "(A)ll, (F)or condition, or number of records to delete -> ";
        GET VALUE
        READ
        **
        DO CASE
           CASE UPPER(VALUE)="A"
              DELE ALL
           CASE UPPER(VALUE)="F"
              ACCE "Condition -> " TO CONDITION
              DELE ALL FOR &CONDITION
           CASE ASC(VALUE)<58
              DELE NEXT VAL(VALUE)
        ENDCASE
        **
```

```
      CASE RESPONSE=246
          COPY TO TEMP
          USE TEMP
          SET DELE ON
          COPY TO &DATABASE
          SET DELE OFF
          INDEX ON &KEYFIELD TO &DATABASE
          USE &DATABASE INDE &DATABASE
    ENDCASE
ENDDO
```

A nice feature of the preceding routine is that it uses the function keys in the tried-and-true way of capturing the key value with a WAIT TO command. You may not be aware of this technique, so allow me this little digression.

The WAIT command in dBASE III Plus can be used to input single-character data into the program. Any character can be received, including graphics characters and those associated with the function keys and control keys. In the preceding listing, I used the WAIT command in this way to capture the values of the function keys, which I redefined for my own purposes.

Readers may wonder why I don't use the III Plus ON KEY command in place of WAIT when I capture function-key input from the user. Quite simple. I need use only one WAIT to capture any function-key input. With ON KEY, similar code would require a DO CASE . . . ENDCASE block of its own, probably external to the existing code. No thanks.

PLUS

Note that the routine doesn't include any error-checking procedures. I don't check for valid files or much else; I am protoptyping. Because the element of error checking is omitted, no attempt is made to prevent screen scrolling. Normally, I SET TALK OFF to prevent dBASE III Plus from telling me what it's doing, and to suppress error messages. The preceding code doesn't provide a means of catching errors via loops or traps; I therefore chose to leave TALK ON.

Now let's check to see whether anything else is missing. Particularly, we must make sure that each variable is either declared or passed. We find that the variables DATABASE, KEYFIELD, FRAMER, and GETTER are used but neither declared nor passed.

We have two useful methods for declaring and passing variables. First, we can include

```
PARAMETER DATABASE, KEYFIELD
```

in our module (read task) and use

```
DO DBACCESS WITH DATABASE, KEYFIELD
```

or

```
DO DBACCESS WITH "database name", "keyfield name"
```

when we call the module. Second, we can simply declare

```
PUBLIC DATABASE, KEYFIELD
DATABASE="database name"
KEYFIELD="keyfield name"
```

before we call the subroutine.

What else is missing? We haven't described our FRAMER and GETTER modules. They are also subroutines, and their names are based on our database. For instance, if our database is called CLIENTS, our framer file could be called CLIENTS.FRA, and our getter file could be CLIENTS.GET. We can build these files off our DATABASE variable using the commands

```
FRAMER=DATABASE+".SAY"
GETTER=DATABASE+".GET"
```

We also need to let our users know what the function keys do. (Key functions for a general-purpose database are given in Chapter 11.) I use the screen shown in figure 4.1.

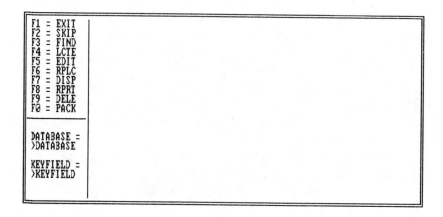

```
F1 = EXIT
F2 = SKIP
F3 = FIND
F4 = LCTE
F5 = EDIT
F6 = RPLC
F7 = DISP
F8 = RPRT
F9 = DELE
F0 = PACK


DATABASE =
>DATABASE

KEYFIELD =
>KEYFIELD
```

*Fig. 4.1. A screen display showing key functions.*

Although it looks like a time-consuming endeavor, this screen is easily generated with the MODI SCRE command. The screen is transformed into this code:

PLUS

```
CLEA
@  1,   2  SAY  "F1 = EXIT"
@  2,   2  SAY  "F2 = SKIP"
@  3,   2  SAY  "F3 = FIND"
@  4,   2  SAY  "F4 = LCTE"
@  5,   2  SAY  "F5 = EDIT"
@  6,   2  SAY  "F6 = RPLC"
@  7,   2  SAY  "F7 = DISP"
@  8,   2  SAY  "F8 = RPRT"
@  9,   2  SAY  "F9 = DELE"
@ 10,   2  SAY  "FØ = PACK"
@ 12,   2  SAY  "DATABASE ="
@ 13,   2  SAY  ">DATABASE"
@ 15,   2  SAY  "KEYFIELD ="
@ 16,   2  SAY  ">KEYFIELD"
@  Ø,   Ø  TO 18, 79      DOUBLE
@ 11,   1  TO 11,  13
@  1,  13  TO 17,  13
```

When using a box screen for database access, we naturally have to make sure that our data fits. The box parameters give us a square with corners at screen coordinates (0,0), (0,79), (18,0), and (18,79). We can easily fit a "personality profile" FRAMER into this area (see fig. 4.2).

```
First Name:
Last Name :

City         :                              State:
                                            Zip  :

Age          :
Profession   :
Hobby        :
Last Book Read:
Latest Accomplishment:
Why they do what they do:
Quote        :
Profile      :
```

*Fig. 4.2. A "profile" FRAMER.*

The FRAMER can be coded as follows:

```
@ 2, 16 SAY "First Name:"
@ 3, 16 SAY "Last Name :"
@ 5, 16 SAY "City        :                                    State:"
@ 6, 60 SAY "Zip       :"
@ 8, 16 SAY "Age          :"
@ 9, 16 SAY "Profession   :"
@ 10, 16 SAY "Hobby        :"
@ 11, 16 SAY "Last Book Read:"
@ 12, 16 SAY "Latest Accomplishment:"
@ 13, 16 SAY "Why they do what they do:"
@ 14, 16 SAY "Quote        :"
@ 15, 16 SAY "Profile      :"
```

The GETTER can be similarly coded.

How does the access module come together? If we are using the CUSTOMER database, we have

```
DATABASE="CUSTOMER"
DO DBACCESS
```

Our work on the database access module is complete. Now we can move on to the other modules.

## Tracing the Logic

Let's look at what we did. We did top-down, or structured, programming. Our logic followed this path:

1. We defined the problem.

2. We broke the problem into modules.

3. We defined the modules.

4. We broke the modules into their constituent modules.

5. We coded the constituents.

6. We ran the constituents and debugged them as necessary.

7. We coded only what was necessary to maintain our task philosophy.

8. We ran the modules and debugged them as necessary.

9. We coded the problem.

10. We linked, or chained, the modules together.

11. We ran the program and debugged as necessary.

12. We were done.

Two new terms appear in step 10: *link* and *chain*. Readers with assembly language or compiler backgrounds now nod knowingly; others pale. No need. dBASE III Plus makes linking and chaining simple.

*Linking* simply means that we get all the separate pieces together in the most logical way possible. Usually we link programs in the order that we use them. Linking in that way can be difficult, however, if some subroutines are called repeatedly; the result is spaghetti code. PROCEDURE files simplify linking to some extent. Repeatedly accessed subroutines are identified by SET PROCEDURE TO.

*Chaining* describes the method that structured programs use: only one part of the program—the necessary part—is in memory at any time. Getting the parts into memory when needed is quite simple: you tell dBASE III Plus to DO something. The PRG file that is the object of the DO is then loaded into memory. Normally a pointer of some kind is placed in the calling program so that dBASE "knows" where to return to.

If you are chaining, you might write a top-level file like this:

```
*** TOP LEVEL PRG FILE
***
DO PROGNUM1
DO PROGNUM2
DO PROGNUM3
DO PROGNUM4

   .   .   .

   .   .   .
```

Structured programming gets us into the habit of modular coding. We code in specific groups. The database access module, DBACCESS, is now a task-oriented module that can be used for many of our database tasks. Likewise, our other task-oriented modules, LISTING, MAILLIST, and so on, can be used for a wide variety of purposes.

The following sections deal, in more detail, with the concept of modular coding.

# Combining the Subroutines

I've spent many words telling you how subroutines can help and hurt a dBASE III Plus program (see Chapter 3, "Subroutines and dBASE III Plus PROCEDURE Files"). I've discussed memory, file and buffer size, disk I/O, and other topics, all pertaining to the efficient use of memory space, disk space, and files. This section and the next are the beginning of the return on our investment. We're going to start hoarding our solutions.

Let's consider an inventory system as an example. Any inventory system will do, any at all. All inventory systems share many characteristics. Part number, part description, quantity in stock, cost per item, total inventory value, and reorder level are practically universal to inventory systems.

Next, we consider what operations are likely to be performed on an inventory. We do our standard manipulations—edit, delete, display, add, and so on—but we also do things unique to inventories, such as

Print purchases
Update inventory as purchases are made
Print stock report (what's moving, what's not, what's left)

These procedures form a fairly complete program for all inventory systems. Well, not quite. What we have mentioned can definitely be used by all inventory systems. Users of larger inventory systems, however, are also interested in location of stock (warehouse number or city) and reorder quantity; and they may need to break out the stock price into a separate database containing price and quantity-discount information.

Our interest here, however, is in the core programs necessary to all inventory systems. We use the INVENTORY database, which is structured as follows:

```
Structure for database   : C:INVENTORY.DBF
Number of data records   : 4
Date of last update      : 07/02/85
```

| Field | Field name | Type | Width | Dec |
|-------|-----------|------|-------|-----|
| 1 | PARTNUM | Character | 10 | |
| 2 | DESCRPTION | Character | 30 | |
| 3 | INSTOCK | Numeric | 10 | 2 |
| 4 | UNITS | Character | 5 | |
| 5 | PERITEM | Numeric | 10 | 2 |
| 6 | TOTALVALUE | Numeric | 10 | 2 |
| 7 | ORDERLEVEL | Numeric | 10 | 2 |

```
** Total **                          86
```

We also use the database PRINTPLT for printing the total customer order. PRINTPLT is structured as follows:

Structure for database   : C:PRINTPLT.DBF
Number of data records  : 0
Date of last update      : 07/02/86

| Field | Field name | Type | Width | Dec |
|---|---|---|---|---|
| 1 | DESCRPTION | Character | 20 | |
| 2 | QUANT | Numeric | 10 | 2 |
| 3 | PARTNUM | Character | 10 | |
| 4 | DISCNT | Numeric | 10 | 2 |
| 5 | SUBTTL | Numeric | 10 | 2 |

** Total **                              61

And, of course, we need the programs that put the subroutines all together. In this case, I've created a menu file that calls up our different routines, one of which also calls up a PROCEDURE file with the necessary subroutines for the ordering screen (see fig. 4.3).

```
F7 = MTNC   INVENTORY DATABASE MANAGEMENT (ADD, DELETE, VIEW, ETC)
F8 = ORDR   ENTER CUSTOMER ORDERS AND PRINT SALES FORM
F9 = EOD    GENERATE END OF DAY REPORTS
FØ = EXIT   RETURN TO WHATEVER
```

*Fig. 4.3. A menu for calling up subroutines and procedures.*

The screen directs the user to press the function key corresponding to the required activity. Typing F7 will cause the user to enter the database access module, DBACCESS. Note that in the following code, which generates the screen and WAITs for a response, I again use the WAIT command to capture a keystroke and place it into a variable.

```
@ 2,  2 SAY "F7 = MTNC   INVENTORY DATABASE MANAGEMENT (ADD, "
@ 2, 49 SAY " DELETE, VIEW, ETC)"
@ 4,  2 SAY "F8 = ORDR   ENTER CUSTOMER ORDERS AND PRINT SALES FORM"
@ 6,  2 SAY "F9 = EOD    GENERATE END OF DAY REPORTS"
@ 8,  2 SAY "FØ = EXIT   RETURN TO WHATEVER"
@ Ø,  Ø TO 10, 79   DOUBLE
@ 1, 13 TO 9, 13
```

```
WAIT "TYPE THE FUNCTION KEY OF YOUR CHOICE " TO RESPONSE
RESPONSE=ASC(RESPONSE)
**
IF RESPONSE>249 .OR. RESPONSE<=246
   RETURN
ENDIF
**
DO CASE
   CASE RESPONSE=248
      DO ORDER
   CASE RESPONSE=249
      DO DBACCESS
   CASE RESPONSE=247
      ? "PLEASE MAKE SURE THE PAPER AND THE PRINTER ARE READY"
      WAIT
      USE INVENTORY INDE PARTNUM
      REPORT FORM EOD1 NOEJECT TO PRINT
      REPORT FORM EOD2 FOR INSTOCK<ORDERLEVEL TO PRINT
ENDCASE
**
**EOF


**ORDER.PRG FILE FOR INVENTORY CONTROL
**
SET PROCEDURE TO ORDRFILE
SELE D
USE PRINTPLT
SELE A
USE INVENTORY INDE PARTNUM
AGAIN=.T.
DO ORDRFMT
**
DO WHILE AGAIN
   SELE A
   STORE 0 TO QUANTITY,DISCOUNT,SUBTOTAL
   PN=SPACE(10)
   DESCRIPTION=SPACE(30)
   @ 15,0 CLEAR
   @ 20,10 SAY "Part Number -> " GET PN PICTURE "XXXXXXXXXX"
   @ 22,10 SAY "Description -> " GET DESCRIPTION
   READ
   **
```

```
       DO CASE
          CASE PN <> ' '
              SET INDEX TO PARTNUM
              FIND &PN
              **
              IF EOF(). AND. PN<>PARTNUM
                 SET COLOR TO G*
                 @ 15, 0 SAY "ITEM NOT FOUND"
                 WAIT
                 SET COLOR TO W, ,
                 LOOP
              ENDI
          CASE DESCRIPTION <> ' '
              SET INDEX TO DESCRIPT
              FIND &DESCRIPTION
              IF EOF(). AND.  DESCRIPTION<>DESCRPTION
                 SET COLOR TO G*
                 @ 15, 0 SAY "ITEM NOT FOUND"
                 WAIT
                 SET COLOR TO W, ,
                 LOOP
              ENDI
          OTHE
              SET COLOR TO G*
              @ 15, 0 SAY "Part Number and/or Description missing"
              WAIT
              SET COLOR TO W, ,
              LOOP
       ENDC
       DO ORDRGET WITH QUANTITY, DISCOUNT, SUBTOTAL
       READ
       REPLACE INSTOCK WITH INSTOCK-QUANTITY, TOTALVALUE WITH PERITEM*INSTOCK
       SELE D
       APPEND BLANK
       REPLACE DESCRPTION WITH A->DESCRPTION, SUBTTL WITH SUBTOTAL, ;
               QUANT WITH QUANTITY, PARTNUM WITH A->PARTNUM;
               DISCNT WITH DISCOUNT
       @ 23, 0 SAY "Order again? " GET AGAIN
       READ
ENDDO
DO PRINTPLT
```

```
**ORDRFILE.PRG PROCEDURE FILE FOR INVENTORY DATABASE
PROCEDURE ORDRFMT
CLEAR
@  3,  3  SAY "Part Number   :"
@  5,  3  SAY "Description   :"
@  7,  3  SAY "(Quantity      x     Unit Cost)  -   Discount(%)  ="
@  7, 54  SAY "          Total"
@  1,  0  TO 10, 79    DOUBLE
RETURN
**
PROCEDURE ORDRGET
PARA QUANTITY, DISCOUNT, SUBTOTAL
@ 3, 19 SAY PARTNUM
@ 5, 19 SAY DESCRPTION
@ 9, 3 SAY SPACE(76)
@ 9, 6 GET QUANTITY
@ 9, 28 SAY PERITEM
@ 9, 44 GET DISCOUNT PICTURE "999"
READ
DISCOUNT=(PERITEM*DISCOUNT)/100
SUBTOTAL=QUANTITY*(PERITEM-DISCOUNT)
@ 9, 44 SAY DISCOUNT PICTURE "99999999.99"
@ 9, 62 SAY SUBTOTAL PICTURE "99999999.99"
RETURN
**
PROCEDURE PRINTPLT
SELE D
SET FILTER TO TRIM(DESCRPTION) <> ' 'CLEAR
CLEAR
ACCE "Customer Name    -> " TO NAME
ACCE "Customer Address -> " TO ADDRESS
ACCE "City, State, ZIP -> " TO CSZ
WAIT "LINE UP THE PAPER AND TYPE ANY KEY WHEN READY"
REPORT FORM PRINTPLT NOEJECT TO PRINT
EJECT
ZAP
SET FILTER TO
RETURN
```

Now we have an inventory-control and order-entry system. Simple, neat. We already have our basic database access module (see Chapter 13). We link the modules with the menu file, again using the function keys and some parameter passing. Linking modules with the menu makes them more universal than unique in scope. With this design, we can incorporate another database, PRICES, if our needs warrant it. We can also make the minor modifications necessary to include a LOCATION field if needed.

Note that we created part of our system much earlier. The part we just created will no doubt be used again and again with few or no modifications. Our calling system, however, may have modifications because the logic flow may be unique to a given environment.

The fact that we can use modules over and over leads us to our next subject.

# Building a Library of Modules

The templates DATABASE ACCESS MODULE, LABEL/ENVELOPE MAKER, WORDSTAR MAILMERGE MODULE, and "WHERE SENT" MODULE, all of which are used to track manuscript markets, are shown in Chapter 13.

You'll notice that the files in Chapter 13 share many subroutines. They do so by DOing the subroutines, passing a parameter or two, or accessing the subroutines through a PROCEDURE file. Originally, all the subroutines were complete programs in themselves. But at some point the light came on, and I realized I had no need for all those duplicate files on disk. The only differences were in the FRAMER, GETTER, DBF, and NDX file names, so I started building a library.

Library files are not new to high-level languages or dBASE III Plus. Many languages (BASIC and MASM, for example) have runtime libraries, which are referenced during running, compilation, or both. This fact, along with the logic of dBASE III Plus, provides a strong argument for the implementation of library files in dBASE III Plus.

Essentially, your building blocks should be linked by function. For instance, you could partition a disk along logical lines like those found in the following TREE listing:

```
DIRECTORY PATH LISTING FOR VOLUME DBASE3BOOK


Path: \OTHER
Subdirectories: none


Path: \DBACCESS
Subdirectories: none
```

```
Path: \ACCOUNTI
Subdirectories: GL
                AP
                AR
                INVENTOR
                PAYROLL
                GJ

Path: \ACCOUNTI\GL
Subdirectories: none

Path: \ACCOUNTI\AP
Subdirectories: none

Path: \ACCOUNTI\AR
Subdirectories: none

Path: \ACCOUNTI\INVENTOR
Subdirectories: none

Path: \ACCOUNTI\PAYROLL
Subdirectories: none

Path: \ACCOUNTI\GJ
Subdirectories: none

Path: \MAILFUNC
Subdirectories: none

Path: \123TODB3
Subdirectories: none

Path: \MPLN2DB3
Subdirectories: none
```

Each directory contains separate modules with functions common to all
the general dBASE III Plus projects. I can modify and use the modules
needed for each project. For a service-oriented business, more
modifications may be necessary to the MAILFUNC modules than to
others. Some businesses that already use Lotus® 1-2-3® or Multiplan®
may need a little juggling of those modules without needing even to
touch the ACCOUNTING modules. A merchandise-oriented business
needs inventory control.

The MPLN2DB3 module was designed to provide a one-way bridge for getting a client's Multiplan files into dBASE III Plus format. Later, another client needed a two-way bridge. The changes were easy enough to install and the modules have been used many times since.

Keeping the routines separate on disk makes it easy to link them for different applications. Because each routine is complete, I don't have to worry about making fancy arrangements to use any one on a particular project. I determine which routines I need, make whatever (usually minor) adjustments are necessary for a project, determine whether the routines should be PROCEDUREized, and I'm done. If a new routine is developed, it goes in the library, with external documentation describing its function, purpose, original environment, and so on. Often I name the linked PROCEDURE files a library designate, such as ACCOUNT.LIB, recognizing the fact that dBASE III Plus defaults to but is not limited to the PRG extension. Thus, my files often contain lines like

```
SET PROC TO ACCOUNT.LIB
SET PROC TO GL.LIB
SET PROC TO MAILLIST.LIB
SET PROC TO 123TODB3.LIB
```

and so on. These files execute with no problem.

I emphasize tasks rather than jobs, modular coding, and writing tight, efficient code, because I enjoy work but am not a workaholic. Readers with a background in mathematics will appreciate the following story, and recognize its truth in the previous discussion.

An engineer walks into a room and sees a fire in a corner and a bucket of sand close by. The engineer dumps the bucket of sand on the fire and puts it out, then leaves the room. A physicist walks into a room and sees a fire in a corner and a bucket of sand close by. The physicist pours a ring of sand around the fire, sits down, and observes the fire. A mathematician walks into a room and sees a fire in a corner and a bucket of sand close by. The mathematician realizes the problem can be solved and walks out of the room.

Advanced programmers don't like to work any harder than they have to. We're all mathematicians at heart.

# 5
# Knowing dBASE III Plus's Strengths

Because you're reading this book, I assume that you have purchased dBASE III Plus or are considering its purchase. Perhaps you purchased dBASE III Plus because you have database work to do and you feel like going with the first and foremost, even though you don't know too much about the program. By now you do know that dBASE III Plus is a logical language and an applications-development language. Now comes the time to investigate the strengths of dBASE III Plus.

Inherent in the preceding statement is an acknowledgment of dBASE III Plus's weaknesses. One of its principal weaknesses—at least according to many detractors—is "slow" execution. I should point out, however, that I do not feel that dBASE III Plus is slower than the competition. If you put any two products side by side, you'll generally find that they do many things the same and some things differently. Hence, the "slowness" has never concerned me. I've learned to code around whatever slowness I feel exists. Much of this chapter is concerned with decreasing execution time.

My explorations in dBASE III Plus have revealed a multitude of strengths, and I'm sure I haven't uncovered all of them. (I would be interested if any readers are willing to share their discoveries.) This chapter deals with those strengths, first on a theoretical level (the design of databases and index files) and then on a practical level (how using or not using certain commands affects the behavior of dBASE III Plus).

The evolution of Ashton-Tate's best-known product is interesting. Originally it was called Vulcan (yes, after Mr. Spock's home world). Then it mutated into dBASE II. dBASE II went through many revisions as the world went from 8-bit machines to multiuser 8-bit machines to 16-bit machines. The advent of the 16-bit PC brought us dBASE III.

When dBASE was released, there were few competitors in the microcomputer DBMS field. There were systems that ran on the PICK operating system, but I doubt that any readers except programmers and developers have heard of it. And there were tremendous systems written for UNIX™; the problem with these systems was UNIX, and the lack of any forgiving interface.

Anyway, more competitors came into being. After all, there are only three things you can do with a computer: word processing, spreadsheets, and DBMS. dBASE III stood at the top of the heap for some time, but it began to lose its edge. dBASE III was, after all, just a 16-bit version of dBASE II. Yes, it had more power and more abilities, but it still had the feel and ring of a primordial system, something still struggling to do what it had to do. The worst problem: dBASE III was still difficult for a neophyte to use. Some of dBASE III's competitors could be run directly from the box (without looking—much—at the documentation). Most people thought that was technically impossible with dBASE III.

PLUS

The next stage of evolution was a product that retained the constructions of dBASE II and III—Ashton-Tate didn't want to lose loyal customers, after all—and yet was much easier to use than was dBASE III itself. The solution was dBASE III Plus. III Plus is unique in its structural proximity to C; anyone reading through the documentation realizes that Ashton-Tate must be preparing to release III Plus or similar products into more arenas than PC and MS-DOS®.

Because of the changes, dBASE III Plus has caught on well with developers and programmers, including those not already familiar with dBASE III. III itself was supported by a number of third-party developers; consider the speed at which support became available for III Plus. While writing the 2nd edition of this book, I looked at several of the hundreds of available add-on packages. I chose those described in Chapter 12 for their ease of use, viability for the developer and programmer, availability, and support.

The fact is that Ashton-Tate has claimed the lead once again in the micro DBMS field. A recent announcement says that they've sold so many packages they're celebrating by offering a Porsche to a lucky person. I should have such luck. But the hoopla speaks eloquently: III Plus is accepted in all areas of microcomputer use.

# Databases with Keyfields and Related Fields

Does database size and structure affect dBASE III Plus's performance? Program I/O takes a great deal of time, but if the code is tight and to the point, program I/O usually occurs only once. The time needed for data I/O, however, is horrendous.

We can choose from several techniques for controlling and minimizing the time required for data I/O. Two techniques have been mentioned earlier: using an electronic disk, and changing the number of available buffers.

But what if neither method is satisfactory? You design the database so that important information can be easily and quickly read. You can minimize data I/O by recognizing how dBASE III Plus looks at databases. The key to minimizing data I/O is INDEXed files. The INDEXing is important, but it is not as crucial as designing the database so as to maximize the benefits provided by INDEXing.

When you are designing a database, especially one that is going to be INDEXed and REINDEXed fairly often, you should follow two rules:

1.  Keyfields go at the top of the database.

2.  Related fields should be grouped together.

The following STUDENTS database applies these rules.

```
Structure for database    : C:STUDENTS.DBF
Number of data records    : 2
Date of last update       : 04/12/85
```

| Field | Field name | Type | Width | Dec |
|---|---|---|---|---|
| 1 | SNAME | Character | 30 | |
| 2 | SADDRESS | Character | 30 | |
| 3 | SCITY | Character | 30 | |
| 4 | SSTATE | Character | 2 | |
| 5 | SZIP | Character | 10 | |
| 6 | SPHONE | Character | 10 | |
| 7 | MAJOR | Character | 10 | |
| 8 | MINOR | Character | 10 | |
| 9 | CLASSOF | Numeric | 2 | |
| 10 | CLUB1 | Character | 10 | |
| 11 | CLUB2 | Character | 10 | |
| 12 | SPORT1 | Character | 10 | |
| 13 | SPORT2 | Character | 10 | |

| | | | |
|---|---|---|---|
| 14 | ASSOC1 | Character | 10 |
| 15 | ASSOC2 | Character | 10 |
| 16 | HONOR1 | Character | 10 |
| 17 | HONOR2 | Character | 10 |
| 18 | PNAME | Character | 30 |
| 19 | PADDRESS | Character | 30 |
| 20 | PCITY | Character | 30 |
| 21 | PSTATE | Character | 2 |
| 22 | PZIP | Character | 10 |
| 23 | PPHONE | Character | 10 |
| ** Total ** | | | 327 |

In this database, student information is kept in one block; next comes alumni information, and then parent information.

What makes this data structure efficient? Primarily, the structure is efficient because it follows the two rules I've stated. dBASE does not have to look through several fields to find an indexkey; INDEXing is faster. Related blocks of data, such as the information needed when the Class of '85 leaves the school, can be COPYed, REPLACEd, or UPDATEd in one operation: dBASE doesn't have to get fields from positions 1, 5, 14, 15, 22, 30, and so on. When databases exceed a quarter megabyte of space, such niceties are appreciated.

How do you design a database this way? Two things come to mind; both have to do with forethought. First, you must recognize one characteristic of most clients: they are "sure" that every record needs 200 fields. Perhaps that is true for one or two functions of the program, but it certainly is not true for all functions. About 90 percent of day-to-day business operations do not use all the data the customers want in their databases. You must know when all the data is necessary and when only selected portions are necessary; then code accordingly.

Second, all dBASEs have a feature you can use to combine into one field what might otherwise take several fields. This feature can decrease database size.

Consider a partial database that keeps track of auto insurance policies. The insurance company keeps track of auto policies with information on MAKE, MODEL, YEAR, and VID. Our structure for the database is

```
Structure for database    : C:AUTOPLCY.DBF
Number of data records  : 1000
Date of last update       : 05/28/85
```

| Field | Field name | Type | Width | Dec |
|-------|-----------|------|-------|-----|
| 1 | MAKE | Character | 3 | |
| 2 | MODEL | Character | 5 | |
| 3 | YEAR | Character | 2 | |
| 4 | VID | Character | 13 | |
| . | | | | |
| . | | | | |
| . | | | | |

Following these are several fields of less interest.

This structure is worthy, but it produces a large database. The insurance agency has told us that this information is looked at once or twice and after that is needed only rarely. The data is neither INDEXed nor SORTed on, but it is nonetheless important when you win the bet with the insurance company and your car is stolen.

A solution follows:

Structure for database　　: C:autoplcy.dbf
Number of data records　 : 1000
Date of last update　　　 : 05/28/85

| Field | Field name | Type | Width | Dec |
|-------|-----------|------|-------|-----|
| 22 | AUTO_INFO | Character | 36 | |

When this field is filled at data entry, we can use the following command line:

```
@ x,y SAY "Auto Information" GET AUTO_INFO;
    PICTURE "mk!!! mdl!!!!! yrXX vid!!!!!!!!!!!!!"
```

We have decreased the size of our database on several fronts. First, the header block of the database has to keep track of three fewer fields. The database itself has three fewer fields to be scanned when looking for other information. The data is always accessible and now is stored in one line that actually makes more sense—to insurance people—than before. Finally, note that I moved the data down to a less important position in the database (field 22).

This entire discussion should give you ideas about how to compress database size and hence speed up applications. The preceding example is but one use of the many PICTURE and PICTURE FUNCTION methods that can be used to decrease execution time. Remember that these two @ GET qualifiers can and will be limited by the dBASE III Plus

CONFIG.DB BUCKET command. You must make sure that your BUCKET is large enough to hold all the PICTURES and PICTURE FUNCTIONS you include in your FMT, SCR, and similar files. A final caveat: Don't go wild when you combine fields with PICTURE and PICTURE FUNCTION qualifiers. Remember that users are human and easily confused.

Is there a decided benefit to using the PICTURE and PICTURE FUNCTION qualifiers? For the answer, check the section "Hiding Pictures in Databases" later in this chapter.

## The Blank Record, or When Nothing is Something

I have a subtle little technique that has impressed clients no end. The technique is simple to use, does not take up tons of room on disk or in memory, can be used on SORTed and INDEXed files with no difficulty, and makes your input, edit, and work screens look jazzy. The best use of the technique has been in applications where someone other than the keypunch operator has to use the database.

What is the technique? Simply place a blank record in your database. The record doesn't have to be totally blank; blank numeric database fields always contain zeros until you fill the fields. Most important is that the keyfield or fields you INDEX on must be blank.

To insert the blank record, you take an INDEXed database and APPEND BLANK. Then you never fill that one blank. Instead, you put new data in other APPENDed BLANKs. The INDEXed file automatically pops that blank record to the top of the file. When you first open (USE) the INDEXed database and DO some FRAMER and GETTER files, you immediately come to a clean, handsome screen. A screen like the one shown in figure 5.1 is much more pleasing than an unhighlighted (SET INTENSITY OFF) screen or a screenful of information that could be confusing, or at least distracting.

This simple technique, when used with any kind of custom data display, adds a highly professional touch.

## Hiding Pictures in Databases

Now that you understand why a blank record can be a useful part of a database, I'm going to tell you the other side of the story. Sometimes, the format of an input screen needs to be changed in accordance with the value in a field or a memory variable.

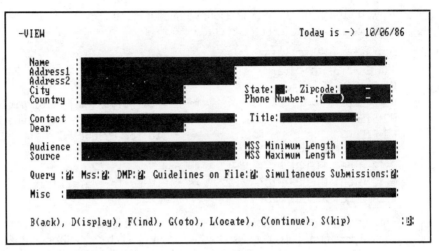

Fig. 5.1. A data-entry screen.

An example can be seen in the insurance industry. Each type of insurance policy—preferred auto, standard homeowner, electronics and data processing, tenant homeowner, and so on—has associated risk, coverage, and underwriter information. The nature of that information is different for each type of policy.

The following database shows an application of this principle.

```
Record#  INDEXFIELD FIELD1            FIELD2               FIELD3
    221  format-1   mkAAA  yr99       lien no xxxxxxxxxxx  lienholder AAAAAAAA
    222  format-2   oldcode  XXXXXX   newcode  XXXXXXX     password XXXXXXXX
    223  format-3   carrier AAAAAAAAAAAA codetype XXXXXXXXXXX frequency 9999 AAAAA
```

Fields FIELD1, FIELD2, and FIELD3 are each 20 characters long. None of those fields holds information about individuals or items; instead, they hold pictures for screen formats 1, 2, and 3.

Before you learn how to use these pictures, consider where I have chosen to hide them. They are not in a memory file or in a database containing various picture formats. Instead, the pictures are in a database containing data—the data that is gathered through the input screens in which those pictures are used.

How are the pictures used? The following code demonstrates the elegance and simplicity of this method.

```
USE database INDEX indexfile
FINDER="format-"+var            ** var is the alpha code 1, 2, or 3
FIND &FINDER
F1=FIELD1                       ** F1 now holds the FIELD1 picture
F2=FIELD2                       ** for the corresponding alpha code;
F3=FIELD3                       ** ditto for F2 and F3.
APPEND BLANK
@ 10,0 GET FIELD1 PICT "&F1"    ** And now F1, F2, and F3 become the
@ 12,0 GET FIELD2 PICT "&F2"    ** PICTUREs for data input.
@ 14,0 GET FIELD3 PICT "&F3"
```

Throughout this book, I emphasize modularity and library building for code. These principles apply also to the design of databases; although it is true that no one database can be transported unmodified into several unique environments. The database must be modified for each environment. (This is true also of vertical market packages, but that is a slightly different arena.)

Here I want to emphasize how hiding pictures in databases can allow you some flexibility in their design without changing their design. Newspeak, huh?

Not really. You can create some specialized "generic" databases that will fit a good number of applications. Such databases could be 40 fields long, with each field about 100 characters. I use these sizes—40x100—because the upper limit on record size is 4,000 bytes. Please note that I don't normally advocate creating records of this size, which is far too large to be used routinely. But 20x100 is acceptable for these types of applications.

In any case, a 40x100 (or 20x100) database is pretty generic. A good variety of information and information types will fit into something of that size. Your job is to create in such a database, records that provide templates for each field. In other words, a generic 20-field database would have 20 field templates. Depending on your needs, these templates could be in 20 separate records or in a single record. Each new application gets a new set of templates, but not necessarily a new database.

This allows you to create a library of databases for quick work, and a "tool bag" for applications on the fly. Once the debugging, modifying, or whatever is done, you can use the templates to generate the database that will be used regularly in the application.

# Masterbases and Smaller Databases

Unless a database is sorted along the lines of our search, the PC spends a lot of time filling buffers with useless information every time we search. Even then, all the information in each record of the database probably isn't needed for every database operation. Forty fields on the screen may seem impressive, but in reality the screen is busy and confusing, and the search is time-consuming to code and generate.

One of the easiest ways around this problem is to use the concept of *masterbase* versus *database*. This is a concept that, frankly, I'm surprised more programmers don't know about.

Imagine a single database that holds an incredibly large amount of information; any metropolitan phone directory is a good example. Specifically, let's consider the Yellow Pages for Boston, Chicago, New York City, or some such locale. This thick rack of information is all-encompassing. As Ed McMahon says to Johnny Carson, "Every number you ever wanted to dial is in that book."

This is probably true, Ed. The listing of phone numbers is so complete that we could call it a master list of phone numbers for the city in question. A master list that includes ALL the information isn't a simple database. It is a masterbase.

But no one, not even dBASE, wants to read from A to Z to find a particular number. Fortunately, the Yellow Pages have been divided into smaller sections with titles like "Auto Repair," "Nurseries," "Schools," "Taxidermists," and so on. Each of these smaller sections is extensive and complete, but only in a certain field of interest. Because these sections don't include ALL information about EVERYTHING, they're not masterbases. They're databases.

How does this apply to dBASE III Plus and the wonderful world of DBMS? Although you may create a file that is all-inclusive for something (students, auto parts, stock quotes), chances are you'll never want to go through the entire file at any one sitting. It is easier for you and dBASE III Plus to COPY the information of interest from the masterbase to a smaller, working database. Do whatever you want to do with the information in the smaller database and then, using UPDATE, etc., transfer the database back to the masterbase.

Although the process of transferring may take a moment longer than you'd like, processing information in the smaller database will make up for the COPY and UPDATE time, and you won't compromise the integrity of your master file should something dastardly happen.

The method of pulling all required records from our masterbase into a smaller database is useful, however, only if we can make certain assumptions about our necessary data:

1. The total number of records of necessary data should be significantly smaller than the entire master database.

2. The structure of the necessary database should be small compared to the structure of the entire database. Small is ten or fewer fields. (More on setting up databases later.)

3. The changes to be made should be different for each record.

This technique may take time at the outset, but we benefit because we then work with a smaller database file, and operations on the data are more time-efficient.

Suppose, for example, that we want to enter new addresses for all 1985 graduates of Whatsamatta U. Out of more than 5,000 students, only 150 managed to graduate; we need to change only those 150 addresses. Our database is called STUDENTS. The database is INDEXed on SNAME, the SNAME field is 30 characters wide, and names are entered according to the following pattern:

LASTNAME, FIRSTNAME, MIDDLE NAME OR INITIAL

The database has the following structure:

Structure for database     : C:students.dbf
Number of data records  : 2
Date of last update        : ~~01/01/80

| Field | Field name | Type | Width | Dec |
|---|---|---|---|---|
| 1 | SNAME | Character | 30 | |
| 2 | SADDRESS | Character | 30 | |
| 3 | SCITY | Character | 30 | |
| 4 | SSTATE | Character | 2 | |
| 5 | SZIP | Character | 10 | |
| 6 | SPHONE | Character | 10 | |
| 7 | MAJOR | Character | 10 | |
| 8 | MINOR | Character | 10 | |
| 9 | CLASSOF | Numeric | 2 | |
| 10 | CLUB1 | Character | 10 | |
| 11 | CLUB2 | Character | 10 | |
| 12 | SPORT1 | Character | 10 | |
| 13 | SPORT2 | Character | 10 | |
| 14 | ASSOC1 | Character | 10 | |

| 15 | ASSOC2 | Character | 10 |
|----|---------|-----------|-----|
| 16 | HONOR1 | Character | 10 |
| 17 | HONOR2 | Character | 10 |
| 18 | PNAME | Character | 30 |
| 19 | PADDRESS | Character | 30 |
| 20 | PCITY | Character | 30 |
| 21 | PSTATE | Character | 2 |
| 22 | PZIP | Character | 10 |
| 23 | PPHONE | Character | 10 |
| ** Total ** | | | 327 |

We want to make changes to the records of all students in the class of '85. The following code does the job.

```
***UPDATER.PRG
USE STUDENTS
COPY TO GRADUATE FIELD SNAME, SADDRESS, SCITY, SSTATE, SZIP, SPHONE;
        FOR CLASSOF=YEAR(DATE())
SELECT 2
USE GRADUATE
INDEX ON SNAME TO GRADUATE
@ 20,0 SAY "CTRL-W to save and continue"
*
DO WHILE .NOT. EOF()
   EDIT
   SKIP
ENDDO
*
SELECT 1
USE STUDENTS INDEX SNAME
UPDATE ON SNAME FROM GRADUATE;
        REPLACE SADDRESS WITH GRADUATE->SADDRESS, ;
        SCITY WITH GRADUATE->SCITY, SSTATE WITH GRADUATE->SSTATE, ;
        SZIP WITH GRADUATE->SZIP, SPHONE WITH GRADUATE->SPHONE
CLOSE DATABASES
ERASE GRADUATE.DBF
ERASE GRADUATE.NDX
```

This method would make no sense if the same changes were made to every set; the REPLACE command would be easier to use in that case. But if the assumptions listed above are valid, we can use buffers quite nicely with this method.

First, we create a temporary database file called GRADUATE, into which we copy all the necessary records (everyone who is CLASSOF '85). We INDEX that temporary file on the student's name to make the file contiguous on a given field. This new database is contiguous in that it contains the records we're interested in: we've taken the separate CLASSOF '85 students and made a new database contiguous on that field. We make our changes and copy our edited database back to our master file. The necessary data is small enough to be kept in buffers, and very little, if any, I/O occurs.

The question comes up whether UPDATER.PRG embodies the best method. That I can't answer. As an alternate approach, however, I can offer some code that uses one of the strengths of dBASE III Plus; the routine is listed as NEWUPDTR.PRG (see the section called "Performing Sophisticated Searches with SET UNIQUE OFF/on" in Chapter 7). Differences between UPDATER.PRG and NEWUPDTR.PRG are discussed after the program listing.

NEWUPDTR.PRG keeps two databases active and works exclusively with INDEXed files. The STUDENTS database is INDEXed on CLASSOF. NEWUPDTR.PRG first FINDs an entry that meets the criterion (the first CLASSOF '85 entry in the database), and then COPYs WHILE that criterion is met. Changes are made to the new database in the same way, but data is written back to the original database according to an NDX ijn the NEWUPDTR.PRG. All in all, the two methods are valid. With larger subsets, I would choose the NEWUPDTR.PRG file.

What I want to emphasize in this discussion is a specific memory-management technique. The technique is to pull the necessary information from a much larger database and put it in a smaller temporary database. Work is done to the data in the smaller database. We create a smaller database that contains what we want, make our changes, then UPDATE the main database. This method makes for efficient data structures, as mentioned earlier.

We can use two or more temporary databases that pull information from a larger database. The only time the entire database in the Whatsamatta U. example is referenced is when records are added and edited. Every other operation references a subset of the fields used. In truth, STUDENTS.DBF is not large enough to warrant this method, but the example holds. This method temporarily decreases the number of files available in memory while minimizing the data I/O execution time.

An extension of this method is to have on disk two or more databases that have similar fields and share information. In many cases, data entry and editing need be done to only one of the databases; the others can be UPDATEd, APPENDed, or REPLACEd from the first. As always, an example follows.

The managers of a local video store want to keep track of VHS, Beta, and disk rentals. The managers also want a comprehensive list giving for each movie the supplier (with all related data), the store's catalog number, rental frequency, other suppliers, date received, and other data that won't really help in this example.

Obviously, the data has two distinct functions. One is keeping in-house records of orders; the other is compiling information on customers. Both functions use the store's catalog number. Data is entered only once—to the larger database at the time of initial data entry. All necessary information can be APPENDed to the second database after the new information has been entered.

In the example, the permanent databases are ALLINFO and SOMEINFO. ALLINFO is INDEXed on CAT_NUMBER. Similar fields in the two databases have identical field names. A third database, TEMPINFO, is used simply as a temporary storage vehicle.

```
USE ALLINFO INDEX INFO
COPY STRUC TO TEMPINFO
USE TEMPINFO

   [DATA IS ENTERED TO TEMPINFO]

APPEND FROM TEMPINFO
USE SOMEINFO
APPEND FROM TEMPINFO
```

Then, when the SOMEINFO database needs to be used, we can

```
USE SOMEINFO INDEX INFO
```

This presents no difficulties whatsoever, provided the value of the keyfield is never changed. We have created an NDX file that operates equally well on two (or more) databases, thus giving quick access. The index key is identical in both DBFs, even though the keyfield needn't have the same priority in both databases (see fig. 5.2).

The true beauty of this method is that, because only one NDX file is opened, I/O is cut significantly.

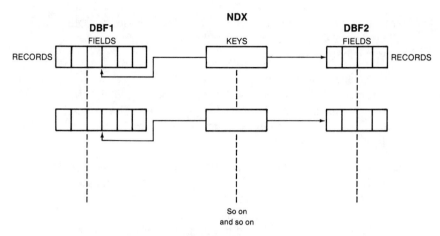

*Fig. 5.2. Using the same NDX file for two databases.*

This method works because of dBASE III Plus's NDX file structure. NDX
files contain two pieces of information relevant to their related DBF files:
keyfield value and record number. A simple representation is

| Keyfield Value | Record Number |
| --- | --- |
| Andover | 1 |
| Boston | 3 |
| Hanover | 10 |
| Hanover | 32 |
| Kingston | 4 |
| Kingston | 16 |
| Kingston | 100 |
| Manchester | 5 |
| Melrose | 6 |
| Melrose | 7 |

We are using primary and secondary keys in a database system (see
Chapter 3). As long as the associated databases are APPENDed in the same
order (as is done in the preceding code) and they share a keyfield, one
NDX file serves all.

# The Database Template

A strong argument can be made for the other side of a masterbase: the
database template. The template concept shows its worth when data is
going to be gathered and flushed, either for shipment of the database to

another site or through ZAPping or PACKing, both of which are permanently destructive operations.

Let's assume that we have a central office receiving information from remote branches. Eventually, the central office decides to create one masterbase from all the different database files received.

Because all the information is to be APPENDed to one masterbase, all of the databases must have the same structure. The central office does not want to keep supplying the branches with clean databases for their work. Instead, at the time of setup, the central office gives each branch location a template. The database contains no records, only structure. When the branch office runs the system, the program first checks to see whether an active database is available. If not, the program creates an active database, as follows:

```
IF .NOT. FILE("database")
    USE template
    COPY TO database
ENDIF
**
USE database
```

Notice that we don't have to COPY STRUCTURE TO database in the preceding code segment. Because the template contains no records, we do not need to specify that we want only STRUCTURE.

Another value of the database template is that it preserves database integrity. Working on our master database is not in the best interests of life. Please take the following rule to heart—engrave it in stone, tattoo it on your mate, whatever, but do remember it. It is JDI's Standard Rule of Programming #1.

Open an important file, and

- lightning will strike;
- an earthquake will come;
- the dam will burst;
- you will be called to eternal rest;
- the dog will pull the cord out when you get up to get coffee;
- you will win the lottery and kick the cord out while pouring coffee on the motherboard.

Because I guarantee that these things will happen, I am going to suggest another use of database templates, as demonstrated by the following code:

```
SELE A
USE database INDEX indexfile  *** THIS DATABASE HAS RECORDS IN IT
FIND var
COPY NEXT 1 TO template
SELE B
USE template

[MAKE ANY NECESSARY CHANGEs, EDITs, ETC.,]

SELE A
REPLACE FIELD1 WITH B->FIELD1, FIELD2 WITH B->FIELD2,...
```

If several records in the database are to be modified, the code can be changed so that REPLACEing doesn't occur at the end of each modification:

```
SELE A
USE database INDEX aindex
COPY STRUC TO template
SELE B
USE template
INDEX ON keyfield TO bindex      ***KEYFIELDS TO A AND B ARE THE SAME
ACCEPT "Find-> " TO var
DO WHILE TRIM(var)#" "
    SELE A
    FIND var
    SELE B
    APPE BLAN
    REPLACE NEXT 1 FIELD1 WITH A->FIELD1, FIELD2 WITH A->FIELD2,...

[MAKE MODIFICATIONS, EDITs, etc., TO THE TEMPLATE]

    ACCEPT "Find -> " TO var
ENDDO
**
GOTO TOP
**
DO WHILE .NOT. EOF()
    SELE A
    SEEK B->KEYFIELD
    REPLACE NEXT 1 FIELD1 WITH B->FIELD1, FIELD2 WITH B->FIELD2,...
    SELE B
    SKIP
ENDDO
```

The third and last use of the database template that I'm going to mention is also based on JDI's rule of the open database. This use has to do with adding new records to the database.

Don't open (USE) your master database simply to add records. In Chapter 13, I demonstrate how to create a template to add new records. Your master database is opened (USEd) only twice during the entire operation: when the template is created and when the new records are APPENDed.

```
USE database
COPY STRUC TO template
USE template

[ADD RECORDS]

USE DATABASE
APPEND FROM template
```

Please note that, in this discussion and the rest of the book, I usually don't have many databases open at the same time. My reasoning is that the more databases I keep active, the more chance I have for a major kibosh. Just because a database is not currently selected doesn't mean the database is safe from damage should the inevitable happen. Hence JDI's Standard Rule of Programming #2:

> There are only two types of computer users:
> Those who have experienced a major disk failure
> Those who are going to experience a major disk failure

# Index Files and Bell Curves

I have mentioned the fact that most data access is not random but follows certain curves (see Chapter 3). These curves give useful information for our clients in their business and for us in our coding. Consider our video store example. Is a curve possible for our primary index, the CAT_NUMBER? We note that our CAT_NUMBER is built on the following criteria:

1. First letter of store location

2. Type of medium (Beta or VHS)

3. First letters of first three significant words in title

4. Number of title in inventory of all titles (remember that each store has a list of all titles in all stores)

From CAT_NUMBER alone, therefore, we can get bell curves that reveal significant information for management. The records for the store that has the most titles in-house (first letter in CAT_NUMBER) can be compared with the total number of titles rented per day, week, or month. Note that, when the database is INDEXed on CAT_NUMBER, all titles from one store will be grouped together. If we find that we have 2,000 titles in our Lebanon store, but only 30 titles were rented from that store, we know that the store is serving as little more than a warehouse. The second letter in CAT_NUMBER can tell what percentage of the titles are of what medium (VHS, Beta, disk). This figure tells management the best medium for the market and how to order.

Other bell curves can be made from the other fields in the database. Which movies go out most often? Which go out least often? Where are most of our customers from? Do more people buy during promotions or not?

Without exception, you will find that the frequency of data access follows a bell curve on several fields. Usually, your client also knows (or at least suspects) this fact. You can ask about curves and ask to see graphs, if any are available, because they will be helpful in constructing programs. The standard bell curve in our example is shown in figure 5.3.

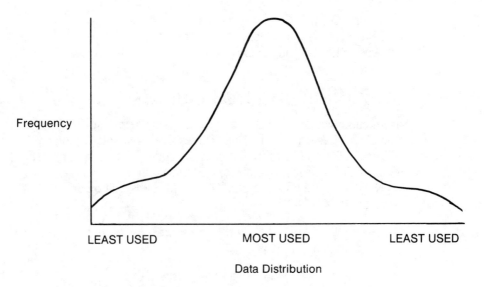

*Fig. 5.3. The standard bell curve.*

This curve helps us to program in two ways. The curve can be used for data entry. The information from the bell curve helps us put the most frequently called functions at the beginning of the front end in a DO CASE . . . ENDCASE command.

The curve also helps us when we INDEX and LOCATE. Let's assume the curve tells us that most of our media are VHS. We want all titles in inventory that are VHS format.

```
SET EXACT OFF
SET PRINT ON
USE MOVIES INDEX INFO
FIND "LV"
? "Lebanon Store has: "
LIST MOVIENAME, CAT_NUM WHILE CAT_NUM="LV"
FIND "HV"
? "Hanover Store has: "
LIST MOVIENAME, CAT_NUM WHILE CAT_NUM="HV"
FIND "NV"
? "Norwich Store has: "
LIST MOVIENAME, CAT_NUM WHILE CAT_NUM="NV"
SET PRINT OFF
```

This code gives us a quick-and-dirty list of requested titles. The list is not especially pretty, but it is a list, nonetheless. Pretty lists are produced by dBASE III Plus's REPORT writer.

The point I'm making is that the LISTing recognizes that bell curves exist. The Lebanon store may have many titles, but we already know that we have more VHS titles than any other. What we do is FIND the first L(ebanon) V(HS) title, and then LIST all the following titles WHILE they are VHS format. This operation is repeated for our Hanover and Norwich titles. The magic is that we've used an "ordered" random search. Many would code a sequential search, as follows:

```
SET PRINT ON
USE MOVIES
LIST MOVIENAME," Lebanon Store ",CAT_NUM FOR CAT_NUM="LV"
LIST MOVIENAME," Hanover Store ",CAT_NUM FOR CAT_NUM="HV"
LIST MOVIENAME," Norwich Store ",CAT_NUM FOR CAT_NUM="NV"
SET PRINT OFF
```

# Operations with Index Files

Several ways of using dBASE III Plus's NDX files can make or break a system. Usually, the larger the environment, the larger the program system. The larger the system, the more databases are used. More databases usually mean more NDX files; hence, a knowledge of how dBASE III Plus treats NDX files is vital to the programmer. This section deals with several aspects of NDX files and their use.

## Using Primary and Secondary Keys

The video rental store provides an example of efficient use of primary and secondary keys in a database system. Let's say a customer wants to rent "The Never-Ending Story" for a VHS VCR. If we know that the information for "The Never-Ending Story" is in record 392, we can get the information simply by entering

```
GOTO 392
```

Unfortunately, we don't know the record number for each of the 5,000 titles in our inventory. What we do know is that "The Never-Ending Story" catalog number is LVNES?????.

That number has an easily remembered syntax, as explained previously. L(ebanon store) V(HS format) N(ever-)E(nding) S(tory), followed by a five-digit code that signifies that the movie is number such-and-such of so many movies in stock.

We don't know the five-digit code, a fact that makes sense because the customer doesn't care that the movie is number 3,019 of the 5,000 movies on our shelves. All we care about, when the customer is right there with money in hand, is whether the Lebanon store has "The Never-Ending Story" in the requested format. We may have five copies of "The Never-Ending Story" in VHS format at the Lebanon store. This method finds them for us:

```
SET EXACT OFF
USE SOMEINFO INDEX INFO
FIND "LVNES"
```

We are using a secondary key to reference the primary key (see Chapter 2).

## Indexing on Concatenated Fields

I want to point out at the start of this discussion that I do not normally INDEX on concatenated fields. I try to keep keyfields between five and eight characters wide. That amount normally is enough to keep records separate.

One exception that comes to mind is a genealogy study conducted by a New York City group. The database consisted of the names of approximately 8,000 relatives spread all over the U.S. and Canada. (The family was both prolific and migratory.) From the start, it was obvious that we would have a tremendous duplication of names. To INDEX using a standard LASTNAME+FIRSTNAME concatenation would have been ridiculous; for instance, several hundred relatives with identical names lived in both NYC and Toronto. Obviously, using CITY was also unsatisfactory.

The solution was the bizarre concoction,

```
LASTNAME+FIRSTNAME+ZIPCODE+RIGH(PHONE, 4)
```

This key worked well enough, except in FINDing and SEEKing; no one polling the database could correctly fit all the keys in an indexkey.

Moral: If you must INDEX on concatenated fields, try this kludge:

1. Determine the field lengths of the INDEXing fields:

Structure for database    : C:test.dbf
Number of data records   : 1
Date of last update         : ~~01/01/80

| Field | Field name | Type | Width | Dec |
|---|---|---|---|---|
| 1 | FIELD1 | Character | 10 | |
| 2 | FIELD2 | Character | 13 | |
| 3 | FIELD3 | Character | 6 | |
| 4 | FIELD4 | Character | 8 | |
| 5 | FIELD5 | Character | 20 | |
| ** Total ** | | | 58 | |

2. Adjust the following template as necessary to get a workable value for FINDing or SEEKing:

```
STORE SPACE(20) TO F1, F2, F3, F4, F5
@ 2,0 SAY "FIELD 1 -> " GET F1
@ 3,0 SAY "FIELD 2 -> " GET F2
@ 4,0 SAY "FIELD 3 -> " GET F3
```

```
@ 5,0 SAY "FIELD 4 -> " GET F4
@ 6,0 SAY "FIELD 5 -> " GET F5
READ
F1=TRIM(F1)
F2=TRIM(F2)
F3=TRIM(F3)
F4=TRIM(F4)
F5=TRIM(F5)
FINDER=TRIM(F1-SPACE(10-LEN(F1))+F2-SPACE(13-LEN(F2))+F3-SPACE(6-LEN(F3));
      +F4-SPACE(8-LEN(F4))+F5-SPACE(20-LEN(F5)))
SET EXACT OFF
FIND &FINDER
```

The only note worth making is that I use TRIM, SPACE, and SET EXACT
OFF to build and use the variable. This simple technique has proved
invaluable.

Note that the SPACE( ) argument is the size of the field (FIELD1 is 10
characters wide, FIELD2 is 13 characters wide, etc.) minus the size of the
search data. These character expressions are then string-summed to the
FINDER variable to ensure proper spacing during searches for the
indexkey.

## Truncating Keyfields

In the previous section, I told you how to FIND and SEEK using
concatenated fields. In that discussion, I said that the best keyfields are five
to eight characters long. Now I explain my reasoning.

Let's consider several kinds of lists. Pick up your local telephone directory.
Turn to any page and scan the names. With the possible exceptions of
Adamses, Smiths, Joneses, and St. Somebodies, few names show
similarities much beyond the eighth character. Those who live in a
metropolitan area may find this experiment more profitable using phone
numbers or addresses instead of names. Within area codes, no seven-digit
phone numbers are repeated. (This is also a good example of knowing
your data before you design the database.) Insurance records are keyed on
a seven-digit code based on the last and first names of their clients.
Account numbers range from four to seven digits. All in all, a keyfield of
five to eight characters is normally safe. Naturally, this brevity improves
the INDEXing speed when an INDEX or REINDEX is necessary.

## Appending from the Start

If you have used the dBASE II, III, or III Plus INDEX command at all, you
know that you can both APPEND and INSERT an INDEXed database. The
new records show up where they should in the file. Pursuing this logic a
step further, we can INDEX an empty database and APPEND and INSERT
forever after. This method produces ordered random data from the first
record entered.

A good idea is always to start a database with an NDX file, even if the
client says an index is not needed. Nine times out of ten the need will
arise. Good judgment in choosing a keyfield can save a lot of time further
down the road.

## Creating Descending Indexes

The dBASE III Plus manual claims that indexkeys can be done only in
ascending order. I disagree. Getting a descending INDEX on a numeric
database field is easy. You merely enter

```
INDEX ON -(numeric fieldname) TO indexfile
```

For instance, to generate an NDX file of checks paid from greatest amount
to the least, you use

```
INDEX ON -AMOUNT TO indexfile
```

Doing this index with character database fields is a bit more difficult. The
theory is the same, but remember that you have no such thing as a
negative character. The trick is to use the ASC( ) function, as in

```
INDEX ON -ASC(character fieldname) TO indexfile
```

The preceding line INDEXes only on the first character in the string, but
the pattern can be used as a guide for building more intricate character
indexes in descending order. This technique, if used properly when the
database is first designed, takes no more execution time than a normal
indexkey.

Rather than have you go nuts trying to figure out how this technique
works, I'll show you. You need a secondary database, appropriately called
LETTERS. As you look at the structure of LETTERS, and the listing of
what's in the file, note that both fields are CHARACTER data types. This is
important, as I explain later.

```
Structure for database    : D:LETTERS.dbf
Number of data records    : 26
Date of last update       : 10/10/86
```

| Field | Field name | Type | Width | Dec |
|-------|------------|------|-------|-----|
| 1 | LETTER | Character | 1 | |
| 2 | VALUE | Character | 2 | |

\*\* Total \*\*                              4

—> LIST

| Record# | LETTER | VALUE |
|---------|--------|-------|
| 1 | A | 01 |
| 2 | B | 02 |
| 3 | C | 03 |
| 4 | D | 04 |
| 5 | E | 05 |
| 6 | F | 06 |
| 7 | G | 07 |
| 8 | H | 08 |
| 9 | I | 09 |
| 10 | J | 10 |
| 11 | K | 11 |
| 12 | L | 12 |
| 13 | M | 13 |
| 14 | N | 14 |
| 15 | O | 15 |
| 16 | P | 16 |
| 17 | Q | 17 |
| 18 | R | 18 |
| 19 | S | 19 |
| 20 | T | 20 |
| 21 | U | 21 |
| 22 | V | 22 |
| 23 | W | 23 |
| 24 | X | 24 |
| 25 | Y | 25 |
| 26 | Z | 26 |

Note that each letter is assigned a two-digit code complementary to its value. *A* has a value of *01*, not *1*. This is necessary for the code that follows.

```
** DESCENDER PSEUDO-CODE FOR REVERSE ALPHA INDEXING
**
SELE 2
USE LETTERS INDE LETTERS
SELE 1
USE dbf
GET field name to reverse index
GET MAX(length of character string to use)
*
DO WHIL .NOT. EOF()
   INDEXVALUE = ""
*
   DO WHIL LEN(field value) # 0
      GET ALPHA VALUE OF LEADING CHAR
      INDEXVALUE = INDEXVALUE + ALPHA VALUE
      field value = RIGH(field value, LEN(field value) - 1)
   ENDD
*
   REPL FIELDVAL WITH -INDEXVALUE
   SKIP
ENDD
```

Note that this pseudocode closely parallels valid dBASE III Plus code. (This will facilitate changes, should you use this block in an application.)

We start by opening the LETTERS database and index file combination in work area 2. Our database of interest is then opened in some other work area (work area 1 in this example). You can open the primary interest database with associated NDX files, provided none of the NDX files are based on the FIELDVAL field. FIELDVAL is a field that isn't normally in the database. It is placed there to facilitate our reverse INDEXing, and serves as a "flag" for the rest of the code. It has nothing to do with the other, application-specific data you would normally find in the database. The FIELDVAL field is NUMERIC, and holds the VALue of the ASC string sum of whatever field you're really interested in. Remember that we're designing something to allow descending ASCII character sorts. We don't want to have to SORT our database each time we use it, and this is the method around that.

The inner DO WHILE . . . ENDDO block does nothing other than determine the alpha sum of the ASCII character values in what we would normally use as a keyfield. We can't perform a descending INDEX on our keyfield, so we do this to determine the ASC value sum of the keyfield value, and then place the negative of that value in FIELDVAL.

Here we come to an interesting point. We can USE our primary interest database with the FIELDVAL NDX file from the first if we design our code to perform a sequential scan of the file. Without that sequential search, we run the risk of getting ourselves in an infinite loop. This loop will occur if we do a random search that shifts the NDX as we're waiting for an EOF flag.

Remember that all INDEXing is done in ascending order. Our FIELDVAL values are the negatives of their true values (100 is entered as −100, 60 becomes −60, and so on). When III PLUS updates the NDX file the ascending order on negative values returns a descending order on our real keyfield. Voilà!

To prove my point, I'm going to show you how this code looks in a real-life application. Consider the following database and listed fields of interest.

```
Structure for database    : D:STUDENTS.dbf
Number of data records    : 51
Date of last update       : 10/10/86
```

| Field | Field name | Type | Width | Dec |
|-------|------------|------|-------|-----|
| 1 | SSNUMBER | Character | 11 | |
| 2 | CLASS | Character | 6 | |
| 3 | FIRSTNAME | Character | 15 | |
| 4 | LASTNAME | Character | 15 | |
| 5 | DAY | Date | 8 | |
| 6 | CLASSGRADE | Character | 1 | |
| 7 | WASHOMEWRK | Logical | 1 | |
| 8 | HOMEWORK | Numeric | 3 | |
| 9 | FIELDVAL | Numeric | 10 | |
| ** Total ** | | | 71 | |

—> LIST ALL LASTNAME

| Record# | LASTNAME |
|---|---|
| 1 | BASS |
| 2 | BICKFORD |
| 3 | BOUCHARD |
| 4 | BRYCE |
| 5 | BOLT |
| 6 | COTE |
| 7 | CRYAN |
| 8 | DAIGNEAULT |
| 9 | DOYLE |
| 10 | DUPUIS |
| 11 | FERRIERA |
| 12 | GANNON |
| 13 | GRANDE |
| 14 | HARNISH |
| 15 | HARVEY |
| 16 | HATHAWAY |
| 17 | HIBBARD |
| 18 | HORNE |
| 19 | KELLEHER |
| 20 | LEVESQUE |
| 21 | LORD |
| 22 | LOVEJOY |
| 23 | MACLEOD |
| 24 | MARTIN |
| 25 | MURRAY |
| 26 | OBARTON |
| 27 | PORTER |
| 28 | RICHARDSON |
| 29 | ROBERGE |
| 30 | ROBINSON |
| 31 | SMITH |
| 32 | TUCCOLO |
| 33 | VANZANDT |
| 34 | BLANDFORD |
| 35 | CONVERSE |
| 36 | CORDI |
| 37 | CORNETT |
| 38 | COTE |

```
39   DEMOND
40   DENONCOURT
41   FICHERA
42   GREGOIRE
43   JOYAL
44   KINSMAN
45   LAFLAMME
46   LAZARRO
47   MOORE
48   PHANEUF
49   SKEEN
50   WARD
51   ZRAKET
```

You'll notice that the names were entered alphabetically. Sorry, I didn't
mean to, it just happened that way. You should note also that record #33
was originally *VAN ZANDT*. The space between N and Z had to go.
Likewise, record #26 was originally *O'BARTON*. Ditto the single quote
between O and B. It wouldn't matter if the names were entered in both
upper- and lowercase. The code, shown below, converts lower- to
uppercase when SEEKing.

```
** DESCENDER. PRG
SELE 2
USE LETTERS INDE LETTERS
SELE 1
USE STUDENTS
MAXCHARS = 255
*
DO WHIL .NOT. EOF()
   MAXCHARS = MIN(MAXCHARS, LEN(TRIM(LASTNAME)))
   SKIP
ENDD
*
1
*
DO WHIL .NOT. EOF()
   INDEXVALUE = ""
   NAME = LEFT(LASTNAME, MAXCHARS)
```

```
*
   DO WHIL LEN(NAME) # Ø
      SELE 2
      SEEK UPPE(LEFT(NAME,1))
      INDEXVALUE = INDEXVALUE + VALUE
      NAME = RIGH(NAME,LEN(NAME) - 1)
   ENDD
*
   SELE 1
   REPL FIELDVAL WITH -VAL(INDEXVALUE)
   SKIP
ENDD
*
INDE ON FIELDVAL TO RLNAME
*
** EOF: DESCENDER.PRG
```

Note that this code doesn't perform the sequential search on an NDXed file. I INDEX after everything else has been done. I used that procedure here because there were only 51 records in the file. Had the database contained more than 100 records, I would have USEd the database INDEXed on the FIELDVAL field. Then I would have performed the sequential search, starting at record #1 and continuing to EOF( ). The results of DESCENDER.PRG are shown below.

—> LIST ALL LASTNAME,FIELDVAL

| Record# | LASTNAME | FIELDVAL |
|---|---|---|
| 51 | ZRAKET | −26180111 |
| 50 | WARD | −23011804 |
| 33 | VANZANDT | −22011426 |
| 32 | TUCCOLO | −20210303 |
| 31 | SMITH | −19130820 |
| 49 | SKEEN | −19110505 |
| 30 | ROBINSON | −18150208 |
| 29 | ROBERGE | −18150205 |
| 28 | RICHARDSON | −18080308 |
| 27 | PORTER | −16151820 |
| 48 | PHANEUF | −16080114 |
| 26 | OBARTON | −15020118 |
| 25 | MURRAY | −13211818 |
| 47 | MOORE | −13151518 |
| 24 | MARTIN | −13011820 |

| | | |
|---|---|---|
| 23 | MACLEOD | −13010312 |
| 22 | LOVEJOY | −12152205 |
| 21 | LORD | −12151804 |
| 20 | LEVESQUE | −12052205 |
| 46 | LAZARRO | −12012601 |
| 45 | LAFLAMME | −12010612 |
| 44 | KINSMAN | −11081419 |
| 19 | KELLEHER | −11051212 |
| 43 | JOYAL | −10152501 |
| 18 | HORNE | −8151814 |
| 17 | HIBBARD | −8080202 |
| 16 | HATHAWAY | −8012008 |
| 15 | HARVEY | −8011822 |
| 14 | HARNISH | −8011814 |
| 42 | GREGOIRE | −7180507 |
| 13 | GRANDE | −7180114 |
| 12 | GANNON | −7011414 |
| 41 | FICHERA | −6080308 |
| 11 | FERRIERA | −6051818 |
| 10 | DUPUIS | −4211621 |
| 9 | DOYLE | −4152512 |
| 40 | DENONCOURT | −4051415 |
| 39 | DEMOND | −4051315 |
| 8 | DAIGNEAULT | −4010807 |
| 7 | CRYAN | −3182501 |
| 6 | COTE | −3152005 |
| 38 | COTE | −3152005 |
| 37 | CORNETT | −3151814 |
| 36 | CORDI | −3151804 |
| 35 | CONVERSE | −3151422 |
| 4 | BRYCE | −2182503 |
| 3 | BOUCHARD | −2152103 |
| 5 | BOLT | −2151220 |
| 34 | BLANDFORD | −2120114 |
| 2 | BICKFORD | −2080311 |
| 1 | BASS | −2011919 |

.XEDNI ahpla esrever A !alioV

## COPYing an INDEXed File To Get a SORTed File

Now that I've explained how to get descending NDX files, I will explain why I developed the method. A particular client (a bulk-mail advertiser) required an application that performed a unique sort. The U.S. Postal Department likes things sorted by descending ZIP code. For bulk mailing, the ZIP codes are further broken down along other lines.

The client's representatives explained the postal regulations, and stated that their database already had more than thirty thousand names. It has since grown. SORTing through that large a database was an overnight job each time mailings had to go out (once a month). Another complication was that their PC was bandaged to a unique printer that put labels directly on the catalogs.

The solution uses the previously described method to generate a complete, descending NDX file. To produce the labels, the database is COPYed rather than SORTed, an operation that saves a lot of time. The labels are generated from the COPYed file.

## Using Multiple NDX Files

With dBASE III Plus, you can use several (up to seven) NDX files with the command,

```
SET INDEX TO indexfile1, indexfile2,...
```

dBASE III Plus uses the SET ORDER TO command to manipulate NDX files that are out of the Dark Ages. This section describes the two procedures for opening NDX files for use. The next section describes ways to manipulate opened NDX files.

> **PLUS**

The ability to keep several NDX files active during a work session is a powerful tool in dBASE III Plus work. Both methods of opening NDX files described here have merits; I prefer the second method, the USE command method. For the first method, you should save the SET INDE TO command for adding another NDX file to an already active NDX file list. Remember, however, that adding another NDX file to an already active NDX file list may invalidate the most recently opened NDX file if changes have been made to that NDX file's keyfield.

A more economical way of activating NDX files is to name them in the same line that USEs the database.

```
USE databasefile INDE indexfile1, indexfile2,...
```

This method automatically brings the first-named NDX file to the front of the system while keeping subsequently named NDX files active. APPENDing, INSERTing, EDITing, and READing of records automatically modifies all active NDX files. Should you wish to bring another of the listed NDX files to the front, you can use the

```
SET ORDER TO n
```

statement, which switches the hierarchy of the NDX files for the FIND and SEEK commands.

You should note the following warnings:

Be careful when EDITing on the keyfield, because you can blow up the referenced NDX file.

Errors can result when you try to open more than seven NDX files. These errors can drop you out of a program.

## Controlling NDX files with the SET ORDER TO Command

The SET INDEX TO and USE dbf INDE ndx commands activate multiple NDX files. In previous versions of dBASE, the capacity to manipulate NDX files was confined to these commands. To bring a particular NDX file to the top of the list, and thus give that file control of the index key for the in USE database, you had to shuffle the NDX files like a deck of cards. This meant that you had to include several SET INDE TO commands in your code. If you didn't activate all the necessary NDX files with the USE dbf INDE ndx command, you had to do a great deal of disk work—SETting and then shuffling the priority of the NDX files during a work session.

No more.

The dBASE III SET ORDER TO command, hinted at previously, gives you the luxury of opening the NDX files in whatever order you choose. For example, the start of your work session requires NDX files in the priority

        NDX1
        NDX2
        NDX3
        NDX4
        NDX5
        NDX6
        NDX7

You can activate the NDX files with either of the following commands:

USE dbf INDE NDX1, NDX2, NDX3, NDX4, NDX5, NDX6, NDX7

or

SET INDE TO NDX1, NDX2, NDX3, NDX4, NDX5, NDX6, NDX7

The latter assumes that a USE command has previously been issued. You can alter the priority of active NDX files by recognizing the order in which they have been activated. Both of the previous commands show the following priority:

| | |
|---|---|
| NDX1 | 1 |
| NDX2 | 2 |
| NDX3 | 3 |
| NDX4 | 4 |
| NDX5 | 5 |
| NDX6 | 6 |
| NDX7 | 7 |

Assume that some work has been done, and now you need to give top priority to NDX6. Enter the command

PLUS

SET ORDE TO 6

dBASE III Plus takes that command and automatically (internally) shuffles the NDX files to create the following priority list:

| | |
|---|---|
| NDX6 | 1 |
| NDX1 | 2 |
| NDX2 | 3 |
| NDX3 | 4 |
| NDX4 | 5 |
| NDX5 | 6 |
| NDX7 | 7 |

What exactly has dBASE III Plus done? The command that originally activated the NDX files put an ORDER on them, as shown in the first priority list. (The order in which files are activated also dictates their original priority.) We use the SET ORDER TO command to shift the ORDER, and hence the priority, of the NDX files. The command

SET ORDER TO 6

is equivalent to

SET INDE TO NDX6, NDX1, NDX2, NDX3, NDX4, NDX5, NDX7

Note that dBASE III Plus takes the sixth NDX file listed in the original command (either the USE dbf INDE ndx or the SET INDE TO command, shown at the beginning of this section), and gives that sixth file top priority. dBASE III Plus bumps all higher priority NDX files (NDX1, NDX2, NDX3, NDX4, NDX5) down one on the list. All lesser priority files (NDX7) retain their previous positions.

**PLUS**

What do you gain with the SET ORDER TO command? The most obvious gain is that you are working in memory rather than on disk. Whenever you SET INDE TO, you run the risk of dBASE III Plus having to farm out some work to disk as the program shuffles NDX file priorities. If you use the SET INDE TO command to activate files, you definitely will force dBASE to hit the disk for information. Totally unsatisfactory. The SET ORDER TO command allows you to activate as many as seven NDX files with either the SET INDE TO or USE dbf INDE ndx commands, and then use a single command to alter the files' order of precedence in a work session.

This feature is particularly useful when you write code that alternates between LOCATEing and FINDing or SEEKing information. No version of dBASE likes to LOCATE something on an INDEXed database. Jumping from one randomly sorted record to the next randomly sorted record simply requires too much work. You are trying to perform a sequential search (the LOCATE command) on a randomly ordered file. (Any dbf with an active NDX file is randomly ordered.) Previous versions of dBASE (with the exception of the dBASE III Developer's Release) forced you to use code such as the following:

```
SET INDE TO              && SHUT OFF NDX FILES
LOCATE statement         && FIND INFO IN NON-KEY FIELD
THATONE = RECNO( )       && STORE FOUND RECORD NUMBER TO VARIABLE
SET INDE TO ndx list     && REACTIVATE NDX FILES
GOTO THATONE             && GO BACK TO ROUND RECORD
```

That type of code was necessary because activating any NDX files repositioned the record pointer. The SET ORDER TO command allows that code to become

```
SET ORDE TO              && SHUT OFF NDX FILES
LOCATE statement         && FIND INFO IN NON-KEY FIELD
SET ORDER TO n           && RE-ESTABLISH NDX FILE PRECEDENCE
```

The SET ORDE TO command doesn't close or reopen NDX files. It merely shifts their priority. Used at the start of the code, the command

```
SET ORDE TO
```

tells dBASE III Plus to disconnect the NDX files from the associated DBF file. Because the command doesn't tell dBASE III Plus to close the NDX files, those files remain in memory and their priority remains established. The files themselves are not reactivated when we SET ORDER TO n.

| PLUS |
| --- |

# Weeding Out Duplicate Records

In this section, I demonstrate two methods of doing the same thing. The first method uses the "Bigger Hammer" method of programming. This method requires a lot of computer time and not too much experience with dBASE; the "Bigger Hammer" can do the job overnight. The second method uses one of the strengths of dBASE III Plus. This method solves the same problem with some clever programming; it requires a little knowledge about how dBASE III Plus works, but not much else. Best of all, this method can do the same job in less than an hour. This second method uses the SET UNIQUE OFF/on command.

Our example originated when a local historical society tried to make a single workable database; they ended up with three different databases, identical in structure. Each database contained duplicates of records in one or both of the other databases. One database ran from A through Z, another ran from A through L, and the third ran from M through Z. Each record of the three databases held several fields. The problem was compounded by the fact that different keypunch operators had entered new information in each database, and no two operators had entered the same information in any one of the three databases.

Begins to sound like one of those old logic problems, doesn't it? The catcher's name was Smith, and he ate strawberries on Sunday. The shortstop shot the conductor. What color is your lunch? The problem gets worse.

One day someone who had never touched a computer wanted to get involved. The resulting error ate one entire database. This one database, which everybody knew held up-to-date membership data, was some 3,000 records long.

Fortunately, the society had backups for all the files. The managers wanted to know whether they could use an easy one-line command to merge all the databases, find the duplicated records and delete them, and then sort the members by identification number into a new database.

Is there a one-line command that can do all that? No. But everything they asked for is possible.

Certain things have to be done no matter which method we use. Merging the databases poses no problem. This operation is straightforward and easily done. Likewise, sorting the merged database is not a big shake. You can use either program I've listed in this section to sort (read INDEX) on any field; the interesting part of this example is the identification number field. The middle request—finding the duplicated records and deleting them—is the key.

The first solution recognizes that dBASE can LOCATE, FIND, and SEEK. This is the "Bigger Hammer" method. Both FIND and SEEK work only on an indexed database, however. Further, these commands always stop at the first occurrence of what they're looking for. You can DELETE a record after it's found, but unless you either PACK the database after each deletion or SET DELE ON before you enter the code, SEEK and FIND still stop at the first occurrence.

The smart people out there are leaning toward LOCATE. Good. Let's investigate the LOCATE method first, using the following solution:

```
SET TALK OFF
CLEAR
USE C:MEMBERS
IF FILE('C:TANK.DBF')
   ERASE C:TANK.DBF
ENDIF
COPY STRUCTURE TO C:TANK
USE C:TANK
**
APPEND FROM C:MEMBERS
APPEND FROM C:MEMBACK
APPEND FROM C:MEMBACKX
**
N = 1
**
DO WHILE N <> RECCOUNT()
   GOTO N
   **
   IF ID_NUM = "-1"
     STORE N+1 TO N
     LOOP
   ENDIF
   **
```

PLUS

```
      STORE ID_NUM TO LOOKER
      SKIP
      LOCATE REST FOR LOOKER = ID_NUM
      **
      IF LOOKER = ID_NUM
         REPLACE ID_NUM WITH "-1"
         DELETE
      ENDIF
**
      DO WHILE .NOT. EOF()
         CONTINUE
         **
         IF LOOKER = ID_NUM
            REPLACE ID_NUM WITH "-1"
            DELETE
         ENDIF
      **
      ENDDO
**
      STORE N+1 TO N
ENDDO
**
PACK
SORT ON ID_NUM TO MEMBER
**
@ 20,10 SAY "Tra-la, Tra-la. It is done."
RETURN
```

TANK is a name I use to define a storage area. In this case, I use TANK to store all the data in the three databases. Rarely does anyone else employ my system of logic. In case someone does, though, I include the first IF . . . ENDIF test. Those lines look to see whether anybody else has used a TANK, and erase it if found.

We have already placed the largest of the three databases in USE. After making sure no other TANKs exist, we COPY the STRUCTURE of the MEMBERS database TO C:TANK. Once this is done, we can input data to TANK exactly as if we were working with the MEMBERS database.

We then proceed to gather all the records into the TANK database. This is done by APPENDing FROM the three other databases (MEMBERS, MEMBACK, and MEMBACKX).

PLUS

The meat of the program is in the DO . . . ENDDO loops. We start with N = 1. While N <> RECCOUNT( ), the program is directed to GOTO record N. We use −1 as a marker to indicate a duplicate record. (I don't think anyone would use −1 as an identification number—at least, I never have.)

We know that the program has already looked through a record IF we find ID_NUM = "−1". If the program has looked through that record, the system LOOPs back and does a GOTO for the next record.

But if dBASE III Plus doesn't find ID_NUM = "−1", the program STOREs the ID_NUM in LOOKER, which is just a variable name. Then the program SKIPs to the next record. RECNO( ) is the dBASE III Plus function that tells us the number of the record being examined. The command

```
LOCATE REST FOR LOOKER = ID_NUM
```

tells dBASE to look from where it is to the end of the database for duplications.

IF LOOKER = ID_NUM, dBASE III Plus has found a duplicate record. The program marks that record for deletion by REPLACEing the ID_NUM with −1 and DELETEing it. Simply DELETEing the record won't do the trick unless we PACK the database at the same time. The "−1" gimmick is a nice bit of fudging that does the job.

Not all duplications are nearby in the database. The

```
DO WHILE .NOT. EOF()
```

ensures a perusal of the entire database by CONTINUEing the search until the program encounters the end of file. Eventually, I complete my search for duplications. The deletions are going to be permanent once I PACK the database.

This operation is a nice exercise that gives you a feel for LOCATE, DO . . . ENDDO, and IF . . . ENDIF programming structures. This method is not what I really want to show you in this section, however; I have discussed this method only to show you what some forethought can do. Now I show you a better way.

The following program meets the same needs as the first program. This program, however, does the job much more quickly, much more neatly, and shows *panache*.

```
SET UNIQUE ON
SET TALK OFF
CLEAR
USE C:MEMBERS
IF FILE('C:TANK.DBF')
   ERASE C:TANK.DBF
ENDIF
COPY STRUCTURE TO C:TANK
*
USE C:TANK
*
APPEND FROM C:MEMBERS
APPEND FROM C:MEMBACK
APPEND FROM C:MEMBACKX
*
INDEX ON ID_NUM TO NEWTANK
COPY TO MEMBER
@ 20,10 SAY "Tra-la, Tra-la. It is done."
RETURN
```

What makes this second method so clever? Well, we use the fact that dBASE itself can keep track of duplications in a file and weed them out. We use that capability in the first line of the second program,

```
    SET UNIQUE ON
```

From there we proceed much as we did in the first program until we have APPENDed the three databases.

With the second program, I don't care about the amount of work because dBASE does the work for me. To delete duplicate files, I INDEX on the field of interest, ID_NUM, to an index file (NEWTANK). The historical society wants a database called MEMBER. Fine, we COPY TO MEMBER. The program is clever—but even more clever, to those paying close attention, is that we got the database sorted without SORTing.

Can we do more than what we've already done? Of course we can. In this case, we want to give the user the option of deciding what information goes into the new database. The code has the form

```
USE dbf1 INDE ndx1
COPY STRUC TO TANK
USE TANK
APPE FROM dbf1
APPE FROM dbf2
(keep on APPENDing as necessary)
SELE 2
USE dbf1 INDE ndx1
SELE 3
USE dbf2 INDE ndx2
SELE 4
USE dbf3 INDE ndx3
(keep SELECTing work areas and USEing files as necessary)
N = 66
SELE 1
INDE ON key field TO TANK UNIQ
*
DO WHIL .NOT. EOF()
    (display TANK information on left of screen)
    WORKAREA = CHR(N)
    SELE &WORKAREA
*
    IF RECC() = 0
        EXIT
    ENDI
*
    FIND A->key field value
    SELE 1
*
    IF FOUN()
        (display work area B information on right of screen)
        WAIT "I(gnore), A(ccept), C(hange)? (I/A/C) -> " TO  WAITER
        WAITER = UPPER(WAITER)
```

PLUS

PLUS

```
*
      DO CASE
         CASE WAITER = "A"
            DELE
            APPE BLAN
            REPL fields in A WITH fields in other work area
         CASE WAITER = "C"
            EDIT TANK's data, but keep other work area's data on screen
      ENDC
*
   ENDI
*
   SKIP
*
   IF EOF()
      N = N + 1
      GOTO TOP
   ENDI
*
ENDD
*
! REN TANK.* TO whatever.*
*
** EOF
```

Note that this is pseudocode that closely resembles valid III Plus code.

What does the code do? It allows the user to create the master DBF file based on information in the other dbf files. This is useful in a situation such as that described earlier in this section. The process takes time, however, and the user must be beyond the infancy stage. The code works by creating a temporary storage vessel, TANK, and an associated NDX file, which contains a UNIQUE sampling of the combined data in whatever files need to be analyzed.

SELECTing work areas involves some fancy footwork. I first had to create a variable, WORKAREA, which is the CHR( ) equivalent of N. Then I used a macro substitution to get the code to SELECT work areas as I needed them. Notice that I use the IF RECC( ) = 0 line to test for DBFs in each work area. If a work area contains no records, no database is active in that work area. No active database means that I've gone through all the necessary files, and can exit the DO WHIL . . . ENDD block.

The rest of the code is fairly obvious. If the SELECTed work area's database has no record corresponding to TANK's record, you SKIP to the next record in TANK. I WAIT to find out what the user wants to do, and then I take action based on that choice. When I hit TANK's EOF, I get ready to SELECT another work area and start over. Finally, I use ! REN because using III Plus's RENAME command would involve at least two lines of code. Poobah to that, especially if I'm RENaming several files!

# Operations with Memory Variables

Memory variables are what their name implies: variables that have nowhere to go but to the the memory of the machine. Memory variables are unlike database fields, which take up space in the database and in files and buffers. The problem is that memory variables are always active until dBASE leaves the routine that uses them, or CLEARs them from memory with the RELEASE ALL or CLEAR MEMORY command.

The question therefore becomes: What can we do to achieve more efficient use of memory and memory variables? dBASE III Plus provides many ways of using memory variables. Unfortunately, most of these ways are overlooked by most programmers.

## The CONFIG.DB MVARSIZ Command

The CONFIG.DB MVARSIZ command isn't really a command or function, but a parameter that dBASE III Plus uses to set up the computer. The command takes the form

```
MVARSIZ= n
```

where n can be any integer between 1 and 31.

The preceding command line can be placed anywhere in the CONFIG.DB file. The command tells dBASE III Plus how much machine memory to use for memory variables. You say that you read "the book," and it says dBASE III Plus has only 6,000 bytes for memory variable storage? Try this experiment. Use a word processor to enter in your present CONFIG.DB file the line

```
MVARSIZ=1
```

If your CONFIG.DB file already contains an MVARSIZ line, just write that line down somewhere. You can always put it back later.

Now start dBASE III Plus and type

```
DISP MEMO
```

Because you have just started dBASE, no memory variables should be
present. You should still see the following information on your screen:

```
    0 variables defined,        0 bytes used
  256 variables available,   1024 bytes available
```

Now quit dBASE III Plus and use your word processor to overwrite the
old MVARSIZ line with

```
  MVARSIZ=31
```

Start dBASE III Plus again and DISPLAY the MEMORY. This time you'll
see the message

```
    0 variables defined,        0 bytes used
  256 variables available,  31744 bytes available
```

As you can see, changing the value of the MVARSIZ line in the
CONFIG.DB file has dramatic affects on the memory management of the
dBASE III Plus system.

"So," you say, "even though I have increased the size of memory
available for memory variables, I still have only 256 variables. What have I
gained?"

You have gained precision. You still have 256 variables, but the precision
of the values can extend to several decimal places when the MVARSIZ is
high. Programmers who work with double-precision real values can
appreciate this feature and will, I hope, make good use of it. This capability
is a great advantage in engineering and scientific applications.

## Three-Dimensional Arrays
## Using Memory Variables

Now that we know the true limit on memory variables is 256 variables
total—not 6,000 bytes of storage—we can investigate ways to raise that
256-variable ceiling.

One method I use frequently is to create three-dimensional arrays. This
construct is valuable because dBASE III Plus itself doesn't directly support
matrix operations. Using three-dimensional arrays makes array and matrix
work (as found in both linear algebra and linear programming) much
easier. I preface this discussion by saying that this method involves some
pretty fancy footwork, but can be a great energy saver for programmers.

First, we have to agree on what an array is. Consider an illustration of a normal database:

|  | FIELD1 | FIELD2 | FIELD3 | FIELD4 | . . . . . |
|---|---|---|---|---|---|
| RECORD1 | R1F1 | R1F2 | R1F3 | R1F4 | . . . . . |
| RECORD2 | R2F1 | R2F2 | R2F3 | R2F4 | . . . . . |
| RECORD3 | R3F1 | R3F2 | R3F3 | R3F4 | . . . . . |
| RECORD4 | R4F1 | R4F2 | R4F3 | R4F4 | . . . . . |
| . . . | . . . | . . . | . . . | . . . | . . . |

If you're wondering what a spreadsheet is doing in a dBASE III Plus book, then congratulate yourself; the diagram is a spreadsheet. A normal database is also a two-dimensional array, just like a spreadsheet.

Consider the everyday dBASE II, dBASE III, or dBASE III Plus database. It holds a collection of records; each record is a collection of fields. The records are numbered from 1 to whatever by dBASE III Plus itself; the numbers then are used as primary keys. The fields are usually given names such as NAME, MAKE, YEAR, CODE, COST, and so on.

The illustration shows numbered fields. Let's assume that the field numbers correspond to field names as follows:

```
FIELD1 = NAME
FIELD2 = MAKE
FIELD3 = YEAR
FIELD4 = CODE
FIELD5 = COST
```

If we want to see the COST and MAKE of the car in record 4, we look in cells R4F5 and R4F2, respectively.

Now we go to three-dimensional arrays. Look at the illustration in figure 5.4. Those of you who studied physics or engineering will recognize that little plot, and you'll groan. But the plot serves as the focus and beginning block for this discussion.

The diagram is nothing more than a three-dimensional coordinate system with x, y, and z axes. This system is nothing to be afraid of. Just recognize that instead of being located by an (x,y) coordinate pair, elements are located by an (x,y,z) coordinate triplet. Pilots and drivers are used to

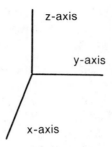

*Fig. 5.4. Axes of a three-dimensional array.*

three-dimensional thinking. If you are 30 miles north of Boston, 20 miles east of Boston, and 2 miles above Boston, you can say your location is (20,30,2) with reference to Boston.

Now we introduce a database, MEMFILES; fields in the database, MFILENAMES; and the memory variables themselves, running from MEMVAR1 to MEMVAR256 (see fig. 5.5).

*Fig. 5.5. Memory variables in a three-dimensional array.*

Let's take a minute to analyze this construct. It is a true three-dimensional array. How so? Let's assume we have 256 memory-variable names available. We want a particular set of values for those variables, say for a certain cylinder rotation (as in a graphing operation) or for a coordinate translation such as changing the x,y,z triplet into a [ $\rho$ ], [ $\theta$ ], [ $\phi$ ] triplet.

We USE the MEMFILES database, which is INDEXed on MFILENAMES, and

```
FIND "XYZ2RTP"
```

This value in the MFILENAMES field is the key to the MEM file that contains the values necessary for translation from the XYZ system to the $[\, \rho\, ], [\, \theta\, ], [\, \Phi\, ]$ system.

The other fields in this database record contain the names of the memory variables that handle the different translations from x,y,z to $[\, \rho\, ], [\, \theta\, ], [\, \Phi\, ]$. This record also contains the names of the variables that handle translations in the other direction. Because 256 variables are available to memory, and 128 fields are available to each database record, one record can handle a large number of translations.

What does this capability gain you? When many memory variables are active or are being juggled and changed throughout your work session, this capability gains you efficiency.

You probably won't remember the names of all the variables, their values (which may change), or the names of the various MEM files you'll create and SAVE throughout the life of your program. But you should recognize that you have created a database template for the input of variables and values. Once this information is entered, your program can work with the information, eventually asking if the calculated values are to be saved for future use. If so, they can be placed in a MEM file. With this method, you can predefine MEM files, variables, and the like, to anticipate most manipulations, simply by recognizing that, no matter how varied the data, it will always fit a certain template. Through clever programming, you can even create your own variable names and MEM files by APPENDing the MEMFILES database and then READing responses to a standard entry screen.

Some code that allows the user to select a MEM file or to scan the MEM file listings is useful in such a situation. The following pseudocode, closely resembling dBASE III Plus code, provides an example:

```
USE memfiles INDE memfiles
ACCE "What memory file do you want (8 char max)? -> " TO THIS
FIND THIS
*
IF .NOT. FOUN()
   YORN = .T.
   CLEA
   @ 1,0 SAY "I can't find that file. Want a list? (Y/N) -> " ;
        GET YORN
   READ
```

PLUS

```
*
   IF YORN
      @ 0,0 CLEA
      ON ESCA EXIT
      SET MESS TO "PRESS THE ESCAPE KEY TO STOP THE LISTING"
      GOTO TOP
      ROW = 1
      COL = 10
*
      DO WHIL .NOT. EOF()
         @ ROW,COL SAY STR(RECNO(),3,0) + " -> " + mfilename
         ROW = ROW + 1
*
         IF ROW = 23
            ROW = 2
            COL = COL + 20
         ENDI
*
         IF COL > 60
            ROW = 2
            COL = 0
            WAIT "I'm about to clear the screen. Press ESCAPE "+;
                 "to stop the listing, any other key to continue"
         ENDI
*
      ENDD
*
      THIS = 0
      ON ESCA
      @ 23,0 SAY "What number file? -> " GET THIS RANG 1,RECC()
      READ
      GOTO THIS
   ENDI
*
   THISFILE = mfilename
   REST FROM THISFILE
*
** EOF
```

PLUS

Note that little has to be done to this code to make it work in your
system. I created the THISFILE variable in case the user doesn't enter the
complete MEM file name when he tries to FIND that file. I usually run
with SET EXACT OFF, which means that, for dBASE III Plus to return a

valid result (if one exists), the user need enter only the first few significant characters of the search string.

This method has been used successfully; it even has been said that this looks like artificial intelligence. That is a generous comment, albeit naive. The only intelligence in this method is on the part of the programmer, and precious little is artificial about that.

## Memory Variables with Similar Names

Often, several variables on the same program level are very similar in intent. Because they are at the same level, the PUBLIC and PRIVATE commands are disabled. Giving each variable a different name adds to the confusion. The solution is to give each variable a similar, yet unique, name.

Once again, you may feel that your author has gone off the deep end. I haven't.

Consider an example with variables representing several cylinder sizes: CSIZE1, CSIZE2, CSIZE3, . . . CSIZE256, and perhaps even more. Cylinder size 2 is based on cylinder size 1; cylinder size 10 is based on cylinder sizes 1 through 9. This progression is typically called an *historical progression.* We don't want to create 256 or more variables and keep them floating in memory, but we do need to keep the cylinder sizes unique as they are created. In particular, we want each CSIZE variable to keep its own history, so that the variable name of the fourth cylinder size tells us the size is derived from the sizes of cylinders 1, 2, and 3.

The solution makes use of dBASE III Plus's MACRO function. We can't keep overwriting the CSIZE variable every time a new cylinder is created—that would wipe out the historical information—so we use the following trick:

```
CSIZE = "CSIZE4"
CHIST = "123"
NEWC  = "&CSIZE.&CHIST"
```

The important trick is the inclusion of the period (.) in the last line of the example. The result is

```
NEWC = CSIZE4123
```

Using this trick, we can create several variables, all with similar yet unique names. These variables carry their history with them—excellent for debugging, if nothing else.

## Databases of Memory Variables

I have already described a method of creating three-dimensional arrays by using MEM files and databases. A similar method is to use databases as storage tanks for memory variables.

dBASE III Plus MEM files are useful constructs, but crude and indelicate ones. A MEM file is loaded once and bypasses the buffers, which are a strength of the PC. One way around this problem is to create a database file to hold our memory variables. With this method, we can add selected memory variables to the program.

The central problem with MEM files is that you can retrieve them only with the RESTORE and RESTORE ADDITIVE commands. The former command destroys any existing values; the latter can create more than the maximum 256 memory variables, thus forcing dBASE III Plus to argue vehemently with you in the middle of an application.

If you use a database to hold memory variables, you gain the following advantages:

1. Quicker access to the variables

2. Repeated access to values even if the related memory variable's value has changed

3. Use of buffers

4. The capability of selectively "restoring" memory variables without overwriting existing variable values

5. Better memory management, because you can "restore" variables as they are needed, not all at once

Of course, we don't want to cloud up our disk with many databases that serve no purpose other than memory variable storage tanks. How do we get around that? With templates, of course.

At the start of every work session, we use a database that has no records. This database has only two fields per record: VARNAME and VARVALUE. We first APPEND a BLANK to the database, and move the memory variable values into the BLANK record; then we use the database for memory variable work. The code looks something like

```
REST FROM memfile
USE dbmemfile
REPL VARNAME WITH variable name, VARVALUE WITH variable value
etc.
```

This is a code-intensive operation. I don't recommend it unless your system depends heavily on memory variables for normal work. Note also that any single DBF holds only 128 fields; memory space allows up to 256 declared variables. Know your constraints before you use this method.

## Database Fields and Memory Variables with the Same Names

I've told you to make more use of database files when you are using memory variables. Now I'm going to show you how to use the same names for database fields and memory variables, and still avoid confusion.

With dBASE III Plus, you can keep up to ten databases active at one time. Correct? Actually, you can have eleven. The eleventh "database" is the memory of the machine, where your memory variables are stored.

With dBASE III Plus, you can reference the separate databases with

```
SELE A
SELE B
SELE C
```

and so on. You can reference the fields in the separate databases with

```
?  A->FIELD1
?  B->FIELD1
?  C->FIELD1
```

and so on.

Now let's assume that you have in USE a database with the field names COST, AMOUNT, and DISCOUNT. You also have memory variables named COST, AMOUNT, and DISCOUNT. dBASE II would get confused in some situations; dBASE III Plus won't, if you remember the following facts:

1.  Without a modifier (the A->, B->, and C->), the current database field value is returned for any query to a particular name.

2.  Database modifiers are A, B, C, through J.

3.  The memory variable modifier is M.

Number three is the most important. The use of M-> is as follows:

```
->use testdbf
```

```
->disp struc
```

```
Structure for database : C:TESTDBF.DBF
Number of data records : 2
Date of last update    : 03/18/85

Field  Field name  Type        Width     Dec
   1   FIELD1      Character    10
   2   FIELD2      Character    10
   3   FIELD3      Numeric      10
** Total ** 31

->disp all

Record#  FIELD1    FIELD2        FIELD3
     1   hello     howdy             25
     2   goodbye   toodles            0

->1

->? field1

hello

->field1='yep, a change.'

yep, a change.

->? field1

hello

->? m->field1

yep, a change.
```

Notice that by including m–> we've separated the memory variable, field1, from the database field, also called field1. This is an important improvement over dBASE II and one worth exploring, if for no other reason than that it provides clarity in variable names.

You may have a database of client accounts with a field called BALANCE. At the end of the month you want to know the total due (the sum of the BALANCEs). You can't use TOTALDUE or SUMOFBAL because these names are used elsewhere in the same program and must be kept active. SAVEing them to a MEM file isn't worth the time. It is far easier to

SUM ON BALANCE TO BALANCE

and then reference the memory variable with M–>BALANCE in subsequent parts of the program.

# Conclusion

In this chapter, we have investigated methods of overcoming weaknesses by discovering strengths. Usually these strengths involve little more than some clever solutions to apparently difficult problems. I want you to remember what a "clever" solution is: something that's intuitively obvious after you have tried everything else and failed. Our clever solutions make use of little-known features of dBASE III Plus in unique ways. Most of this book shows techniques that have been developed laboriously. But the point is simple enough: Wherever there is a weakness, there is a strength to overcome it.

# 6
# Powerful but Overlooked Commands

Many dBASE III Plus commands are poorly documented or rarely used, and wrongly so in both cases. These commands have been useful in my work, and a knowledge of them can be helpful to yours. So saying, I invite you to sample, experiment, and enjoy.

## The Speed of SET CONSOLE ON/off

One dBASE III Plus command gets much less use than it should; that command is SET CONSOLE ON/off. Normally, the CONSOLE is SET ON, and that setting is fine for 99% of the work dBASE III Plus does. At times, however, we have no need for the screen to be on. Also, DOing a program and monitoring the console takes more time than just DOing a program.

We notice the greatest savings of time in programs that need little user input, and hence don't have to keep the user informed. This consideration leads us to another important one: the psychology of the user. Users like to know that something is going on. When a machine appears dead, they likely will either kick it (reboot)—or they themselves will expire. Fortunately, for both the user's and the machine's mortality, the SET CONSOLE ON/off command gives some flexibility.

This command doesn't alter what is already on the screen. SET CONSOLE ON/off merely prevents dBASE from checking to see whether each subsequent command has to send information to the console. The nature of the command means that we can write code like the following:

```
SET COLOR TO BG*
TEXT
   WW    WW   OOOOOOO   RRRRRRRR  KK    KK  IIIIIIII  NN      NN  GGGGGGGG
   WW    WW   OO    OO  RR     R  KK  KK       II     NNN     NN  GG      G
   WW    WW   OO    OO  RR     R  KK KK        II     NN N    NN  GG
   WW WW WW   OO    OO  RRRRRRRR  KKKK         II     NN  N   NN  GG    GGG
   WW WW WW   OO    OO  RRRR      KK KK        II     NN   N NN   GG      G
   WW WW WW   OO    OO  RR RR     KK  KK       II     NN    NNN   GG      G
   WWWWWWWW   OOOOOOO   RR    RR  KK    KK  IIIIIIII  NN     NNN  GGGGGGGG
ENDTEXT
SET COLOR TO W, ,
?"                 !!PLEASE DO NOT DISTURB!!"
SET CONSOLE OFF

     [block of working code]

SET CONSOLE ON
```

This display ensures (we hope) that the computer is left to work uninterrupted; the code gives dBASE III Plus the added speed that can be gained from not monitoring the console at each step in the program.

Invariably, people who have absolutely no idea of what the computer is doing or how the program works will decide that they know what is best for man and machine. In other words, they'll mess up.

PLUS

You can guard against such problems by including

```
ON KEY DO NOTHING
```

at the top of the code and

```
ON KEY
```

at the end. NOTHING can be either a separate PRG file or part of a PROCedure file. In either case, it has the form

```
** NOTHING.PRG FILE
** EOF
```

# REPLACEing with Provisions

For those who aren't familiar with the REPLACE command, the basic syntax is

```
REPLACE [range] fieldname(s) WITH value(s) [FOR/WHILE condition]
```

REPLACE is used to change the values in specific fields in the USEd database.

Experience has shown me that this command is not as widely used as it could be. The best use of the command, aside from REPLACEing values that have been entered incorrectly and so forth, is for finishing the job of data entry. This section presents an example of a central office that gets disks of data from remote sites.

The object of the lesson is to speed entry and manipulation of data by requiring the keypunch personnel to enter only the data that changes in each entry, not data that is the same for record after record. This technique is obviously useful in that it speeds up data entry; it is also useful in that it reduces errors. Unless your keypunch personnel are vegetables, entry of repetitious data will cause their minds and hearts to wander to golden beaches or snowcapped peaks—anywhere but the CRT.

I have often used the concepts of masterbase and database in this book. Now I turn to the other side of the balance, and explain the logic for the database template.

Let's go back to the example of a central office with branch offices reporting to it. The branches gather data about their areas, and the form of the data gathered is the same no matter what the location. The database file structure might be as follows:

```
Structure for database    : C:REMOTES.DBF
Number of data records    : 0
Date of last update       : 12/30/84
```

| Field | Field name | Type | Width | Dec |
|-------|-----------|------|-------|-----|
| 1 | NAME | Character | 30 | |
| 2 | DEAR | Character | 15 | |
| 3 | HADDRESS | Character | 30 | |
| 4 | BADDRESS | Character | 30 | |
| 5 | PHONE | Character | 8 | |
| 6 | CITY | Character | 20 | |
| 7 | STATE | Character | 2 | |
| 8 | ZIP | Character | 5 | |
| 9 | AREACODE | Character | 5 | |
| ** Total ** | | | 146 | |

Each branch office has a DBACCESS module much like the one in Chapter 13. The DBACCESS module handles the bulk of database functions. The separate parts allow for addition of records, deletion of records, PACKing the database, viewing the database, EDITing records, and similar functions. The FRAMER and GETTER modules produce a screen like the one shown in figure 6.1.

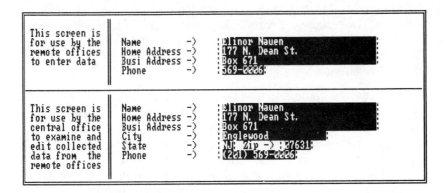

*Fig. 6.1. Data-entry screen for remote sales.*

At some point, the disk must be shipped from the branch to the central office. On the Main Menu, put the following option:

```
F9 -> SHIP DISK
```

Make sure that your client knows this option doesn't RUN the DOS PARK or SHIPDISK program. Selection of that option causes the following block of code to run:

```
CASE response=247
    CLEAR
    SET COLO TO R*
    @ 10,0 SAY SPACE(20)+"FIXING"
    REPLACE ALL CITY WITH cityname, STATE WITH stateid,;
            ZIP WITH zipcode, AREACODE WITH areacode
    SET COLO TO G*
    @ 10,0 SAY SPACE(20)+"LOCKING"
    !ATTRIB
    SET COLO TO W, ,
    CLEAR
    @ 10,0 SAY SPACE(20)+"PLEASE REMOVE DISK"
```

This code makes use of the DOS ATTRIB.COM file to change the attributes of a file. Attributes are changed to make the file R/O (READ ONLY). Other files, such as Norton's FILEATTR.COM or the dBASE Programmer's Utilities' CHMOD.EXE, can be used to make the file

HIDDEN. In either case, the purpose is to ensure that the file is unalterable until someone makes a special effort to "unlock" the file. Note that this procedure has nothing to do with using III PLUS on a network, nor is it similar to the LAN FLOCK( ), LOCK( ), and RLOCK( ) functions or the UNLOCK command.

This code provides a simple example of the REPLACE command. Stronger uses of the REPLACE command are shown in Chapters 7 and 8.

# STRING Operators in Place of LOGICAL Operators

Suppose that, in a certain comparison test, two conditions are given. The result of a test on those conditions is valid if either condition exists. The two conditions cannot coexist, so we don't worry about that possibility. What is the easiest and safest method for coding that comparison test? Most people would choose

```
IF "&var"="condition1" .OR. "&var"="condition2"
```

Right? Wrong!

A better way to code the comparison is with one of these equivalent statements:

```
IF AT('&var','condition1 condition2')#0
```

or

```
IF '&var' $ 'condition1 condition2'
```

The space between *condition1* and *condition2* is intentional. It prevents true statements from occurring when the value of var equals an unintended combination of the conditions. An example would definitely help.

```
var='radar'
condition1='adar'
condition2='adar'
```

We want to know if the value of var is equal to either the value of condition1 or condition2, but not a combination of the values.

```
IF '&var' $ 'condition1 condition2'
```

becomes

```
IF 'radar' $ 'adar adar'
```

which is false. On the other hand,

    IF '&var' $ 'condition1 condition2'

becomes

    IF 'radar' $ 'ada*radar*'

which is logically true, but programmatically false.

The first example returns a value greater than zero if **var** can be found in either condition. The second example returns a logical value of .T. if **var** can be found in condition1 condition2. It returns a logical .F. if **var** can't be found in condition1 condition2.

The most obvious use of this kind of test is in systems that ask the user to enter information for comparison to data in a database. The test is also used as a request for data from a database (see Part III).

In this example, the test is used with string variables and operators. Similar tests can be used with numeric variables by first converting them to their STR equivalents.

One use I want to emphasize has the form

    ANSWER$"A B C D E..."

where the ellipses mean that anything can follow. This form can be followed by . **NOT**. This form is very useful in CASE statements.

By setting up a situation in which the user can select one of several menu options, you open up the possibility that the user may select several invalid options. To test for such an occurrence, use

    CASE .NOT. ANSWER$"A B C D E..."

at the top of a DO CASE . . . ENDCASE block, followed by looping instructions.

# Arithmetic on DATE Fields

Programmers can use the DATE( ) function and DATE variables to add a certain degree of sophistication to programs. We can do arithmetic with DATE variables and fields, but the operations are limited: we are limited to adding and subtracting numbers to and from DATEs, and subtracting one DATE from another.

These capabilities can be used to determine when databases should be created or closed. The typical example is a polling system. Most polling systems close out at regular specified intervals: 7 days, 30 days, 120 days, and so on. We don't have to rely on the operator to know when a particular polling database should be closed. We can let the program determine that time for us.

The following code assumes the existence of a system clock or some other reliable way of ascertaining the date.

```
starter=.T.
CLEAR
@ 10,10 "Does today start a new polling session (Y/N)? -> " GET STARTER
**
IF starter
   REST FROM BEGIN
   startdate=DATE()
   SAVE startdate TO BEGIN
ELSE
   REST FROM BEGIN
ENDIF
**
IF DATE()=startdate+pollperiod        ** POLLPERIOD IS THE
   USE database                       ** LENGTH OF THE POLL.
   COPY STRUC TO newdatabase           ** IT IS STORED IN THE
                                      ** BEGIN.MEM FILE
   [POSSIBLE COPYING OF STRUCTURE TO A NEW DISK, ETC.]
ENDIF

[WORKING BLOCK OF CODE]
```

Arithmetic operations on DATE variables also can be used to solve some typical accounting problems. We can test for past-due accounts simply by having a DUEDATE field in each record in our RECEIVABLES file, and testing with

```
IF DATE()-DATEDUE<0
DO NOTICE2 WITH DATEDUE, BALANCE
```

Past-due accounts can then be flagged, and messages can be sent.

# Using DISPLAY and GOTO with SET RELATION TO

Many programmers hesitate to use dBASE III Plus's work areas because they think the work areas provide little more than do the SELECT

PRIMARY and SELECT SECONDARY commands. In this section and the next, I present often overlooked ways of using several databases, using the concept of primary and secondary keys (see "Primary and Secondary Keys" in Chapter 2).

The computer uses a primary key to keep track of information; we mortals use the secondary key to keep track of things. Let's imagine that we have one masterbase, DBA, and several databases containing related information—DBB, DBC, DBD, and so on. All of the related databases have information in common with DBA but not with each other. The exception is one keyfield that is also the indexfield for DBA (see fig. 6.2).

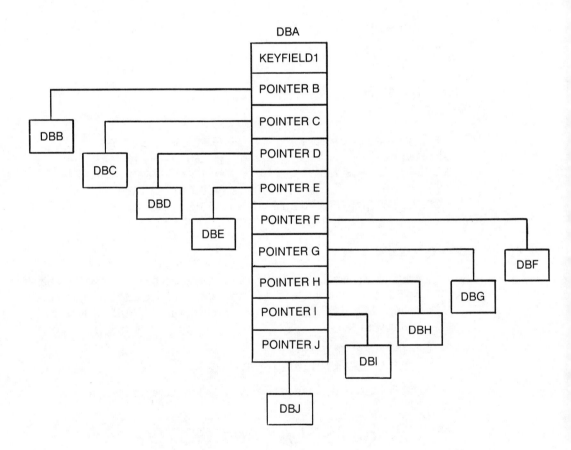

*Fig. 6.2. A masterbase and related databases.*

Remember that, because of the RELATIONs we set up, DBA is both *pointing to* and *being pointed to by* every other file. In the following code, each file shares the field AFIELD1. Only DBA is INDEXed on that field, however. Each of the other databases is INDEXed on its individual pointers. For example, DBB is INDEXed on POINTER B, DBC is INDEXed on POINTER C, and so on.

```
USE DBA INDE NDXA
SELE B
USE DBB INDE NDXB
SET RELA TO AFIELD1 INTO A
SELE C
USE DBC INDE NDXC
SET RELA TO AFIELD1 INTO A
SELE D
USE DBD INDE NDXD
SET RELA TO AFIELD1 INTO A
```

and so on, down to DBJ. Remember that AFIELD1 is in every database and is the keyfield for DBA. We reference databases DBB through DBJ by using the fields of our pointer file. To find in DBG information that is related to information in DBC, we can use

```
SELE C
FIND key field value in work area C
SELE A
FIND C->AFIELD1
SELE G
FIND A->POINTER G
```

This capability, which is useful in many ways, is directly useful for overcoming dBASE III Plus's normal single RELATION per work area constraint.

This code is an example of "pointing." We know the indexkey in database DBA. We want to find the related information in database DBG. We FIND the INDEXKEY in DBA, switch to DBG, and instruct dBASE III Plus to GOTO the RECNO( ) pointed to by the database record in work area A.

The ability to point to one work area from another work area is a powerful construct; I strongly recommend that you experiment with it in your own applications. It can save many program steps.

As another method of making the other databases point to DBA, we can use

```
DISP A->AFIELD10, GFIELD10, GFIELD5, . . .
```

Again, to compare values or related fields in different databases, we can

```
SELE A
FIND var
RECORDNUM = RECNO() A
SELE G
GOTO RECORDNUM
SELE C
GOTO RECORDNUM
SELE F
GOTO RECORDNUM
DISP A->AFIELDx, G->GFIELDy, C->CFIELDz, F->FFIELDt
```

This is another powerful but overlooked construct in dBASE III Plus. I advise you to experiment before using this construct in a program; you may have to make a few trial runs to achieve the desired result.

# The Difference between SEEK and FIND

SEEK and FIND are the dBase III Plus commands used to quickly GOTO INDEXed records. Both commands are based on indexkeys and keyfields. First, we look at similarities, then at differences.

Assume that you have a 2,000-record database of clients INDEXed on the NAME field. You've entered the names carefully, so each is unique. Now you want to find Jack Jickjock's name and pull his record. Using FIND, you could do either

```
FIND Jack Jickjock
```

or

```
STORE 'Jack Jickjock' to ANAME
FIND &ANAME
```

Using SEEK, you either

```
SEEK 'Jack Jickjock'
```

or

```
STORE 'Jack Jickjock' to ANAME
SEEK ANAME
```

As you can see, both commands do the same job, only differently. One of the problems with using SEEK instead of FIND results from a programming prejudice based on the dBASE III Plus manual.

The dBASE III Plus manual says that we cannot use macros within control structures. More precisely, we are warned that using macros within control structures causes the program to execute more slowly, and also may cause confusion. I believe the reference is to users' being confused by a program listing.

The dBASE III Plus control structures are DO WHILE . . . ENDDO (with or without EXIT or LOOP), DO CASE . . . ENDCASE (with or without OTHERWISE), and IF . . . ENDIF (with or without ELSE). The brave ones among you have already realized that you can use macros inside control structures without headache.

For many applications (obviously those where cross-referencing is vital), the SEEK command is the method of choice. It can be used in all applications (at least those I've tried) without restriction.

Using SEEK instead of FIND in a dBASE III Plus control structure has an advantage in time of .002 seconds. Hardly significant; after 1,000 passes, FIND increases execution time by only two seconds. If you are a purist, however, this economy can be meaningful. If you're programming massive amounts of code, with repeated requests for information from an INDEXed database, the advantage may be worth having.

The reason for using SEEK is that it makes less work for the computer. SEEK eliminates one manipulation: conversion of FIND &VAR into the proper form. That omission also eliminates one chance for making a mistake.

So much for using SEEK and FIND on the same database to find the same information. There is one more highly significant difference between FIND and SEEK. To demonstrate this difference, I again use the concept of database and masterbase. Assume that the database has 2,000 records with 10 fields. The masterbase has 2,000 records with 50 fields. The masterbase was INDEXed when we created it (even though there were no records to INDEX) with the keyfield MFIELD1. The database also was INDEXed from the first, so each APPENDing updated the index file accordingly. The database's keyfield is DFIELD1. DFIELD10 corresponds to MFIELD1.

```
USE database INDEX dindexfile
FIND var
SELE B
USE masterbase INDEX mindexfile
SEEK A->DFIELD10
```

For those who feel that the code is quicker than the eye, I've used the database to FIND something. The database, which holds information parallel to that in the masterbase, is INDEXed on DFIELD1. The tenth field in the database, DFIELD10, holds information parallel to the masterbase's keyfield, MFIELD1. In other words, DFIELD10 = MFIELD1 for each parallel set of records in the two databases.

Now, "parallel records" doesn't necessarily mean "parallel order." Parallel records simply means that for each record in the masterbase there is a corresponding record in the database. For example, the data in masterbase record #237 may be in database record #631 (not database record #237).

We've found something of interest in the database. We know that DFIELD10 is parallel to MFIELD1. We use that knowledge to

SEEK A→DFIELD10

The preceding line tells dBASE III Plus to use the value in DFIELD10 as the key value in the SEEK command in the masterbase.

To further demonstrate this powerful construct, let's assume that we have seven active database-indexfile combinations. They are linked in a way similar to the method described in the previous section. This time, however, the fields in DBA contain the indexkeys for databases DBB through DBG.

Database DBA is INDEXed on field DBA-1, DBB on field DBB-1, and so on. Further,

| | | |
|---|---|---|
| DBA-2 | corresponds to | DBB-1 |
| DBA-3 | corresponds to | DBC-1 |
| DBA-4 | corresponds to | DBD-1 |
| DBA-5 | corresponds to | DBE-1 |
| DBA-6 | corresponds to | DBF-1 |
| DBA-7 | corresponds to | DBG-1 |

Our primary database is DBA, which is also a powerful indexfile to databases DBB through DBG. If all seven database-indexfile combinations are active, we can use the following code:

```
USE DBA INDE AINDEX
SELE B
USE DBB INDE BINDEX
SELE C
USE DBC INDE CINDEX
SELE D
USE DBD INDE DINDEX
SELE E
```

```
USE DBE INDE EINDEX
SELE F
USE DBF INDE FINDEX
SELE G
USE DBG INDE GINDEX
```

We can access data in DBE, for example, when all we know is the related keyfield for DBA.

```
SELE A
FIND var
SELE E
SEEK A->DBA-5
```

Also note that any of the databases can be used to define the SEEK field for any of the other databases, provided that the field being sought is the keyfield.

# The RANGE Delimiter as an Error Check

Most dBASE II, dBASE III, and dBASE III Plus programmers have worked to death the limits of @ SAY . . . GET and @ SAY . . . GET PICTURE. One valuable option, however, is rarely used. The limits of data input can be predetermined through use of the RANGE delimiter, as in the following line:

```
@ SAY ... GET RANGE lowvalue, highvalue
```

This command works with all dBASE III Plus variable types and can provide a useful one-line error check. By using the system date, we can provide a means of limiting the dates of entry with

```
@ x, y SAY "Date of transaction -> " GET transdate RANGE;
DATE()-100, DATE()+100
```

Another useful check is to ensure the proper range for data entry of numeric variables:

```
@ x, y SAY "Percentage rate -> " GET prate RANGE 0, 100
```

You can use expressions, constants, or database field values as RANGE arguments. The RANGE command is also capable of accepting arguments from other active databases, such as

```
@ x, y SAY "New value -> " GET var RANGE A->AFIELD, B->BFIELD
```

The power of the RANGE delimiter is that it can take any valid dBASE III Plus value or argument and use it as part of the error check. Accounting systems can check that entries are made between the start of the month and the system date; engineering systems can determine if valid temperature ranges are entered based on given scales of measurement; and so on.

## Using IIF( ) for Conditional Commands

IIF( )—a new function with dBASE III Plus—should be used much more than it is. I want to demonstrate that dBASE III Plus can execute macro commands based on IIF( ). This is slick; sit back and enjoy.

First, how would you tell dBASE III Plus to take one action path rather than another? Well, you would probably use either an IF . . . ENDIF block or, if there were a significant number of action paths, a DO CASE . . . ENDCASE block. The DO CASE . . . ENDCASE block is discussed in Chapter 7; here we'll discuss using an IF . . . ENDIF block.

Let's say that there are two action paths to take, each of which is based on the veracity of a condition during processing. The normal code for such decision making is

```
IF condition
    DO path one
ELSE
    DO path two
ENDI
```

But why not code it as

```
COMMAND = IIF(condition, "DO path one", "DO path two")
&COMMAND
```

By golly, we've saved ourselves three lines of code. What's more, IIF( ) also processes impressively faster than the equivalent IF . . . ENDIF block—IIF( ) (for "Immediate IF") is one of the most appropriately named functions in all of dBASEdom. And there is more.

As coded in the preceding example, IIF( ) handles an *either/or* structure. You can code it as

```
COMMAND = IIF(condition1, "DO path one", IIF(condition2, ... ))
```

and so on. This allows you a multiple either/or structure that can replace

```
IF condition1
   DO path one
ELSE
*
   IF condition2
      DO path two
   ELSE
*
      IF...
*
   ENDI *2
*
ENDI *1
```

As always, I encourage you to experiment.

## Getting Two CASEs for the Price of One

I have already shown that you can do some fancy footwork with IIF( ). Now I will show you how to use IIF( ) to get four CASE statements where there are only two, ten where there are only five, and so on.

The dBASE III Plus CASE statement is designed to hold only one logical argument at a time. The form is

```
CASE condition
```

where "condition" must equate to True or False. However, we know that, based on its own internal condition, dBASE III Plus's IIF( ) function will return a True or False. What happens if we write something like

```
CASE IIF(condition, .T., .F. )
```

Well, for one thing, we've created two CASE statements—although we've written only one. Placing two such CASEs in a DO CASE . . . ENDCASE block, with nonexclusive conditions (condition1 → condition2), generates the following Truth Table:

|            | condition1 | condition2 |
|------------|------------|------------|
| condition1 | T          | T          |
| condition2 | F          | T          |

Thus, in this example, two CASEs generate the equivalent of three TRUE tests and one FALSE test. Again, careful readers will note that using IIF( ) in this way is a waste of code. And again, I chide you. We can use CASE and IIF( ) in forms such as

```
CASE field or variable = IIF(condition, value1, value2)
```

or

```
CASE IIF(condition, .T., IIF(...))
```

The first line is another example of doubling the function of the code by using IIF( ). This is especially useful when a single path is to be taken due to two different outcomes. The second line demonstrates the use of IIF( ) to create a logical nest.

# Determining Disk Space before Saving a File

One form of the dBASE III Plus ERROR( ) function tells you that a disk has no more room for a disk write operation. This is nice, but I'd rather know *before* I begin the writing process that I won't be able to save a file to disk. Fortunately, other functions allow just that.

PLUS    These functions are DISK( ), RECC( ), and RECS( ). You start by determining the size of the file you want to save to disk. This is done with the following algorithm:

```
IF DISK() > RECC() * RECS() + file header size
   save file
ENDI
```

You use the information found in Appendix D of the "Learning and Using dBASE III Plus" manual to determine file header size. Note that the file header size changes, albeit slightly, as records are added and removed. Also note that the DOSes do use space to save information in the disk's FAT and DIR areas.

# 7

# Rare Combinations

Just as dBASE III Plus has some powerful but overlooked commands, it also has several powerful but overlooked combinations. Some of these combinations simply add pizzazz to a data input screen; others can serve as useful error checks, or allow wider FIND and SEEK tolerances.

## Cross-Referencing Other Databases

The dBASE III Plus work areas and the COPY STRUCTURE EXTENDED command can provide a particularly clean error check. This check takes advantage of dBASE III Plus's capability of evaluating expressions in one work area by comparing them to expressions in another work area.

Assume, for instance, that you have designed a system that checks immediate information against a larger body of past information. An example of this type of system is the check-cashing machine that uses a "secret number" to make sure that you are who you claim to be. These devices check your given reference against a historic reference.

A similar system is feasible with dBASE III Plus. The system can be used to check memberships, member status, affiliation, or any other information that can be referenced from one database to another. Such a system requires two databases: one to contain the master file information, and one to store the structure file of the first database. You create these databases with

```
USE adatabase
COPY STRUC EXTENDED TO bdatabase
```

The following code can then perform the error check:

```
USE adatabase INDEX IDS
ACCE "CODE-> " TO id
FIND &id
SELE B
USE bdatabase INDEX PWS
ACCE "PASSWORD -> " TO pw
FIND &pw
**
DO WHILE .NOT. EOF()
   IF id=A->&ID_NUM
      ? "ACCEPTED"
      EXIT
   ENDIF
   SKIP
ENDDO
```

We are using two separate databases. One of the databases, adatabase, contains ID numbers and other nonvolatile data. For the purposes of the preceding code, the other data isn't even referenced. For an example similar to the magic money machine example, you could set the adatabase to count the number of accesses in one day, the amount of deposit or withdrawal per access, the number of incorrect entry attempts, and so on.

Once we find immediately necessary information in adatabase, we get more information from bdatabase. Notice that each database checks the other's data. Each database is keyed on a different item, but their data overlaps for the purpose of validating entry.

# Collapsing Databases
# with ZAP and PACK

dBASE III Plus provides two commands whose function is, in essence, to collapse databases. One command is ZAP, and the other is PACK. You can use ZAP if you want to collapse all the records in your database quickly. If you use PACK on a large database, the process can be slow. You didn't buy your computer to slow down your work, so the moral here is "Don't PACK."

You frequently will want to back up an important database, even if you plan to delete some of the database records. Instead of PACKing, use the commands RENAME and COPY TO:

```
database=DBF()
oldbase=left(DBF(),AT(".",DBF()))  +  "OLD"
CLOS DATA
RENA &database TO &oldbase
SET DELE ON
USE &oldbase
COPY TO &database
USE &database
```

PLUS

This routine is simple, clean, and neat. We've created a backup file and "packed" the work file, in about the same time required to PACK the database normally.

## Creating Database Subsets by COPYing with a FILTER

The COPY TO command also can be used with the SET FILTER TO command. This combination, used in conjunction with the method described in the last section, can help you design some uniquely "packed" databases. This is a strong combination because you can SET FILTER TO anything: a value, a database field or fields, the database fields of other work areas, and so on.

The best use of this command is to create subset database files. Consider the video-store example of Chapter 5. If you want to create a database for the records of everyone in the Hanover area, you would

```
USE customers
SET FILTER TO CITY="Hanover"
COPY TO hanover
USE hanover
```

The syntax used to reference another work area's database field is the same as in the method presented earlier:

```
SELE D
SET FILT TO CITY=A->CITY
COPY TO acity
```

The SET FILTER TO command also allows for the use of multiple conditions:

```
SET FILT TO CITY="Hanover"+LASTNAME=A->LASTNAME+...
```

In this way, you can perform highly selective COPYs.

Note: The SET FILTER TO command requires logical operators, such as <>, =, +, and .NOT.

PLUS

The QRY file, a new feature with dBASE III Plus, allows you to build FILTER conditions on a menu-driven system. I mention this file type because it can be used by programmers during the development phase.

Consider a situation in which your clients don't really know how they want their database FILTERed at first. They have an idea, albeit vague, of what they want done. You start by analyzing their database with them. The QRY menu system allows you to build on your clients' verbal concepts as the database is displayed before them. This is even more useful when you combine it with the

   CREA VIEW FROM ENVI file name

PLUS

command. After the proper FILTER and QRY conditions have been adequately expressed, the entire system can be qualified and placed in a VUE file for future use. Although you may have to spend more time with the client than you might like, this process can save you a great deal of time coding FILTERs when you program the job.

# Performing Specialized Searches with SET UNIQUE OFF/on

Imagine that we need to send a mailing to a small subgroup of the people named in a database, and that the records for each of those people share a common item in a common field. In this situation, we can see the power of the SET UNIQUE OFF/on command. By combining that power with the power of the FOR and WHILE qualifiers, we can produce some fancy searches.

In the historical society example, SET UNIQUE ON was used to weed out duplicate records. Now we'll use SET UNIQUE ON to create an NDX file that is kept active with a large database. The database may have a thousand repetitive records. The important consideration is that the keyfield is somewhat repetitive throughout the database. The indexfile can have as few as twenty or thirty pointers, depending on how often the keyfield changes. The key is that the NDX file is not representative of the entire database; it is more like a series of road signs.

How do we use the NDX file as a series of road signs? First, we create the NDX file:

```
SET UNIQUE ON
USE database
INDEX ON keyfield TO indexfile
```

At this point, the indexfile contains the road signs that are needed for the job at hand. We want to send letters to everyone whose record meets the condition

```
keyfield=indexkey
```

All we need is this routine:

```
FIND "indexkey"
DO WHILE keyfield="indexkey"
[WORKING CODE]
SKIP
ENDDO
```

Depending on how the records are to be pulled and where they are found in the database, we can substitute one or more of dBASE's one-line loops for the DO WHILE . . . ENDDO structure.

We can make the search even more specific by including a FOR qualifier. The WHILE qualifier ensures that only contiguous records with keyfield="indexkey" are accepted. The WHILE qualifier is a logical tool; the FOR qualifier is a sequential tool. The FOR qualifier can select several special cases from the subgroup, as in this routine:

```
SET UNIQ ON
USE database
INDEX ON keyfield TO indexfile
FIND "indexkey"
DO WHILE keyfield="indexkey"

   [WORKING CODE] FOR FIELDx="var"  ** If a looping  command is
                                    ** used, the syntax would be
   SKIP                             ** [WORKING CODE] NEXT 1 FOR;
ENDDO                               ** FIELDx="var"
```

An alternative to this method is, of course, to design the indexfile with more than one keyfield. That method would produce code like this:

```
SET UNIQ ON
USE database
INDEX ON keyfield1+keyfield2+...  TO indexfile
FIND "indexkey"
DO WHILE keyfield1="(first part of indexkey)" .AND. keyfield2=;
      "(second part of indexkey)" .AND. ...
```

```
[WORKING CODE]

    SKIP
ENDDO
```

The indexkey in the example must be the entire keyfield construct, unless the SET EXACT OFF option is used. This may not be what we want, however: dBASE will find only the best match, not necessarily the right match.

The problem of Whatsamatta U.'s Class of '85 provides a useful example. We can use SET UNIQUE and WHILE to make a quick-acting block of code if we have used SET UNIQUE ON in creating the NDX file.

```
*** NEWUPDTR.PRG
USE STUDENTS INDEX GRADYEAR
FIND YEAR(DATE())
COPY TO GRADUATE FIELD SNAME, SADDRESS, SCITY, SSTATE, SZIP, SPHONE;
        WHILE CLASSOF=YEAR(DATE())
SELECT 2
USE GRADUATE
INDEX ON SNAME TO GRADUATE
@ 20,0 SAY "CTRL-W to save and continue"
*
DO WHILE .NOT. EOF()
  EDIT
  SKIP
ENDDO
*
SELECT 1
SET INDEX TO SNAME
UPDATE ON SNAME FROM GRADUATE;
        REPLACE SADDRESS WITH GRADUATE->SADDRESS, ;
        SCITY WITH GRADUATE->SCITY, SSTATE WITH GRADUATE->SSTATE, ;
        SZIP WITH GRADUATE->SZIP, SPHONE WITH GRADUATE->SPHONE RAND
! DEL GRADUATE.*
```

Remember that the GRADYEAR NDX file in line 2 was created using SET UNIQUE ON. The NDX file therefore only contains pointers to the first record found for each year. The STUDENTS database may contain several thousand records with CLASSOF field values from 66 to 90, but the NDX file will contain only twenty-five pointers: one for the first entry for CLASSOF=66, one for the first entry for CLASSOF=67, and so on. The DBF file, however, is still organized so that all CLASSOF=66 entries are together, all CLASSOF=67 entries are together, and so on.

In line 3, we FIND the first record that meets our search criterion. The WHILE clause in line 4 can be used because all desired records are contiguous. We switch NDX files in line 16 merely to allow UPDATEing in the SNAME field, which is our field of primary interest and was our keyfield in the GRADUATE database. Line 18 is just a quick way of getting rid of temporary files.

What is the difference between NEWUPDTR.PRG and UPDATER.PRG? Because I have designed a similar system for a local college, I know that the university plans to INDEX on more than one field for different updates. NEWUPDTR.PRG takes that knowledge into account.

The people at the university added memory to their machines, so I could RUN DOS, BASIC, and ASSEMBLER programs from dBASE III Plus. Is this faster than UPDATER.PRG? I don't know. But the program did what the customer wanted, made the customer happy, and earned a paycheck for me. And those are the three things that count.

# Performing Sophisticated Searches with a FILTERed INDEX

Take any large file with duplicated records—such as the genealogical study—and we can use the SET FILTER TO command to perform searches so highly defined that we can pick one desired record out of a crowd. Although this command doesn't alter the size of the index file, SET FILTER TO does change the size of the output.

We begin, as in the last example, INDEXing with SET UNIQUE ON. The difference is the output.

```
SET UNIQUE ON
USE database
INDEX ON KEYFIELD TO indexfile
SET FILTER TO filter1, filter2, ...
FIND "indexkey"
DO WHILE KEYFIELD="indexkey"

    [WORKING CODE]       ** This can include the 'FOR'
                         ** qualifier
ENDDO
```

You can use the SET FILTER TO command with the precision of a surgical blade to winnow out individuals or small groups. Remember, however, that SET FILTER TO is a *logical* construct. The code shows commas (,) separating the filters. You must link them logically.

# Fancy Data Entry with SET DELIMITER TO and SET COLOR TO

I have often wondered about the psychology of data entry. I know that the task is, at best, tedious and boring. I didn't like to enter data; I performed this function for the Navy for several months, using IBM keypunch equipment. Even the development of the inexpensive CRT has not lessened the tediousness of the job. Data-entry people still tend to forget to enter all the data in all the fields, or at least to enter the important data in the fields of major interest.

These tendencies became a major problem when one of my clients needed an incredible volume of information entered into a database. Four keypunch operators worked eight hours a day for one month; such is the lot of the undergraduate work-study student. I needed to develop a method that would alert the operators when they had left something out. The solution was a combination of the SET DELIMITER TO, SET DELIMITER ON, and SET COLOR TO commands. This combination created a screen like the one shown in figure 7.1.

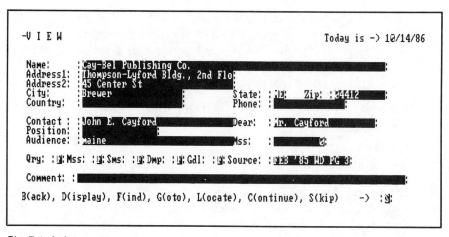

Fig. 7.1. A data-entry screen.

Unfortunately, I can't show you the full impact of the screen in this book. I therefore suggest that you write some matched FRAMER and GETTER routines, and then enter the following program.

```
SET DELIMITER TO ">C"  ** The delimiters can be anything you want.
SET DELIMITER ON
DO &framer
SET COLOR TO BR*          ** Determine which blinking color is the
DO &getter                ** most obnoxious for your monitor
SET COLOR TO W, ,         ** Set the color back to the standard
READ                      ** display
```

You can see the two-color effect when editing and adding data. The adding screen shows blinking delimiters; the colors change when you enter new data. The editing screen shows the old data, blinking in a horrid color. The fields stop blinking and change color as new data is entered. The result is quite effective.

# FINDing Data with SET EXACT and AT

Many programmers use dBASE III Plus's SET EXACT ON/off command to "unqualify" the FIND and SEEK commands in their programs. The SET EXACT ON command instructs dBASE III Plus to FIND only strings or values that match exactly. For example, you can FIND or SEEK an indexkey such as *Hel*, when the actual keyfield value is *Hello*. *Hello* equals *Hel* when SET EXACT is OFF.

This command is obviously useful when you are searching for information in an INDEXed database: you don't need to know the entire keyfield value to use an indexkey. Unfortunately, the SET EXACT ON/off command finds only the first characters of a string. If a FIND or SEEK returns a NO FIND argument, you can use

```
LOCATE FOR AT(partial keyfield value, KEYFIELD)<>0
```

This method takes more time than does using a FIND or SEEK, but the method can help you find records when you know only a part of the keyfield. You can make the code work faster by adding SET ORDER TO with no argument in order to "disengage" all index files.

PLUS

# REPORTing with the SET RELATION TO Command

REPORT used with SET RELATION TO is a useful combination. It allows you to CREATE or MODIFY REPORT forms so that they can use information from other databases. All you need to do is to specify the

unselected database and its field in the FIELD CONTENTS section when
CREATEing or MODIFYing the REPORT, as is shown in figure 7.2.

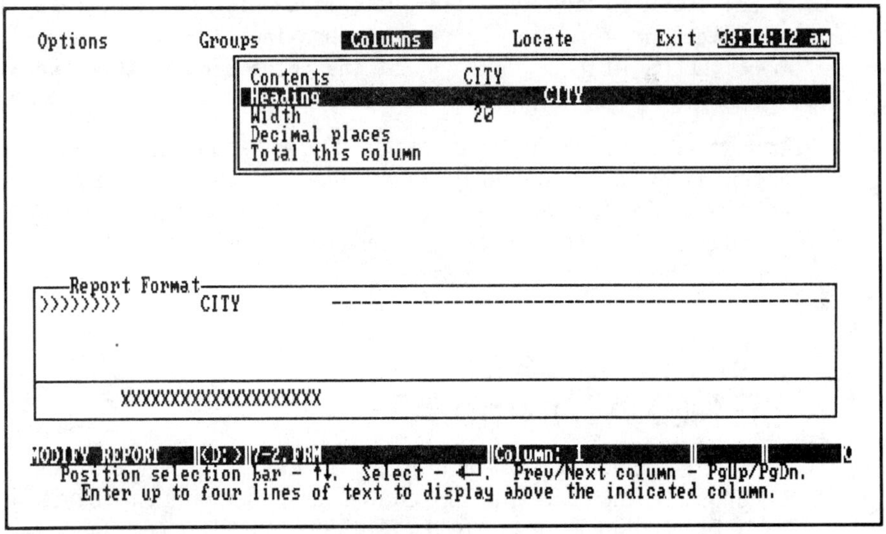

*Fig. 7.2. Referencing an unselected database.*

This combination, when used with SET RELATION TO, creates a
powerful cross-referencing report generator. An example of its use is the
creation of reports from an advertising agency's lists of media and clients.
The client database includes a MARKET field, which stores information on
the client's market audience. The media database has a TARGET field,
which stores information on the target audience. The information is listed
under different field names in the two databases, but the information is
the same in both places.

If we are REPORTing on the CLIENT database, we can use the following
routine:

```
USE MEDIA INDEX TARGET
SELE B
USE CLIENT
SET RELA TO MARKET INTO MEDIA
REPORT FORM MARKETS
```

Depending on what REPORT FORM is used, this structure generates reports that match several fields from one database with fields in the related database.

In a similar example, you can match manuscripts with magazines, based on audience, by using an MSS (manuscript) database and a MAGAZINE database that has an AUDIENCE field.

Figures 7.3 and 7.4 demonstrate how simple this combination is to execute. Figure 7.3 shows a FIELD CONTENTS description based on the field of interest in our primary use database. The same REPORT form can then access information from another, unselected database, as is shown in figure 7.4. dBASE III Plus permits only one RELATION per work area. However, ten RELATIONS can be in use at one time. This capability, with some clever database design, allows for several cross-references.

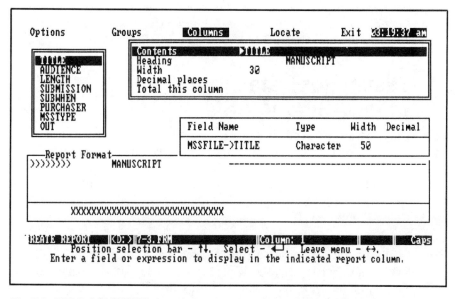

*Fig. 7.3. FIELD CONTENTS description for the primary database.*

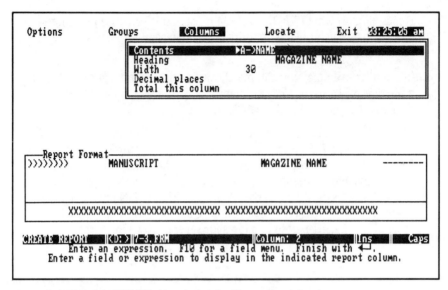

Fig. 7.4. FIELD CONTENTS description for the second database.

# Testing for Data Input with CASE and ASC

The CASE and ASC combination can be used to test for any type of data input. The effectiveness of the combination derives from the fact that the dBASE III Plus CASE command checks for only one condition. That condition, however, can be defined by means of the =, <, and > operators. The condition can also incorporate any of the other arithmetic or logical tests.

We can use the CASE command with the ASC( ) function to determine whether a user's response is numeric, alphabetic, a control code, or a function key. Fortunately, the ASC( ) function is not particular about the argument it receives. ASC( ) simply returns the ASCII character code of the first character of the argument.

Assume that the user can press one of several characters to perform certain operations on the database: C for CHANGE, E for EDIT, or S for SKIP. In addition to these alphabetic inputs, the user can enter numeric characters to call selected records from the same database or from another; 1 and 2 will then have the following meanings:

1 for SELE 1, 2 for SELE 2

1 to put one database in USE, 2 to USE another database

1 for GOTO 1, 2 for GOTO 2, etc.

By using ASC( ) and CASE, we can test such options as follows:

```
***JDIMAIN. PRG
***DESIGNED BY JOSEPH-DAVID CARRABIS, APRIL '85
**
CLEAR
SELE A
USE NEWINS INDE NEWINS
SELE B
USE NEWPLCY INDE NEWPLCY
DO NEWFRAME
**
DO WHIL .T.
   SELE A
   DO NEWGETS
   SELE B
   DO CPOLFRAM
   DO CPOLGETS
   CLEA GETS
   @ 21,0
   ACCE "(C)hange  (R)evise  (N)ext  (B)ack  (P)rint  (E)nd" to A
**
   DO CASE
      CASE ASC(A)<49
         @ 21,0
WAIT "Valid selections are 1-9, C, R, N, B, P,  or E. Press any key to continue"
**
      CASE ASC(A)<58
         STORE RECNO() TO NEWINSREC
         STORE "P"+STR(A, 1, 0) TO P_FIELD
         STORE &P_FIELD TO POL_TYPE
         STORE REC TO FINDER
         DO JDIPLCY
         SELECT A
         USE NEWINS IDNE NEWINS
         SELECT B
         USE INS INDE INS
         CLEAR
         DO NEWFRAME
```

```
**
           CASE ASC(A)>57
              STORE UPPER(A) TO A
**
           DO CASE
              CASE A="C"
                 @ 21,0 CLEAR
                 ACCE "What is the new client code? -> " TO CLI_CODE
                 STORE UPPER(CLI_CODE) TO CLI_CODE
**
                 IF CLI_CODE="NEW"
                    DO MISC
                 ELSE
                    USE INS INDE INS
                    FIND &CLI_CODE
                    COPY NEXT 1 TO INSTANK
                    SELE A
                    APPEND FROM INSTANK
                 ENDIF
**
              CASE A="R"
                 DO NEWSOME
                 DO CPOLGETS
                 @ 21,0 CLEAR
                 @ 21,0 SAY "Type Ctrl-W to exit"
                 READ
**
              CASE A="N"
                 SKIP
**
              CASE A="B"
                 SKIP -1
**
              CASE A="P"
                 SET DEVICE TO PRINT
                 DO NEWINS.FMT
                 SET DEVICE TO SCREEN
**
              CASE A="E"
                 RETURN
**
              OTHE
                 @ 21,0
```

```
WAIT "Valid selections are 1-9, C, R, N, B, P, or E. Type any key to continue"
        ENDCASE
**
    ENDCASE
**
ENDDO
```

I created the first DO CASE . . . ENDCASE set to determine whether the variable A is alphabetic or numeric. If A is alphabetic, the CASE statements pass execution to the second DO CASE . . . ENDCASE set.

# Using IIF() with REPORT and LABEL Forms

PLUS

I'm going to show you one of the neatest tricks in the business. This is something that you won't find in other books (nothing like throwing down the gauntlet, huh?). Not, at least, in any books that I've seen. The trick has to do with the IIF( ) function and the dBASE III Plus form generators.

By the way, this trick will work with CLIPPER files but is totally incompatible with dBASE III. You must use a III Plus-compatible system. I haven't tried the trick yet on Wordtech systems.

The trick is simple, but I'm going to explain why I did it before telling you what it is.

Sometimes the REPORT and LABEL forms we create aren't exactly what we would like them to be. No matter how hard we try, things just don't line up correctly, or extra lines appear between text on our labels. Yuck! Is there a way around this? Oh my, yes.

Figure 7.5 shows the trick. Note that I've included an IIF( ) function in the CONTENTS field of the REPORT FORM. Can you actually do that? Yes, with wonderful results. This example shows a part of the REPORT FORM with several headings, each of the form T#n, where $n$ is a number from 1 to 6. These headings represent database fields named TIERn (again, $n$ is a number from 1 to 6). Each TIERn is a LOGICAL field (either .T. or .F.).

Our client wants to be told which TIERs each customer has. Some customers have TIER1, TIER4, and TIER5. Others have TIER2, TIER3, and TIER4. Some might have only one TIER, others have all.

We could design the REPORT FORM so that it simply would enter .T. or .F. under each T#n heading. This solution is acceptable when you're at

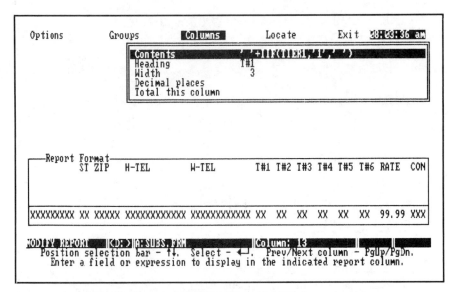

Fig. 7.5. Using the IIF( ) function in REPORT and LABEL forms to place
executable code inside the form itself.

the top of the report form, have the headings immediately visible, and can
eyeball things with fair accuracy. But what do you do when you're trying
to read the report's 35th line and you see the TIER list as

.T..F..F..T..F..F.

Foo. You can't scan that list quickly and understand it. But we can use
IIF( ) in the CONTENTS field of the REPORT FORM as

IIF(TIERn,'n','   ')

When the report is generated, IF TIERn = .T., the FORM will have the
value *n* under the proper heading. The logic list becomes

1          4

That's much easier to scan quickly and interpret correctly, don't you
think? I've given you an example. You can use IIF( ) to create far more
complex CONTENTS.

So much for REPORT FORMs.

What about LABELs?

Have you ever generated a six-line label form such as

```
NAME
COMPANY
ADDRESS1
ADDRESS2
CITY + ', ' + STATE
SPACE(LEN(TRIM(CITY + STATE)) + 2) + ZIPCODE
```

and tried to fill it with only three lines of data? You end up with a LABEL such as

```
Mr. Joseph-David Carrabis

PO Box 3861

Nashua, NH
          03061-3861
```

Not the prettiest or most professional looking label in the world.

PLUS

We use IIF( ) and the capability of some printers to do a reverse line feed. (Note that your printer must be in nongraphics mode and that it must be able to perform reverse line feeds.)

We start with the knowledge that there's data in the NAME, ADDRESS1, CITY, STATE, and ZIP fields in each record in our address database. If we know the control character that tells the printer to do a reverse line feed, we can include LABEL FORM lines such as those shown in the following listing:

```
IIF(COMPANY = SPAC(30), CHR(n) + ADDRESS1, ADDRESS1)
IIF(ADDRESS2 = SPAC(30),CHR(n)+CITY+', '+STATE,CITY+', '+STATE)
ZIP + IIF(ADDRESS2 = SPAC(30), CHR(m), '') + ;
      IIF(COMPANY = SPAC(30), CHR(m), '')
```

and in the CONTENTS expression of the LABEL FORM (see fig. 7.6).

What does this do? Remember that dBASE III Plus and the LABEL FORM don't keep track of physical printer lines. They only tell the printer to throw a line and form feed. The first line of the previous listing translates to "If there is no COMPANY name, reverse line feed and print ADDRESS1. If there is a COMPANY name, stay on this line and print ADDRESS1." The second line of the listing performs in the same way, but uses the ADDRESS2 field. CHR(n) represents the control character used to perform a reverse line feed in both cases.

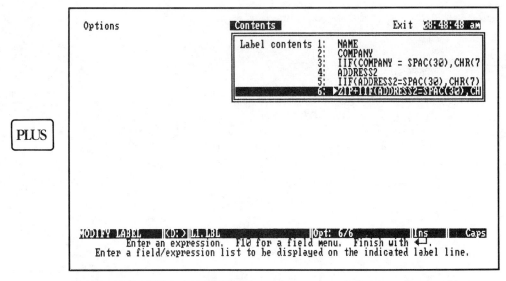

PLUS

Fig. 7.6. Using IIF( ) in LABEL FORMs to close up space between lines and to perform other magic.

Well, now that we've robbed the LABEL FORM of one or two lines, how do we make sure that each LABEL is still six lines long? The third line in the listing tells dBASE III Plus to print the ZIP field in the "sixth" line. This might be the fourth or fifth physical line of the LABEL FORM—we don't really know. But we do know that the ZIP field is printed on the fourth physical line IF both ADDRESS2 and COMPANY are blank fields. IF both ADDRESS2 and COMPANY are blank fields, III Plus throws a line feed to the printer (represented here by CHR(m)). If either ADDRESS2 or COMPANY has data, only one CHR(m) is sent to the printer.

Slick.

# Using FOR and WHILE Qualifiers

Be especially careful when you use the FOR and WHILE qualifiers. When you use WHILE, you will see either the data you requested or nothing, depending on the setting of the database pointer. For example, assume that you want to REPORT something WHILE a condition is true. You use

```
REPORT FORM reportfile WHILE condition
```

If the database pointer is on a record where the condition is not true, no REPORT is generated, although there may be several other records in the database that meet the condition. To solve this problem, you can use a random one-line loop, such as

```
REPORT FORM reportfile FOR condition
```

This command starts from the database pointer location and proceeds until EOF( ) is True, checking every record for "condition"=.T.

You can also get around this problem by using a method listed earlier. Use an NDX file to FIND or SEEK the first occurrence of "condition." Once the first occurrence of "condition" has been found, you can use the WHILE qualifier to poll the selected records.

dBASE III Plus commands that allow both FOR and WHILE qualifiers are

AVERAGE determines the mean value of any number of fields. These fields don't have to be in the SELECTed database. For example, look at the following code:

```
USE ADATABASE   ** Which has 200 records
SELE B
USE BDATABASE INDE BNDX  ** Which has 2000 records
SELE A
SET RELATION TO afieldx INTO B
AVER B->BFIELD1
```

This program returns the mean value of the two hundred related BFIELD1 entries in BDATABASE. Combinations of conditions based on the fields in SELECTed work-area databases can be used. For example:

```
USE adatabase
SELE B
USE bdatabase INDE bndx
SELE A
SET RELA TO afieldx INTO B
AVER B->bfieldx FOR 1st condition in A .AND. 2nd condition in A
```

Note that you can use user-assigned input, memory variables, etc., as part of the FOR or WHILE qualifiers. You must use LOGICAL expressions, however, to link the separate FOR or WHILE arguments. You can use AVERAGE to produce random samplings of a database based on the entries in another database.

CHANGE allows selective editing of a database WHILE or FOR a user-supplied condition. This command can be combined with SET RELATION TO to provide conditional CHANGEs based on two criteria: the user-supplied condition, and the entries in a database in a nonSELECTed area.

An example of this, actually put in use, is

```
** CHANGER MODULE
**
ACCE "What is the condition for changing -> " TO CONDITION
SELE B
USE bdatabase INDE bndx
SELE A
USE adatabase INDE andx
SET RELATION TO afieldx INTO B
SET MESS TO "PRESS F1 TO TOGGLE THE MENU"
CHAN FIEL field list based on application ;
    FOR afieldx = CONDITION ;
    WHILE bfieldx = condition based on application
```

Note that the EDIT command is identical to the CHANGE command, and can be used in this code with no problem.

COPY       can be used with qualifiers on both the SELECTed and nonSELECTed database. For example,

```
USE ADATABASE
COPY TO BDATABASE FOR/WHILE &condition
```

determines the condition based on the FIELDS in the database ADATABASE. The following code determines the condition based on the last referenced field in CDATABASE:

```
SELE C
USE CDATABASE INDE CNDX
SELE A
USE ADATABASE
SET RELATION TO afieldx INTO C
COPY TO BDATABASE FOR C->&condition
```

This combination can provide for some useful conditional COPYs. Conditions can be precisely defined, and databases in several areas can be used.

COUNT      determines the number of records in the SELECTed database that match the condition.

```
SELE B
USE bdatabase INDE bndx
SELE A
USE adatabase
SET RELA TO afieldx INTO B
COUN TO var FOR afieldn = bfieldm
```

The thing to see here is that **afieldn** is not the field used in the SET RELATION TO command. The SET RELATION TO command allows **bdatabase** to track **adatabase** during the COUNTing procedure.

DELETE     marks records to be DELETEd in the SELECTed database based on conditions in either the SELECTed or nonSELECTed database. The syntax for DELETEing records based on conditions set in nonSELECTed databases is similar to that used for the COPY command. The result can be some useful conditional deletions.

```
SELE B
USE bdatabase INDE bndx
SELE A
USE adatabase
SET RELA INTO afieldx INTO B
DELE FOR IIF(bfieldm = condition, .T., .F.)
```

Note that this form can be used also for COPY, etc.

Note my use of IIF( ). The results of my IIF( ) test are themselves logical arguments. Careful readers will argue that, as the code stands, there is no need for IIF( ). I agree, but chide you on your shortsightedness. Each logical argument can be replaced by its own IIF( ). This layering of IIF( )s allows you a control that can't be duplicated by any combination of .AND., .OR., and .NOT.

DISPLAY     sends user-defined information to the screen, one screenful at a time, based on user-defined conditions in the SELECTed or nonSELECTed database, or a combination of the two.

Note that the DISPLAY command can follow the same use patterns as the DELETE command. This means that you can use a command such as

```
DISP field list FOR IIF(b field condition, .T., .F.)
```

PLUS

once proper RELATIONS have been set.

PLUS

| | |
|---|---|
| LABEL FORM | This command follows a syntax identical to that of the DISPLAY command, including the use of both FOR and WHILE qualifiers. You can use IIF( ), as shown in earlier examples, and you can include fields from more than one database in each LABEL. Such a construct requires setting up in one work area a database that is related to a DBF in another work area, which in turn is related to a database in another work area, and so on. Each field in the LABEL can be from a different database. Use the SET RELATION TO command to ensure parallelism and keying off the single master file in the primary-use work area. |
| LIST | This command is identical to DISPLAY except that LIST doesn't pause when it sends data to the screen. Note that although this command allows everything that the DISPLAY command allows, LIST is used primarily with the TO PRINT qualifier. This qualifier tells dBASE III Plus to send the information to the printer, but doesn't stop for page breaks. |

If you're using tractor-feed paper, you can include your printer's paper-feed character (usually Ctrl-L) as the field to display, and set your printer in nongraphics mode. Thus, when your printer tries to LIST the data TO the PRINTer, you get a form feed. Note that for this trick to work, your printer must be in nongraphics mode.

LOCATE      This command, because of its AI-like capabilities, is one of the more interesting one-line loops. The LOCATE command follows all the syntax rules of DELETE, but you can do some interesting things with the FOR qualifier. For example, you can include a line such as

```
LOCA FOR condition$field
```

which goes far beyond the capabilities of FIND and SEEK, even when those commands are used with SET EXACT OFF. FIND and SEEK with SET EXACT OFF still limit the keyfield search to the first significant characters of an alpha keyfield. In this example, the LOCATE command tells dBASE III PLUS to look in a specific field for a specific condition, but to look anywhere in that field. Whether the data of interest is at the beginning, the end, or lost in the middle, this code finds it. Furthermore, the same search condition holds for the CONTINUE command, should you need it after the first LOCATE.

RECALL          The RECALL command is the "other side" of the DELETE
                command. With RECALL, as with DELETE, you can use the      **PLUS**
                FOR and WHILE qualifiers singly or in combination. For some
                finesse, you can use the IIF( ) function.

REPLACE         This command bridges the chasm between CHANGE/EDIT
                and UPDATE. It provides a user interface in the form of a one-
                line loop. Note that conditions can be set from menus; then
                REPLACE can go to work on its own.

REPORT          This command is identical to REPLACE. The method of
                particular interest, mentioned in the section on combining the
                REPORT and SET RELATION TO commands, allows
                multidimensional REPORTing and is worth investigating.

The APPEND and JOIN commands can be used with the FOR qualifier
only.

APPEND          This command shares the syntax of COPY, but is used with
                the FOR qualifier to increase the APPEND range. Note that
                FOR will always perform a sequential search. This feature
                rarely presents a problem because you can't APPEND from
                an active DBF file.

JOIN            JOIN uses only the FOR qualifier. I warn you about using it:
                the JOIN command is a record multiplier. By that I mean
                that JOINing two databases, one with 10 records and the
                other with 20 records, usually will produce a single JOINed
                database with 200 records. You seldom want to JOIN that
                much data or, if you do, you should be making a
                masterbase for your system.

The NEXT n and REST qualifiers can be used with the FOR and WHILE
qualifiers.                                                               **PLUS**

NEXT n and      These two qualifiers are used a great deal with
REST            one-line loops. The NEXT n command tells dBASE III Plus
                to perform the one-line loop for the NEXT n records. (*n* can
                be any valid dBASE III Plus numeric value or expression.)
                By using this qualifier with FOR and WHILE, you can
                perform operations on an evaluated number of records. For
                example, suppose that you do some calculations which
                determine that only the NEXT 100 records should be
                modified. Without causing any problems for dBASE III Plus,
                you can include as NEXT's argument the expression that
                evaluates to 100.

PLUS

REST, which is new with dBASE III Plus, allows you to specify the remainder of the DBF as the range of operations. You can EDIT REST; you will be led from the current record pointer through the remaining records. REST and NEXT work with all of the one-line loop commands that perform some work on the currently active database.

# 8

# Parameters and
# Public Variables

This chapter offers a theoretical discussion of the PUBLIC, PRIVATE, DO PARAMETERS, and RELEASE commands. Like the rest of this book, this chapter is meant to provide a foundation for you to build on. This chapter also offers a discussion of how these commands work.

The main point of this chapter is that a variable declared in a calling program can be used in a called program and returned to the calling program. The variable can return to the program changed in value and—if you're not careful—changed in type.

## Accessing PUBLIC Variables

dBASE III Plus needs to know which variables are local to one program and which variables can move back and forth between programs. The simplest way to make a variable capable of moving back and forth is to declare the variable PUBLIC.

Declaring a variable PUBLIC is similar to using the COMMON command in BASIC. The dBASE III Plus manual describes the command as *global*; some programmers may remember the term. The PRIVATE command is comparable to the LOCAL command of some other languages.

Figure 8.1 shows a hierarchical program structure composed of three programs. Their names indicate their position in the hierarchy. TOP calls MIDDLE, which then calls BOTTOM, but TOP cannot directly call BOTTOM. Each of the memory variables, V1, V2, and V3, is declared in its respective program.

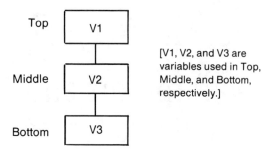

Fig. 8.1. A hierarchical program with variables at different levels.

Assume that we want to pass some information among the programs; there's no point in linking programs that cannot pass data back and forth.

We'll begin with a simple case: passing information from TOP to BOTTOM. This case most closely resembles the method of dBASE II, and requires no special commands. Once declared, all variables are accessible to all routines at all levels. You can always pass information down levels.

Variable V1 can be accessed by all three programs. Variable V2 can be accessed by the two lower programs. Variable V3 can be accessed only by the last program.

Read the last three sentences again. A message is hidden there.

The message is this: *What is accessed can be changed.* If BOTTOM makes changes to V1 or V2, the changes are transferred through the hierarchy. Variables declared in lower-level programs are hidden from higher-level programs, however, because variables are LOCAL to the programs, subroutines, and procedures that call them. The TOP program therefore gives you an error message if you query about V2 or V3. The MIDDLE program gives you an error message if you query about V3.

All variables are automatically RELEASEd when program execution ends. RELEASE is a dBASE IIIism for *destroy*; memory variables declared in a program cannot be accessed after the declaring program ends. You therefore cannot access V2 after MIDDLE has ended, or V3 after BOTTOM has ended.

What if you want to use V2 and V3 in TOP? You can declare all three variables at the beginning of TOP, making them available to any program. That is the easiest way to give all three programs access to the variables.

If you want the variables to remain available after all three programs are terminated, you can declare the variables PUBLIC either before you DO any of the programs or at the beginning of TOP. For example, assume that you want V3 to remain after the TOP, MIDDLE, and BOTTOM programs have executed. Before you can access V3, you must include the command PUBLIC V3.

You will receive an error message if you make a variable PUBLIC after it has been declared. PUBLIC variables assume a LOGICAL value (.T. or .F.) until declared.

# Accessing PRIVATE Variables

The opposite of the PUBLIC command is the PRIVATE command. Whereas the PUBLIC command makes a variable available to any level of the program, the PRIVATE command keeps a variable within a certain level. If V1 is declared in TOP, then ordinarily TOP, MIDDLE, and BOTTOM are able to manipulate the variable. But what if you want to use the variable name V1 in the MIDDLE program without using the value assigned to V1 in the TOP program? Then you use

    PRIVATE V1

in MIDDLE before you use the name V1.

Then you need to declare V1 again, or you will receive an error message. What is the hidden meaning this time?

To understand the answer, assume that you enter the

    PRIVATE V1

command at the tenth line of the MIDDLE program, and that you worked with V1 before issuing that command. Figure 8.2 graphically illustrates that assumption.

The value returned to TOP at line 21 of MIDDLE is the value assigned in line 9 of MIDDLE. All manipulations done on V1 after it is declared PRIVATE in line 10 of MIDDLE are not RETURNed to TOP when MIDDLE finishes execution. The value of V1 RETURNed to TOP, however, is not the same as the one passed to MIDDLE. Even though V1 is declared PRIVATE in line 10 of MIDDLE, all manipulations done on V1 prior to that declaration are RETURNed to the calling program, in this case TOP.

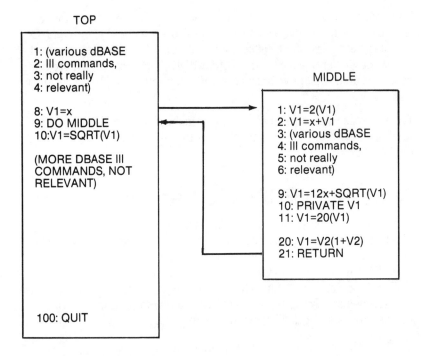

*Fig. 8.2. Interaction of the programs TOP, MIDDLE, and BOTTOM.*

The other message is that making a variable PRIVATE only stops the value stored in the variable from flowing up, not down. If the BOTTOM program uses a variable named V1, the value of the variable is determined in MIDDLE, not in TOP.

You should never use more memory variables than necessary, because the variables tie up valuable memory space. After the program is executed, all PRIVATE variables are released. Periodically (especially if you have a large system), you need to "clean out" your memory with

    RELEASE ALL LIKE variabletype

or

    RELEASE variable1, variable2, . . .

dBASE III Plus provides a bridge between PUBLIC and PRIVATE in the DO WITH . . . PARAMETERS command set. You can use these commands to send information to a subroutine "incognito." In this case, you want the subroutine to perform tasks with the value of a variable without using the variable name. You can do this easily.

Suppose that you have a fourth program, called OTHER, which is not listed in the diagram of figure 8.1. With OTHER included, the diagram appears as in figure 8.3.

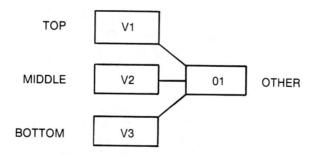

*Fig. 8.3. A program passing data to a hierarchical program structure.*

OTHER has the variable O1. OTHER manipulates data necessary to TOP, MIDDLE, and BOTTOM. You need to pass along to OTHER the value of V1, V2, and V3 without OTHER's using the variable names. You can DO OTHER WITH V1 (or V2 or V3, as the situation requires) to call OTHER.

The first command in OTHER must be PARAMETERS O1. No further declarations are necessary. Then OTHER can manipulate the value of V1 (or V2 or V3), as stored in O1, without actually affecting V1. All changes are made to the variable O1. This trick is useful when you want to compare a value (V1) with an anticipated value (O1) that is determined by performing calculations on V1.

The hidden message here is that the value of O1 is passed to V1 upon termination of OTHER. Even though V1 remains unchanged while OTHER is working, V1 takes the value of O1 when OTHER is terminated. Because of this fact, you must be careful.

The dBASE III Plus documentation (and probably every other book you've read about the program) tells you that the PARAMETER command must be the first command in the receiving file. Even I may have told you that. If I did, I'm glad you've read this far. I lied.

The truth is that you have some flexibility in how you use the PARAMETER command. The PARAMETER command can go anywhere in the receiving PRG or PROC file. You can create a receiving file with a structure like

```
** BOF
executable commands
PARAMETER parameter list
executable commands
** EOF
```

Note that the PARAMETER command is in the middle of the file. This location is significant. What does placing the PARAMETER command in the middle (or end, or anywhere other than in the first line of the receiving file) do to the receiving file?

First, it tells dBASE III Plus not to use the passed value until the PARAMETER command is executed. In truth, dBASE III Plus can use the variable's calling value in much the same way as it would normally. What happens is really simple. Whenever dBASE III Plus DOes something WITH a variable list, a special buffer is created. That buffer holds the passed variables and their values. Thus, using dBASE III Plus's inherent hierarchical variable-passing ability as discussed earlier, you could use a variable in a called routine in the standard way and execute some commands using the normally passed value. Then, when dBASE III Plus executes the PARAMETER command, it looks in the buffer for the passed value, and uses that value for the rest of the calculations.

What value is passed back? After a parameter is passed, assigned values are returned. But the power of placing the PARAMETER command somewhere other than in the first line of the receiving file allows you to use a variable's value as it would normally be passed, without name changes or such shenanigans, and then use the passed value for other work. Slick!

# One-Line Loops with dBASE III Plus

A loop is a block of code that performs a task repeatedly. dBASE III has several commands that perform loops. An example of a one-line loop is

```
COUNT TO NUMBER
```

This simple one-line loop actually accomplishes the same result as the following code sequence:

```
NUMBER=0
GOTO TOP
DO WHILE .NOT. EOF()
   NUMBER=NUMBER+1
   SKIP
ENDDO
```

Note that you would normally use RECCOUNT( ) to COUNT every
record in the DBF. COUNT is best used with FOR or WHILE qualifiers.

In the same way, the one-line loop

```
TOTAL TO SUMMARY ON FIELD1,FIELD2 ...
```

performs the same function as the following lengthy block of code:

```
STORE 0 TO F1,F2, ...
USE DATABASE
COPY STRUC TO SUMMARY
DO WHILE .NOT. EOF()
   F1=F1+FIELD1
   F2=F2+FIELD2

      .     .     .

      .     .     .

      .     .     .

   SKIP
ENDDO
USE SUMMARY
APPEND BLANK
REPLACE FIELD1 WITH F1,FIELD2 WITH F2, ...
```

The final example of a one-line loop uses the SUM command. The one-
line loop

```
SUM FIELD1,FIELD2 ...  TO F1,F2 ...
```

replaces the entire code block

```
STORE 0 TO F1,F2, ...
GOTO TOP
DO WHILE .NOT. EOF()
   F1=F1+FIELD1
   F2=F2+FIELD2

      .     .     .

      .     .     .

      .     .     .

   SKIP
ENDDO
```

If my point is obscure, I apologize. I want you to know that you don't need to reinvent the wheel. The one-line loops listed illustrate two points I want to make in this section:

1. Make the maximum use of minimum code.

2. If a loop is necessary, keep it small.

The point is to code your loops to perform only a specific function. If you code for any contingency, you will create a time-consuming and unwieldy loop. If you read my recoding of the one-line loops, you'll notice that the commands contain only the necessary instructions.

# II
# Turnkey Systems with dBASE III Plus

The time required to write a fully implemented turnkey system is often gauged in programmer-months; you can expect it to run to programmer-years. The reason is simple: you are writing a program that will do everything but turn the machine on and off.

Only rarely will a programmer undertake such a project alone. It involves creating multilevel error traps and text- and code-sensitive help screens. The program must be "forgiving" and, to some extent, even "intelligent." (Notice that I haven't even begun to talk about the code!)

Conversely, you shouldn't design and implement a turnkey system for one client, unless you will be paid incredibly well, or you are a martyr. Development time for the average turnkey system is 12 months. Getting all the bugs out will usually take another two years. By that time your customer(s) will be ready for an upgrade. You'll be ready for a padded cell.

A turnkey system is a program designed so completely that all the user does is activate the system. Every module has been planned to the smallest detail; accounting formulas, access menus, and databases have all been designed and implemented.

If you are hired to create a turnkey system for a client, prepare yourself for headaches, nausea, exhaustion, and incredible pressure. Because a turnkey system is an expensive purchase financially and psychologically, you will find that your client is more fastidious in choosing a system than in choosing a spouse.

This section deals with the theory of designing turnkey systems. If you have never attempted such a system, use these rules as codes to live by:

JDI's Standard Rule of Programming # 12

Inertia controls programming. Once you start working on something, you can't stop. The project gets you out of bed in the morning and away from the dinner table in the evening. You may even find yourself writing notes in the tub. These things are true even after you finish the project.

JDI's Standard Rule of Programming # 13

When you are estimating how long a project will take, convert the estimated time period to the next larger unit and multiply by two. For example, if you think a project will take two weeks, give yourself four months:

2 weeks → 2 * 2 months

Months are the next higher time value. Convert weeks to months and multiply by two.

JDI's Standard Rule of Programming # 14

When you design a turnkey system, use Rule #13, add 10, and convert to the next larger unit. If you give yourself two months, the project will take 14 years:

4 months → (4 +10) years

# 9

# Hardware and Software Considerations

The nomen *turnkey system* implies that you're not just responsible for writing a lot of code. You are responsible also for providing (or at least specifying) the computer hardware your programs will work with.

"Very good," you say. "The clients must use a PC, an AT, or a clone."

Wrong, I say. What size drives? Floppy or hard disk? Do they need a streamer? A print spooler? A printer? A graphics printer or letter-quality? Or will a DMP suffice? How much memory? What type of memory? What kind of boards?

All of this is further complicated if you design a forward-looking system. I personally don't think you should be a consultant unless you *do* design forward-looking systems, but that's my personal prejudice. The definition of "state-of-the-art" is "tomorrow's guess—today's plan—yesterday's business." You should be abreast of such developments as CD-ROM, WORM, Telecomm, networking, security, and other considerations for the system under development.

I strongly support CD-ROM and WORM technologies in information-intense operations. Such operations, traditionally part of the medical and legal professions, recently have appeared in the security industries.

Other packages, although they may provide quicker, more direct access to information than dBASE III Plus does, won't afford you all of the control and power that dBASE III Plus offers. Situations that are information-intense require a synthesis of different packages. Again, dBASE III Plus shows its elegance with the RUN/!, LOAD and CALL commands.

PLUS

I direct your attention also to the C-Tools series, developed by Jeff Cooper of J.T. Cooper & Co. for Ashton-Tate, and available through Ashton-Tate's mail-order department. The two C-Tools packages allow you to use C language routines as part of the dBASE III Plus package. By so doing, you can develop your own prototypes for high-speed access and then run them directly on dBASE III Plus DBF and DBT files. This is useful when you must translate a CD-ROM of data into something that dBASE III Plus is more comfortable with.

**PLUS** Telecommunications—also known as *primordial networking*—is another big consideration. Several of the companies that I've consulted for communicate with their offices through direct phone lines. Running a communications package under dBASE III Plus's supervision entails some juggling with dBASE III Plus. This isn't difficult, but remember that we're working with PCs that will talk over phone lines to other PCs or perhaps to a "mainframe." (I enclose "mainframe" in quotation marks because someone once showed me a mainframe and it was a '286 machine. Fast, sure. But a mainframe?)

Linking PCs over the TOPS systems would be ideal; but it doesn't appear that DEC and IBM will go buddy-buddy soon. We're stuck with dedicated phone lines. As I write this 2nd edition, the best dedicated switching-station lines are at 9,600 baud. The advent of optical systems will no doubt allow for faster dedicated lines, but be wary. The communications software and the modem have to do some intense error checking, and transmissions that are that fast usually work with a compacting algorithm. Caveat Emptor!

Networking finally (and inevitably) is catching up with PCs. Ashton-Tate attests that dBASE III Plus works with two commercially available networks. Several other network authors claim that they, too, can work with dBASE III Plus—DON'T BELIEVE IT!

For one thing, Ashton-Tate supports technical calls about only the Novell® and IBM networks. All other support calls have to go through the other networks' technical staff. This staff is trying to answer calls on every package under the sun. Do you think they know much about dBASE III Plus—or about any one package, for that matter—on their network? Heck, no. They may have come up with some kludges that work in specific situations. I love kludges and this book is a catalog of sneaky petes; but I know also that you can't trust kludges and you can't code for their eccentricities. Stick with the networks that Ashton-Tate supports—you'll be better off for it.

**PLUS** The final consideration is security. The dBASE III Plus package includes a utility, PROTECT.EXE, that is useful but far from the last word in database security. I discuss PROTECT.EXE later in this book, and include an incredibly simple method for disabling all the good work it performs. I strongly suggest that you either purchase a commercial scrambling package or write your own scrambler. A simple scrambler is included in this book, but it is *simple*.

All of these are system considerations. If the system must have a printer, then the computer must either know that the printer is active, or be ready to bypass any error messages when they occur. The computer might also need to check RAM to make sure that all memory is active and usable by the program, especially if the program creates its own RAMdisk or spooler. Because these things usually involve some non-dBASE III Plus coding, I merely mention that they must be considered; here, I discuss only those things that can be handled easily and that don't require a book in themselves.

I would be lax, however, if I didn't direct your attention to BIO.COM, DOS.COM, and COMMAND.COM—the three boot files for every PC and clone. You can make minor alterations to these files that will make life easier for you and dBASE III Plus. Slight modifications to these files will instruct the PC to start with something other than a BAT file, hence making the system more secure. Altering these three files to change the names of the operating system's housekeeping routines will give you a greater degree of surety that someone won't mess up your hard work.

## The CONFIG.SYS File

The CONFIG.SYS file plays a major role in any turnkey system (see Chapter 2). When you use the CONFIG.SYS file, you need to make sure that all system parameters and device drivers are loaded. This is especially important if you plan to attach special equipment to the system.

Such devices are becoming more popular as PCs contend for desk space with mini-machines. You should be aware that the CONFIG.SYS file tells the PC about MOUSE, ANSI (for nonMASM screen code control), and other drivers. You should also know the differences between the 2.xx and 3.xx versions of DOS. If nothing else, dBASE III Plus requires more memory to run on a DOS 3.xx machine than on a DOS 2.xx machine. A 3.xx system, however, may give you greater flexibility in what goes where and why.

PLUS

For complete discussions on designing device drivers, read the IBM (or IBM-compatible) *Technical Reference*, and read thoroughly the *DOS Programmer's Reference.* Pay special attention to the sections about installing device drivers and the request header.

# The AUTOEXEC.BAT File

After the computer has read the CONFIG.SYS file, DOS looks for AUTOEXEC.BAT files. This file initiates the work of the turnkey system's user interface unless you've modified DOS to start the turnkey system. AUTOEXEC.BAT asks the user questions and passes the answers as parameters to lines further down. This program also checks system conditions and obtains date and time information from the system clock or the user.

The simplest turnkey system boots up automatically. The user simply places a disk in a drive and turns the computer on. The following example shows a simple AUTOEXEC.BAT file.

```
ECHO OFF
CHDIR\DBASE
PROMPT $P$G
BREAK ON
  .
  .
  .
  .   ****************************************************************
  .   *                                                            *
  .   *                                                            *
  .   *                                                            *
  .   *                                                            *
  .   *     PLEASE PLACE THE DBASE SYSTEM DISK IN DRIVE A          *
  .   *                                                            *
  .   *                                                            *
  .   *                                                            *
  .   *                                                            *
  .   ****************************************************************
  .
  .
PAUSE
DBASE master
```

The file name "master" identifies a master menu or program file that is executed as soon as dBASE III Plus is loaded.

This AUTOEXEC.BAT file is for a floppy-based system or for a hard disk system that does not have a copy of dBASE III Plus on the hard disk. Note that DOS 3.xx doesn't allow the "." in place of the REM command.

Here I will digress. No matter how you start a dBASE III Plus work session—whether you run your application through DBC and DBL, use the CONFIG.DB COMMAND command, or start with a line like

DB3 MASTER

at the DOS prompt—you will get the dBASE III Plus sign-on screen.

Changing the dBASE III Plus program in any way is illegal. But, should the sign-on screen and its request for a RETURN displease you, any commercially available tracing/debugging tool can be used to determine where the sign-on message starts and stops . . . This is as unethical and illegal as deciding to give your car a new paint job. Both changes are cosmetic and don't affect how the separate vehicles perform.

The AUTOEXEC.BAT file can perform a number of sophisticated functions before dBASE III Plus is even loaded on the computer. You can test for the existence of certain files with code such as the following:

```
IF NOT EXIST *.dbf GOTO NODBF
   .
   .
   .
:NODBF
. THE DATABASE FILES ARE MISSING.
. PLEASE PLACE THE PROPER DISK IN DRIVE B:
PAUSE
IF NOT EXIST B:*.DBF GOTO NODBF
COPY B:*.DBF
```

This code also copies missing files to where they are needed. Note that the previous example uses a recursive command to ensure that the right disks are put in the drives. You may want to include a "Ctrl-C to exit" line in the preceding loop.

The FOR command can be used with the IF command to guide the user with message files:

```
IF %1==JOSEPH GOTO JOSEPH
IF %1==DAN GOTO DAN
:JOSEPH
FOR %%A IN (M1.JDC,M2.JDC,M3.JDC,....) DO TYPE %%A
```

Although you have seen only a few examples, remember that BATch files have more applications in a turnkey system than those typical of the AUTOEXEC.BAT file.

# Other BATch Files

Some programmers argue that BATch-file commands are a kind of programming language. Frankly, I don't care one way or the other. BATch files are useful tools that Microsoft designed for programmers, so let's spend some time studying them.

Turnkey systems are seldom left as they are; upgrades are inevitable. That fact and the fact of users' cyberphobia make a strong argument for the UPGRADE.BAT file. The majority of users will panic when an upgrade goes poorly and their $10,000 baby gets sick. The users will call you, usually at 2 a.m., to wail about the loss of their upgrade and the existing files. Usually, such a loss has not occurred, but the users' fear is real.

The UPGRADE.BAT file should check whether the most recent update is on the disk. You can make the file perform such a check either by changing the name of the programs every time you upgrade the system or by performing an ERRORLEVEL check with a compiled subroutine. The subroutine might look for a flag in the program file. If the flag is not where it's supposed to be, then the upgrade is executed; if the flag is where it belongs, then nothing happens. Error code ØEh is not used, and can be set by a program if no update is necessary. A batch-file line that tests for that condition is

```
IF ERRORLEVEL 14 GOTO NOUPDATE
```

You can also pass parameters to the batch file by using the *%n* syntax. A check for valid disk drives would start with a message, and then proceed as follows:

```
ECHO OFF
IF NOT TEST==%2TEST GOTO GOOD1

        .           YOU DIDN'T TELL US WHICH DRIVE WE'RE WORKING WITH.  TRY

        .           AGAIN, AND SPECIFY DRIVE A:, B:, OR C: AS YOUR TARGET
GOTO END
:GOOD1
IF %1==%2 GOTO ONEISTWO
IF %1==A: GOTO GOOD2
IF %1==B: GOTO GOOD2
IF %1==C: GOTO GOOD2

        .           YOU ONLY HAVE A:, B:, OR C: AVAILABLE

        .
```

```
GOTO END
:ONEISTWO
  .
  .         YOUR SOURCE DRIVE HAS TO BE DIFFERENT FROM YOUR TARGET DRIVE
  .
GOTO END
:GOOD2
COPY %1*.* %2
:END
```

Note: Not all versions of the BATch-file processor allow the use of the period in place of the REM command. Your listing will read more clearly if your version supports use of the period.

Notice that I test to see whether a drive has been selected (TEST==%1TEST) before I test the validity of the drive.

Another use of BATch files is to set up initial subdirectories for different users:

```
IF %1==2 GOTO TWO
IF %1==3 GOTO THREE
IF %1==4 GOTO FOUR
IF %1==5 GOTO FIVE
:TWO
FOR %%A IN (%2,%3) DO MD %%A
FOR %%A IN (%2,%3) DO COPY A:*.* \%%A
GOTO END
:THREE
FOR %%A IN (%2,%3,%4) DO MD %%A
FOR %%A IN (%2,%3,%4) DO COPY A:*.* \%%A
GOTO END
:FOUR
FOR %%A IN (%2,%3,%4,%5) DO MD %%A
FOR %%A IN (%2,%3,%4,%5) DO COPY A:*.* \%%A
GOTO END
:FIVE
FOR %%A IN (%2,%3,%4,%5,%6) DO MD %%A
FOR %%A IN (%2,%3,%4,%5,%6) DO COPY A:*.* \%%A
:END
```

You can start the preceding program from the DOS prompt by entering

```
SETUP 3 JOSEPH SUSAN JIM
```

# The CONFIG.DB File and Turnkey Systems

The CONFIG.DB file is also important to a dBASE III Plus turnkey system. dBASE III Plus uses this file to set the operating parameters, many of which are the same as the SET ON/OFF commands. This file should be kept on the disk used to boot dBASE III Plus.

Some important CONFIG.DB commands in the design of a turnkey system are ALTERNATE, COMMAND, DEBUG, DEFAULT, ESCAPE, F2 through F10, MAXMEM, MVARSIZ, PATH, and WP.

When the system is first set up, ALTERNATE should be both set and active. The initial setups always have some "bugs" that need to be fixed. With ALTERNATE active, all work done by the users will be captured. The debugging team will be able to re-create the errors that brought the system to a halt. You should keep the ALTERNATE file on a disk that can be sent back to the programming house if necessary. Once the turnkey system is running without problems, you can remove the command.

The COMMAND command provides a method of bypassing the AUTOEXEC.BAT command line *DBASE programname*. COMMAND gives you the option of placing the main program name in the CONFIG.DB file, and executing the program from there. If one main program performs all the jobs, this method works well. If, on the other hand, several sections reside on separate disks or in different directories, it is better to use the BATch-file method discussed earlier.

Another invaluable command is DEBUG. I suggest, however, that you slightly alter the command. It is more valuable if the CONFIG.SYS file sets up the system so that certain things ordinarily sent to the printer are instead sent to a disk file. DEBUG used in this way is very useful. The programmer can simply check the disk to find the problem, instead of looking through pages of print.

A technique I've found useful is to send the DEBUGged printer output to a disk file and have my clients ship me the disk when they feel there's a problem. Before dBASE III Plus, I did this by jiggling the BIO file to differentiate the DEBUG buffer from the normal PRINT buffer and to redirect the contents of the DEBUG buffer to disk. dBASE III Plus includes the CALL and LOAD commands, which allow you to create a custom BIN file that users can switch-set. When they feel there's a problem or they contact you with a known problem, you can tell them the key combination that activates the DEBUG-to-DISK transfer. Then you wait for the disk to arrive in the mail.

DEFAULT should be used only if database, index, format, and other files reside on a disk other than the one used to boot dBASE III Plus. You should set ESCAPE to *off*, unless you want to let your clients quit the program in a way that you can't control. That is always a risky way to exit a program; it should be avoided. Valuable files might be damaged, and the integrity of data files is vital in any DBMS.

Later in this book, I describe how to program the function keys with dBASE III Plus. You can also set these keys to initial values with the CONFIG.DB file. Then the function keys can be used to interrupt the programs, terminate execution, return to DOS, RUN programs external to dBASE III Plus, or change modules.

MAXMEM tells dBASE III Plus the amount of available memory within the computer. If there is enough memory space, dBASE III Plus sets up larger files and buffers, places more data in memory, and writes to disk less frequently. The good part of MAXMEM is that the command causes dBASE to run faster. The bad part is that the more data you keep in memory, the more your data is susceptible to surges, spikes, and other power supply problems. Another problem is that you will be unable to run a COM or EXE file external to dBASE if MAXMEM is set to more than 100K within the system's total memory, because dBASE will use all the memory.

MVARSIZ tells dBASE III Plus how much room to allow for memory variables. This use of this command is entirely dependent on the application. If the application relies heavily on manipulation of memory variables and less on database work, you should allow a large share of memory for the variables. You can also store memory variables in an unused database area, eliminating the need for MEM files or memory variable allocations.

PATH is a command that is useful when necessary files are kept in subdirectories. Note that dBASE III Plus searches the directory from which it was booted before searching any other. If dBASE finds the file name close to the original directory, the search stops there, even if the file isn't the correct one for the application.

Suppose, for example, that dBASE III Plus resides in the subdirectory C:\dBases\d3, and that several auxiliary programs are in C:\dBases\d3\d3stuff. Your latest upgrade of TESTER.PRG is in the d3stuff subdirectory. An earlier nonworking version is in subdirectory d3. Even though dBASE knows that a PATH exists to d3stuff, it will use the earlier version of TESTER.PRG when you DO TESTER.

If you plan to use memo fields often, WP is a useful command. In most applications, if you need to use word processing, you might be wiser simply to use

```
RUN wordprocessor
```

than to create MEMO fields.

The following CONFIG.DB file includes all of the commands I've explained. You can use these commands in any valid combination, such as

```
DEFAULT = C:
BELL = OFF
TALK = OFF
HEADINGS = OFF
SAFETY = OFF
DELIMITER = ON
DELIMITER = ><
CONFIRM = OFF
ALTERNATE = C:DEBUG
DEBUG = ON
EXACT = OFF
WP=STAR
MAXMEM=320
MVARSIZ=10
```

The CONFIG.DB file performs the following functions:

| Command | Function |
| --- | --- |
| DEFAULT = C: | Set the default drive to C: (I normally work with an IBM PC XT™). |
| BELL = OFF | The BELL is extremely annoying. Shut it off. There are more civil methods to alert users to errors. |
| TALK = OFF | Don't bore or frighten the user by displaying everything dBASE does. Turn off that display with TALK. |
| HEADINGS = OFF | Turn off the HEADINGS and SAFETY so that you can create your programs with headings and backup procedures. |
| SAFETY = OFF | See HEADINGS. |
| DELIMITER = ON<br>DELIMITER = >< | DELIMITERS are a matter of personal choice, as previously mentioned. |

| | |
|---|---|
| `CONFIRM = OFF` | Because the programs handle most situations, you do not need to CONFIRM anything. |
| `ALTERNATE = C:DEBUG`<br>`DEBUG = ON` | When customers call me with a problem, I ask them to send a copy of the DEBUG disk, so that both DEBUG and ALTERNATE are listed. |
| `EXACT = OFF` | I don't trust the user to remember exactly what was entered. I instruct dBASE to find approximately, not EXACTLY, what the customer looked for. |
| `WP=STAR` | I use a modified version of WordStar. |
| `MAXMEM=320` | The system has 640K of RAM. I limit dBASE III Plus to half that capacity with MAXMEM. |
| `MVARSIZ=10` | I use several active memory variables during the execution of my program. A MVARSIZ of 10K should do the trick. |

Now we've programmed for the computer and dBASE III Plus. Despite the research that may be involved in these parts, they are the easiest parts of designing a turnkey system. After all, we can be fairly certain that the machine—which we either provide or specify—is not going to be changed or modified without our knowledge. Usually, Ashton-Tate is pretty good about letting the public know when they're going to monkey with dBASE. The next chapter introduces the tough parts.

# 10
# Programming for Your Audience

This chapter returns to the psychology of the user. I base it not on studies, but on my 15 years' experience in performing variations on a theme.

Now that you have tools to assist you in your dBASE III Plus programming, you should realize that the user doesn't care about the tools you use. Suppose that you develop a slick system for accepting both numeric and alpha input from the user. This is all background programming to the user, who won't care a whit how you put the program together. You may have been hired for your background programming abilities, but they don't matter when the customer sits down to use your program.

When you are hired as a programmer, you need to spend time in the environment for which you are programming—especially if you are planning to attempt vertical-market software, which is dBASE III Plus's strong point and every turnkey system's potential.

You may want to develop a menu screen like the one shown in figure 10.1. That's all well and good, as long as you keep in mind that the menu screen will work only in one office, and will work only because you know the owner of the business and because she has a sense of humor. The menu screen will not work in a vertical-market application, even if the program works better than any other product on the market.

The next consideration is that you may enjoy being the hired gun, "The Pro from Dover." Hired guns are impressive, but only when others have already been working for some time at the problem the "gun" is hired to kill. They've done most of the work. You can be effective in this capacity

```
┌─────────────────────────────────────────────────────────┐
│         M A I N    M E N U    P R O G R A M              │
│    ─────────────────────────────────────────────        │
│                                                          │
│         0.  EXIT TO DOS                                  │
│                                                          │
│         1.  PERSONAL AUTO                                │
│         2.  COMMERCIAL AUTO                              │
│                                                          │
│         3.  HOMEOWNER                                    │
│                                                          │
│         4.  DISCREPANCY NOTICE                           │
│         5.  CONFIRMATION                                 │
│                                                          │
│         6.  MISCELLANEOUS                                │
│                                                          │
│         7.  OPTION SEVEN NOT YET DEFINED                 │
│         8.  OPTION EIGHT EQUALLY UNDEFINED               │
│         9.  SEE OPTION EIGHT                             │
│                                                          │
└─────────────────────────────────────────────────────────┘
```

*Fig. 10.1. A menu screen.*

because of your distance from the problem and because of your wider experience.

Yes, it's nice to be a pro. Say hello to JDI'S Standard Programming Rule #22:

> If you design a program for one group, you're paid once. If you design a program for an environment, you are paid over and over again.

I first hinted at this fact when I suggested that you program in modules and tasks in order to build a library. Once you've built the library, the magic is easy. The real magic, however, comes from linking the library modules so they can be used in several similar environments, also called *vertical markets*.

I have found that the only way to know a market is to spend time in it. A good start is to spend some time interviewing clients and staff. The Main Menu shown earlier works well in one particular office, but the same menu would not necessarily work in all similar offices.

You need to determine how much work you can transport from one environment to the next. Ponds are all small bodies of water, but they contain different organisms depending on where they are in the world. The insurance industry is an example: Some things are unique to east-coast agencies, and are not used anywhere else in the country.

Your immediate audience is the client who pays your bill, so pay primary attention to his or her needs. Also remember that your fee will not keep you in kippers very long, and that you will have to eat next month, too. Can this environment's work be carried elsewhere?

Now you have determined your audience and started to code. Most clients are very particular about the way the program works. They will tell you how they want the information to appear on screen and in print, how they want to access data, who can manipulate data, and so on. Pay careful attention to their wishes and make them a priority. Unless you've spent time in their environment, your clients know the industry better than you do. And after all, they are paying your salary, so they know better than you do even when they don't.

# Before You Begin

I consider a file-check subroutine mandatory in a turnkey system. Other programmers, however, often overlook this step. I like to know that I have all the pieces before I put a puzzle together. Nobody wants to get half done with a puzzle and suddenly find part of a tree or, even worse, part of a face missing. This same rule applies to dBASE III Plus; all necessary files need to be available when the program begins.

Why would I need to make sure that all the files are available? Because once upon a time, two people in two separate locations decided to learn DOS by ERASEing some necessary files.

My file-checking routine uses its own database, FILECHEK, with the following structure:

```
Structure for database : C:FILECHEK.DBF
Number of data records :     28
Date of last update    : 11/30/84
Field  Field name  Type      Width    Dec
   1    FILENAME    Character    12
** Total **                      13
```

The routine itself is short and direct:

```
USE FILECHEK
? "Missing files"
DO WHILE .NOT. EOF()
**
     IF .NOT. FILE('&FILENAME')
         ? FILENAME
     ENDIF
**
     SKIP
ENDDO
```

Improvements to this routine might include the ability to check other
directories and disks. The completed version might be as follows:

```
USE FILECHEK
FINDFILE=FILENAME
DO WHILE .NOT. EOF()
    IF FILE('&FINDFILE')
        SKIP
        FINDFILE=FILENAME
        LOOP
    ELSE
        CLEAR
        ? FINDFILE+' NOT FOUND.'
        ? 'NEW PATH [DN:\DIRECTORY\(DIRECTORY\...  )]'
        ? 'NEW DISK [PLEASE TYPE THE DISK DRIVE (A:, B:, C:,... )]'
        ? 'SKIP TO NEXT FILE [S]'
        ACCE 'YOUR CHOICE -> ' TO CHOICE
        IF UPPER(CHOICE)='S'
            SKIP
            FINDFILE=FILENAME
            LOOP
        ENDIF
        FINDFILE=CHOICE+FINDFILE
        IF .NOT. FILE('&FINDFILE')
            LOOP
        ELSE
            RUN COPY &FINDFILE
            SKIP
            FINDFILE=FILENAME
        ENDIF
    ENDIF
ENDDO
```

This routine places on the user's shoulders some of the burden of
specifying search paths. The entire subroutine could be coded in BASIC.
In BASIC, however, the data file would be a straight ASCII file,
FILENAME.TXT:

```
DB3-01.BAK
MYNAME.JOE
HERNAME.SLK
WHATELSE.IS
THERE
DB3-01.DB3
DB3-01.2
```

The BASIC program is equally simple:

```
5 REM FILECHEK. BAS
10 OPEN "FILENAME. TXT" FOR INPUT AS 1
20 ON ERROR GOTO 100
30 WHILE NOT EOF(1)
40      INPUT#1, FILE$
50      OPEN FILE$ FOR INPUT AS 2
60      CLOSE#2
70      REM
80 WEND
90 SYSTEM
100 IF ERL=50 THEN PRINT FILE$; " MISSING"
110 RESUME 70
```

Both the dBASE III Plus and BASIC routines are elegantly simplistic. Just remember to customize.

# Setting the Function Keys
# To Rule the World

Another helpful routine redefines the function keys. F1 is permanently set to call up the dBASE III Plus HELP screens. F2 through F10 are ours to use, however, and with a little ingenuity we can even claim F1 for our own use.

F2 through F10 can be redefined to send arbitrary character strings, which is an excellent feature when you are working for someone else. Remember that the users would rather use the function keys than the keyboard.

For example, you can redefine the function keys to send the simple character strings

    E for EDIT
    N for SKIP (as in NEXT RECORD)
    B for SKIP −1 (as in BACK 1 RECORD)
    D for DELETE

Because dBASE has etched F1 in stone, we place our redefinitions on the bottom keys:

    F7 → B      F8 → N
    F9 → E      F10 → D

A preliminary sketch of the code for the screen would appear as follows:

```
                                   +=============================+
SET COLOR TO G+                    |+===========================+|
@ 10,0 SAY 'F1 -> HELP  F2 ->    '||                             ||
@ 11,0 SAY 'F3 ->       F4 ->    '||            M E N U          ||
@ 12,0 SAY 'F5 ->       F6 ->    '||                             ||
@ 13,0 SAY 'F7 -> BACK  F8 -> NEXT'||          B L O C K         ||
@ 14,0 SAY 'F9 -> EDIT  F10 ->DELE'||                             ||
                                   |+===========================+|
                                   +=============================+
```

Note: The MENU BLOCK is not a part of the code above. The block is simply a symbol that more code will eventually fill that space.

This method requires that you write much more code than you need to get the job done, but this is the other side of the balance. In this case, the other side of the balance is ease of use for the customer, which must be a priority. What exactly is the balance? You've no doubt noticed that I stress keeping code as compact as possible, and only coding what is necessary to get a job done. Here I say to go to any length imaginable to code for the customer, which means to write lots of code that might never be used if the customer never creates an error condition.

With a little premeditation, you can adapt the following program, MENUCALL.PRG, to a variety of environments. The program creates a colorful function-key default box.

```
***MENUCALL.PRG
***BY JOSEPH-DAVID CARRABIS
**
PUBLIC KEYWORD2, KEYWORD3, KEYWORD4, KEYWORD5
PUBLIC KEYWORD6, KEYWORD7, KEYWORD8, KEYWORD9
PUBLIC RECNUM, MENUNAME
SET PROCEDURE TO FKEYFILE
**
MENUNAME="TEST"
DO ASSGNKEY
**
DO WHILE .T.
   DO MENUSHEL
   DO MENUFILL WITH RECNUM
   DO FNCKEY WITH RECNUM
   WAIT
ENDDO
```

Because I have mentioned procedure files so often, I felt obligated to use them here. All the DO's in MENUCALL.PRG are found in the procedure file FKEYFILE.PRG.

```
***FKEYFILE.PRG PROCEDURE FILE FOR FUNCTION KEY BASED MENU GENERATORS
***BY JOSEPH-DAVID CARRABIS
**
PROCEDURE ASSGNKEY
SELECT 10
USE KEYVALUE
LOCATE FOR KEYFIELD="&MENUNAME"
SKIP
STORE RECNO() TO HERE, RECNUM
THERE=HERE+8
N=2
DO WHILE HERE<THERE
   GOTO HERE
   KEYFUNC='KEYWORD'+STR(N,1,0)
   STORE KEYDESCRP TO &KEYFUNC
   SET FUNCTION N TO TRIM(KEYFIELD)
   N=N+1
   HERE=HERE+1
ENDDO
SET FUNCTION 10 TO "EXIT;"
RETURN
**
PROCEDURE MENUSHEL
CLEAR
TEXT
@  1, 27  SAY "M E N U    S Y S T E M"
@  4,  2  SAY "F1 » HELP  F2 »          F1 » ACTIVATE THE III PLUS HELP MENU SYSTEM"
@  5, 26  SAY "F2 »"
@  6,  2  SAY "F3 »         F4 »        F3 »"
@  7, 26  SAY "F4 »"
@  8,  2  SAY "F5 »         F6 »        F5 »"
@  9, 26  SAY "F6 »"
@ 10,  2  SAY "F7 »         F8 »        F7 »"
@ 11, 26  SAY "F8 »"
@ 12,  2  SAY "F9 »         FØ »        F9 »"
@ 13, 26  SAY "FØ » EXIT TO III PLUS"
@  Ø,  Ø  TO 15, 79     DOUBLE
@  2,  1  TO  2, 78     DOUBLE
@  3, 24  TO 14, 24
ENDTEXT
```

```
RETURN
**
PROCEDURE MENUFILL
PARAMETER HERE
SET COLOR TO 2+
@  5, 17 SAY KEYWORD2
@  7,  7 SAY KEYWORD3
@  7, 17 SAY KEYWORD4
@  9,  7 SAY KEYWORD5
@  9, 17 SAY KEYWORD6
@ 11,  7 SAY KEYWORD7
@ 11, 17 SAY KEYWORD8
@ 13,  7 SAY KEYWORD9
SET COLOR TO W, ,
N=6
THISHERE=HERE
THERE=HERE+8
SELECT 10
DO WHILE THISHERE<THERE
   GOTO THISHERE
   @ N, 27 SAY WHATITDOES
   THISHERE=THISHERE+1
   N=N+1
ENDDO
RETURN
**
PROCEDURE FNCKEY
PARAMETER HERE
SELECT 10
@ 22, 0
WAIT "YOUR CHOICE -> " TO KEYIN
KEYIN=ASC(KEYIN)
   DO CASE
      CASE KEYIN=254
         GOTO HERE+1
         DOIT=COMMAND
         &DOIT
      CASE KEYIN=253
         GOTO HERE+2
         DOIT=COMMAND
         &DOIT
```

```
        CASE KEYIN=252
            GOTO HERE+3
            DOIT=COMMAND
            &DOIT
        CASE KEYIN=251
            GOTO HERE+4
            DOIT=COMMAND
            &DOIT
        CASE KEYIN=250
            GOTO HERE+5
            DOIT=COMMAND
            &DOIT
        CASE KEYIN=249
            GOTO HERE+6
            DOIT=COMMAND
            &DOIT
        CASE KEYIN=248
            GOTO HERE+7
            DOIT=COMMAND
            &DOIT
        CASE KEYIN=247
            GOTO HERE+8
            DOIT=COMMAND
            &DOIT
        CASE KEYIN=246
            CANCEL
    ENDCASE
RETURN
**
***END OF FKEYFILE.PRG PROCEDURE FILE
```

The joy of using MENUCALL.PRG and FKEYFILE.PRG is that they make it easy to alter function keys. The database file, KEYVALUE, has the following structure:

```
Structure for database : C:KEYVALUE.dbf
Number of data records :     11
Date of last update    : 01/01/80
Field  Field name  Type       Width    Dec
   1   KEYFIELD    Character   100
   2   KEYDESCRP   Character     4
   3   WHATITDOES  Character    40
   4   COMMAND     Character    20
** Total **                    165
```

Note: In these routines I did not redefine the dBASE III Plus HELP key assignment (F1), and I included an EXIT key assignment at F10.

How does the whole shebang work? Let's start with the database file. KEYFIELD stores a command line that is assigned to a key. For example, F2 can be redefined to

```
DISP STRUC; WAIT; DISP MEMO; WAIT; DISP STAT; WAIT; DISP ALL;
```

The semicolons represent carriage returns in the command line. You may think it unnecessary to display all those things. I agree. I have, however, found a need to assign such things as

```
SELECT 2; FIND &VAR; DO [FORMAT FILE]; DO [GETTER FILE]; READ;
```

Now that is a worthy command line! It demonstrates some of the flexibility of the function keys. The FORMAT and GETTER files mentioned in the example are merely files that paint the screen (FORMAT) and then retrieve information for the memory or the database (GETTER).

KEYDESCRP holds the four-letter mnemonic that I use to fill in the menu next to each function-key assignment. WHATITDOES becomes the actual MENU line that describes each key's function.

Now I'll show you some devious programming.

Notice that I include the database field COMMAND. I include COMMAND as a database field because I can assign a short, one-line command to that field. That executable command is then read to a variable:

```
DOIT=COMMAND
```

Then I execute the command with

```
&DOIT
```

in PROCEDURE FNCKEY.

Essentially, I have given the function keys two sets of definitions. I place one set of definitions with the command line

```
SET FUNCTION N TO TRIM(KEYFIELD)
```

The line can be as long as memory allows because of the use of the semicolon, which works as a carriage return in the command line. Those function-key definitions remain until the keys are reassigned.

You should be aware of how much information you can place in the Fkey buffer. Each function key can hold a 30-character string; therefore, the maximum number of characters that can be placed in the buffer is 270 characters (remember—we're not including F1). You can create a single Fkey line that is 270 characters long, but you normally mix and match your Fkey lines to make sure that you don't go over the 270-character maximum. I have noticed that some machines allow more than 270 characters in the Fkey buffer, so I advise you to experiment.

The other set of definitions, which is taken from the COMMAND field, can be used immediately. These definitions are shorter than the KEYFIELD definitions because you cannot insert RETURNs in a macro statement with the semicolon, CHR(13), or CHR(13)+CHR(10).

The PROCEDURE FNCKEY subroutine uses an interesting feature. You can use the line

```
WAIT TO variablename
```

to place the function-key assignments in variables without executing them. The ASC( ) values of the function keys are listed in Appendix F.

I have one more routine that I have not included in the FKEYFILE PROCEDURE file. I place the routine wherever I need it, at various points in my programs. Because of the way I use the routine, I can't guarantee that the proper procedure file is open at the time the routine is called. This routine simply changes the function-key values on the fly.

```
***CHNGEKEY.PRG
***
ANOTHER=.T.
DO WHILE ANOTHER
    CLEAR
    NEWDEF=SPACE(80)
    INPU "Which key do you want to change (2,3,...10)? -> " TO NEWKEY
    ? "Enter the new key definition below"
    @ 5,0 GET NEWDEF
    @ 20,0 SAY "Do another (Y/N)? -> " GET ANOTHER
    READ
    SET FUNCTION NEWKEY TO TRIM("&NEWDEF")
ENDDO
```

I know what you're thinking: "This is all well and good, but what does it really do, JD?" You can use these routines to design turnkey systems that, with the exception of data entry and manipulation, are controlled completely from the function keys. Impressive and nice.

# Displaying Help Screens

Recognize that users are not as sophisticated as you'd like them to be. Your clients will freeze at the keyboard for no apparent reason, and if help is not available at the keyboard, they will call you for help.

Fortunately, dBASE III Plus makes it possible to help the user without clouding the program with unnecessary code. The method is to create a database of MEMO fields, each record containing help screens for different parts of the program. As each module is accessed, it positions a pointer to the corresponding help-screen database. Now the program can set one of the function keys to the string

```
SELE J; GOTO recordnumber of help screens; DISP help screen fields;
```

so that the user has easy access to the help screens at all times.

Note: Make sure that the memo fields are no more than 22 lines long. This prevents the help message from rolling off the screen.

An alternative method is to set one of the keys to

```
CLEAR; DO HELPER WITH PROGNUM;
```

The HELPER module is a subroutine with a PARAMETER command that passes PROGNUM, the calling program's number. PROGNUM is a variable that changes according to which module is in USE. The database is similar to the one described in the preceding paragraph, except that a numeric field is used for INDEXing purposes, and one record contains all the help screens for a particular section. The HELPER program becomes

```
PARAMETER CALLER
SELE J
USE HELPSCRN INDEX CALLER
FIND &CALLER
SELE I
USE HSSTRUC            ** A STRUC file corresponding to the
**                        help screen database file
DO WHILE .NOT. EOF()
    FIELD=FIELD_NAME
    SELE J
    DISP &FIELD
    WAIT "(C)ontinue, any other key to exit" TO MORE
    IF UPPER(MORE) <> "C"
        RETURN
    ENDIF
    SELE I
    SKIP
```

```
ENDDO
**
RETURN
```

The structure file serves as a counter of the help screens in the example. When the last help screen has been DISPLAYed, HELPER RETURNs to the calling program. After reading the information, the user can RETURN by pressing any key except C. A possible improvement is to use the REPORT command to add the capacity of printing the help screens.

Note: When MEMO fields are passed through the REPORT command, the listings are 50 characters wide.

A nice feature of dBASE III Plus is its ERROR( ) and MESSAGE( ) functions. These two functions allow you to perform error checks for both system errors and dBASE III Plus working errors. Naturally, this takes much of the burden off your shoulders when you're developing a system. You need only code for errors that are unique to your application. I suggest that you develop two error systems: one that works on the ERROR( ) and MESSAGE( ) functions, the other for your immediate needs. You can test the error status, as shown earlier, to determine whether you should branch to a system/III Plus error array or to one of your own working. Note that you can test for the value of the ERROR( ) function, but you can't test for the ERROR( ) function itself; for example, you can test IF ERROR( ) = 5, but you can't test IF ERROR( ). Once an error is detected and a value is placed in the ERROR( ) buffer, that value stays there until you exit dBASE III Plus or until a new error value is entered.

|PLUS|

# Conclusion

In the previous chapter, we discussed coding for both the computer and for dBASE III Plus. This chapter involved coding for the user. The length of the chapters and the number of topics discussed should indicate which of the two jobs is harder.

A closing monologue about coding for your audience: Users aren't as sophisticated as you are. If they were, they would write their own code, or at least help you when you code. Because they aren't as sophisticated, be careful and gentle. Remember the prof who used to fill a board with equations and say, "It's intuitively obvious to the casual observer . . ."? Don't do that to your clients. The easier the system is to use, the more likely you'll be able to sell it elsewhere. And—let's face it—aesthetics won't pay your rent.

# 11
# dBASE III Plus in the Office Environment

When a program is written for an office, unique problems arise. The problems usually have little to do with the programmatic aspect of dBASE III Plus; they arise more from dBASE III Plus's integration into the office, and from the work habits of the office staff. You must acknowledge that people make mistakes (usually during data entry); you should realize that dBASE III Plus is not the only program on the disk; and you must recognize that more than one person may want to use the computer at the same time.

## Creating Error Traps and Loops

dBASE III Plus's TYPE( ) function tells us the variable type and the validity of a CONDITION with regard to the database in USE and the referenced variable. This ability to determine the validity of a user-defined condition provides an error-checking method that is applicable in many turnkey systems. Unfortunately, the TYPE( ) command is poorly documented, as was TYPE( )'s dBASE II predecessor, TEST( ).

You can use TYPE( ) to determine whether the type of a memory variable is CHARACTER, LOGICAL, NUMERIC, or DATE. Remember that you cannot use MEMO variables because TYPE( ) works with memory variables, not field types.

Before you design an error trap using TYPE( ), you need to sit down at the computer and study the properties of the command. Start by designing a database as follows:

```
Structure for database : C:CUSTOMERS.dbf
Number of data records :        5
Date of last update     : 07/31/85
Field  Field name  Type        Width    Dec
  1    FIRSTNAME   Character     30
  2    LASTNAME    Character     30
  3    ADDRESS     Character     30
  4    CITY        Character     30
  5    STATE       Character      2
  6    ZIPCODE     Character     10
  7    PHONE       Numeric       10
** Total **                     143
```

If you enter the line

```
? TYPE('FIRSTNAME')
```

you get *C* as a result because FIRSTNAME is declared in memory as a CHARACTER data field. For this example, you would use

```
? TYPE('FIRSTNAME="Joseph-David"')
```

and get *L* because that is a logical use of the variable type. If you enter

```
? TYPE('FIRSTNAME=29.33')
```

you receive a *U* because that is an illogical (or *U*nknown) use of the variable type.

In a program, this error check becomes

```
ACCE "Locate condition -> " TO condition
IF TYPE('&condition')="U"
     ? "That is an invalid condition."
     WAIT
     LOOP
ENDIF
```

The same error loop with a CASE command would appear as

```
ACCE "Locate condition -> " TO condition
**
DO CASE
   CASE TYPE('&condition')="U"
     ? "That is an invalid condition."
     WAIT
     LOOP
```

As a programmer, you must make sure that the user can escape if a condition cannot be met. You need to offer the user the option of looping to the error check a number of times or exiting without harming other files.

The option of looping to an error check a number of times can best be handled by including a counter with the error message. After a number of unsuccessful attempts, the program might pull up a text-sensitive help screen, written either as a TEXT . . . ENDTEXT environment or as a specific MEMO field in a database of error messages. If an input error indicates denied access, you want to drop the user back to DOS without harming files. Simply QUITting dBASE should be enough to preserve database integrity. You may wish to use a CLOSE DATABASE command, just to be sure. (For examples of the TYPE( ) command as an error check, see Chapter 13.)

# Error Checks in Network Systems

PLUS

dBASE III Plus's networking capability is the main thing that separates it from previous versions of dBASE III. The good news is that you don't need a network to make use of some of dBASE III Plus's interesting network features, especially the file and system-protection features.

You should be aware that to use the dBADMINISTRATOR package, even in single-user mode, you need a hard disk *and* 612K available in memory. This is a must. Remote stations, if any, must have a minimum of 384K per station.

Furthermore, you will have to make some changes to the CONFIG.SYS file. You'll need to add an FCBS command such as

```
FCBS = n, m
```

(Note that *n* must be greater than *m* in this command.) The FCBS is the multiuser version of the FILES command used in single-user CONFIG.SYS files. FCBS tells the PC how many files it can open and share at a given time. You should include also a LASTDRIVE command, because the dBASE III Plus network controller needs to know which drive everyone will be working from. The system's last logical drive is usually the drive of choice in such applications.

I advised earlier in the book that your best bet is to go with a network endorsed by Ashton-Tate. I repeat my warning, which comes from experience. I was asked to install dBASE III Plus on a network that already existed on the equipment. I told the client ahead of time that my kludging and calling the network authors would cost more than a new network system. My client didn't believe me—then.

PLUS

The latest version of dBASE III Plus isn't copy protected, so the usual hidden copy-protection files won't go on your disk, but installing the dBADMINISTRATOR does some things to the disk that should be noted. First and foremost, you'll find a new directory located off the root directory. The directory listing looks something like this:

```
C:\>cd dbnetctl.300

C:\DBNETCTL.300>dir

Volume in drive C has no label
Directory of  C:\DBNETCTL.300

  .              <DIR>      23-09-86   7:44
  ..             <DIR>      23-09-86   7:44
4379855D SUB <DIR>         23-09-86   7:44
EE0E7338 HCL    11968      23-09-86   7:44
EE0E7338 COM     1984      23-09-86   7:44
DBA      CTL      208      23-09-86   7:44
4379855D VDW     1184      23-09-86   7:44
DBA      LOD   144384      23-09-86   7:43
      8 File(s)  11610112 bytes free

C:\DBNETCTL.300>cd 4379855d.sub

C:\DBNETCTL.300\4379855D.SUB>dir

Volume in drive C has no label
Directory of  C:\DBNETCTL.300\4379855D.SUB

  .              <DIR>      23-09-86   7:44
  ..             <DIR>      23-09-86   7:44
VDF0300  HUM        0      23-09-86   7:44
      3 File(s)  11610112 bytes free
```

These files and directories contain information on what goes where, who gets to go there, and why such things should be allowed. Removing the entries in these directories causes dBASE III Plus to respond with

```
Check Network drive specification (E)
Network load failure C(18 00)
```

when you try to start the system. There are other messages, none of them relevant except in the sense that they leave your work session on the launching pad without so much as an ignition.

# Running Other Programs under dBASE III Plus

You don't always need to develop an entire system application with dBASE III Plus, because there are many software packages available. The packages may perform 90 percent of the functions your customers need, and you can add the other 10 percent by making slight modifications to the program.

One way to get the other 10 percent is to open the package. This method is usually unsatisfactory for several reasons:

1. At best, you can only decompile the package. If you're not comfortable with assemblers and reverse compilers, decompilation can be painfully intimidating.

2. You are forced to follow someone else's logic, which is virtually impossible. Nobody else thinks the way you do, and you don't think the way anyone else does.

3. You will make the warranties invalid. The warranties may or may not be enforceable, but if you alter the program, the manufacturer can refuse you assistance unless you're a value-added dealer.

4. When you are finished, no one else can modify the program without going through the same headaches that you went through.

5. The bugs in your work will show up at the *worst possible time.*

The other method, which negates all the listed objections (and most others I've encountered), is to program the desired functions using dBASE III Plus. Usually, when another package is the primary-use package, the only other necessary function is to massage the data in whatever ways the primary package can't. Just remember that dBASE III Plus can read files in many more formats than the usual SDF.

dBASE III Plus's APPEND FROM TYPE, COPY TO TYPE, IMPORT, and EXPORT commands let you take in files that you would have to write special code for in dBASE III and other versions of dBASE.

PLUS

Provided that you know the file structure, and that the data either is in ASCII characters or can be translated into ASCII, you can program the primary program's file delimiters into a dBASE III Plus search routine. Such a routine would first scan for a delimiter, and then check the ASCII value of the next character. If the next character is not a delimiter, the program considers that character and successive characters to be data. Data is assumed to stop when the next delimiter is detected. A simple flow chart of this logic shows how easy such an algorithm is to code in any language (see fig. 11.1).

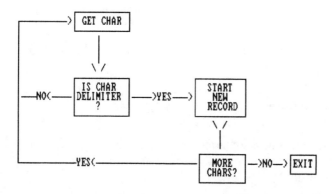

*Fig. 11.1. The flowchart for translating delimited, non-III Plus data fields into a III Plus database.*

The question arises of how you determine another program's data-file structure. If the primary-use package is capable of writing and reading ASCII text files, you don't have to perform this step. Both the primary-use package and dBASE III Plus can work with ASCII files, with dBASE III Plus accessing them as SDF files. But what if the primary-use package can't read and write ASCII text files?

The answer is to use the DOS DEBUG program to determine the data-file's structure. Once that is done, you can write a dBASE III Plus program to read the other program's data, as mentioned earlier, and reverse the process slightly to write data back to a usable file.

Another question arises: how do you make the primary-use package comfortable with dBASE III Plus? Fortunately, dBASE III Plus allows you to RUN other programs, provided that you have more than 256K of memory; this fact is a strong argument for having more than the minimum memory. Having enough memory to RUN other programs also provides easier access to external programs (and the primary-use package) for your client.

# Using dBASE III Plus as an Umbrella

What does an umbrella have to do with dBASE III Plus? The term *umbrella* refers to the capability of dBASE III Plus to act as an integrator for a series of software packages.

For example, let's say that you have a customer with several different packages on disk. dBASE, however, is the turnkey system and the backbone of the entire application. The users know the call names for the individual packages and are aware that arguments must be passed to the packages. Hence you only need to code a menu selection, such as

```
9 -> RUN ANOTHER PROGRAM
```

with follow-up code such as

```
CASE response=9
     CLEAR
     ACCE "What program do you wish to run? " TO program
     arguments=SPACE(50)
     ACCE "With? " TO arguments
     RUN &program &arguments
```

Most errors that cause the other program to trash will only leave the user inside dBASE.

A better example of dBASE III Plus as umbrella entails assigning different programs to each of the function keys, as in figure 11.2. You can use this method to pass SDF files back and forth between programs. If you are extremely industrious, you can take the time to find out how various programs set up their work files. Don't bother. Most programs can write their working files as ASCII text files. If you use that capability, you can guarantee minimum work for yourself and maximum flexibility in system design.

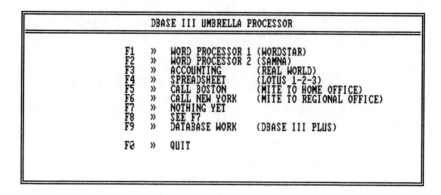

*Fig. 11.2 The menu screen for an umbrella system.*

# Running a Word Processor under dBASE III Plus

Most word processors work according to set rules. One rule is that you can use the DOS TYPE command to display a word-processing document on the monitor. The document may contain some garbage characters, as a WordStar® document does, or it may be pure ASCII text.

In either case, you need to create a two-way street in order to RUN a word processor under dBASE III Plus. You need to get information from dBASE to the word processor for merging (see Chapter 13), and you need to move information from the word processor back to dBASE III Plus.

At some point, your customers may wish to pull information from a document to a database. This transfer of information is not difficult if

1.  The database has already been designed, and you can teach the users its basic structure

2.  You and the users agree ahead of time on a datafield DELIMITER

3.  You agree on a "flag" string. The flag string is any group of characters that you use to tell dBASE III Plus that the following lines are not text, but data to be included in the database file.

When the three conditions are met, you are ready to write the program. Assume that you have created a document entitled 10JUN85.LTR and a database called JUN10VAL. The users know that the flag is a string of three asterisks (***) and that the DELIMITER is a comma (,).

```
USE JUN10VAL
APPEND FROM 10JUN85.LTR SDF DELIM WITH ,
GOTO TOP
DO WHILE .NOT.EOF()
     IF FIELD1<>"***"
          DELE
          SKIP
          LOOP
     ELSE
          DELE
          SKIP
          DO WHILE .NOT. EOF()
               IF FIELD1<>"***"
                    SKIP
                    LOOP
               ELSE
                    RECNUM=RECNO()
                    EXIT
          ENDDO
          DELE
          GOTO RECNUM+1
     ENDIF
ENDDO
PACK
```

The result is shown in figure 11.3.

```
To: The Word Processing Division
From: The dBASE III PLUS Division
Re: The information you requested


This letter will demonstrate the dBASE III PLUS program used to
strip text from a letter or other document and get it into the
required format for inclusion in a dBASE III PLUS database file.
The thing to note is that a "flag" is used. The requested data
comes before and after. The flag is "***".
***
Joseph    Carrabis   Nashua      NH
Jack      Jickjock   ManchesterNH
Someone   Else       Another     ST
Someone   In         PEI         CN
Ablast    from the   Past        2
Joseph    Carrabis   Nashua      NH
Jack      Jickjock   ManchesterNH
Someone   Else       Another     ST
Someone   In         PEI         CN
Ablast    from the   Past        2
***
```

Fig. 11.3. Delimiters marking data for extraction from a text file.

With this routine, you can move information from a file to a database file, even if the word processor does not use pure ASCII.

One common situation requires bit-stripping for nonASCII characters; an example (that has been worked to death) occurs with WordStar files. You can convert WordStar documents to straight ASCII files by stripping the high-order bit from each character; you can do similar things with other word processors. The best of them use straight text. My choices for the best transportable word processors are Final Word® (egotistic, to say the least), Perfect Writer (better, but equally egotistic), and XyWrite (a good one!). If your client won't follow your advice to get one of these programs, try to persuade him to get Framework™ II. I'm not selling Ashton-Tate products, but I know that Framework II comes configured to merge word-processing files with everything else, has a serviceable spreadsheet in the package, and can execute dBASE III Plus without trashing itself. Framework can save you a lot of work.

The result of running the preceding program is shown in figure 11.4. If you analyze the code, you can see that the entire document is copied to the database. The flags indicate the beginning and the end of data for the database. Only the records between the flags are kept. All other records are DELETEd and PACKed when the code is completed.

```
 1  Joseph    Carrabis   Nashua      NH
 2  Jack      Jickjock   ManchesterNH
 3  Someone   Else       Another     ST
 4  Someone   In         PEI         CN
 5  Ablast    from the   Past        2
 6  Joseph    Carrabis   Nashua      NH
 7  Jack      Jickjock   ManchesterNH
 8  Someone   Else       Another     ST
 9  Someone   In         PEI         CN
10  Ablast    from the   Past        2

->
```

*Fig. 11.4. Data extracted from a text file.*

# Creating Secure Systems

Very often, programmers are told that certain files are sensitive and should be made "snoop proof." Voila! We are now in the computer security business. The easiest method of securing files is to encrypt them. Fortunately, you can RUN a program for data and program security from dBASE III Plus. The PROTECT.EXE file, which comes with the dBASE III Plus package and is discussed later, is an example of such a program.

PLUS

The methods of data encryption can range from the sublime to the ridiculous. You have to consider public versus private key encryption methods and decide who assigns the keys, among other things. Often these questions become political issues; you may want to leave the decision to the customer.

Several useful programs on the market can handle this job for you. When a customer asks specifically for one encryption method, you may want to recommend some off-the-shelf software, unless security is your business. Most of the programs are impractical, however, because the programs require several K and boot from a disk. For this reason, these programs are difficult to use on dual floppy systems and inconvenient, at best, on hard disk systems.

The logic of data encryption is basic enough. Figure 11.5 shows a simple scrambler with obvious defects. Some of the defects are intentional; others are simply there. Ideally, this program would be coded in a language that can be compiled.

When pressed, I have compiled the following BASIC code and put it into service. I decided to write the code in BASIC instead of dBASE III Plus because III Plus handles these functions with the skill of a ballerina wrestling a lumberjack.

```
10 REM CRYPTOR. BAS
20 REM
30 P=0
40 INPUT "Your initials -> ",N$
50 INPUT "E(ncrypt) or D(ecrypt) -> ",ED$
60 INPUT "Your password (5 characters) -> ",PWORD$
70 FILE$=N$+".FLE"
80 OPEN FILE$ FOR INPUT AS 1
90 FOR X=1 TO 5
100      P=ASC(MID$(PWORD$,X,1))+P
110 NEXT
120 WHILE P>127
130      P=P-128
140 WEND
150 WHILE NOT EOF(1)
160      INPUT#1,XLATE$
170      OPEN XLATE$ FOR INPUT AS 2
180      OPEN "XLATE" FOR OUTPUT AS 3
190      WHILE NOT EOF(2)
```

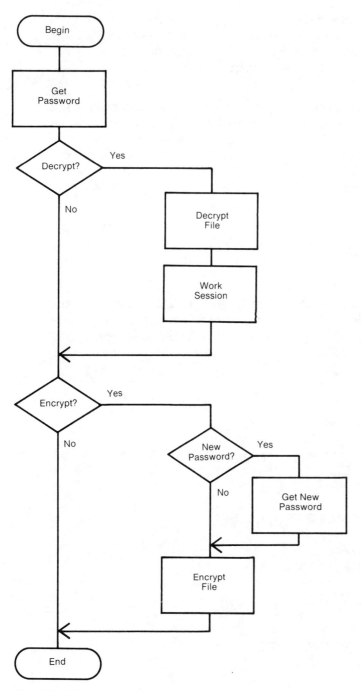

Fig. 11.5. A flowchart for a simple data-encryption system.

```
200                 IF ED$="e" OR ED$="E" THEN C=ASC(INPUT$(1,#2))+P
210                 IF ED$="d" OR ED$="D" THEN C=ASC(INPUT$(1,#2))-P
220             PRINT#3, CHR$(C);
230         WEND
240         CLOSE#2
250         CLOSE#3
260         KILL XLATE$
270         NAME "XLATE" AS XLATE$
280 WEND
290 SYSTEM
```

This code is meant to be a template. I strongly advise you to modify or rewrite the code to suit your own purpose. This program was not written to deter the truly interested from accessing sensitive data; it was written only to prevent the nosy from seeing what they should not.

Now to explain the code. First, we initialize the encrypting variable P (line 30), and then we get the user's initials. The initials plus the extension .FLE constitute a file name (lines 40, and 70 through 80). The file is simply an ASCII text file containing a list of the files that a particular user can access. Next, we find out whether the files are to be encrypted or decrypted (line 50), and we request the password (line 60). The program then determines an encrypting value by working some simple arithmetic with the characters in the password (lines 90 through 110). Notice that this method is nothing more than a transposition of ASCII character values. The source file is not compressed or altered in any way. Then the source file is read and translated character by character (lines 190-230). The rest of the code simply keeps things rolling until there are no more files to encrypt or decrypt.

When the BASIC program is compiled, it creates a staggering 18K file.

Note: Files and data can be lost if you use an incorrect password. This danger puts a great burden on you, the programmer, to provide safe, foolproof backup capability. Remember the definition of foolproof: "Give a fool a 'foolproof' system, and he'll proof you wrong."

This scrambler/descrambler program has several uses. It can descramble files either when they are first accessed or when a user starts to work. You also can use this code to scramble and descramble PRG, NDX, FMT, and other files, although I usually don't bother unless I'm asked. Clients usually are most interested in protecting data.

CRYPTOR.BAS is RUN from dBASE III Plus in the usual way. For the compiled version, the command is

```
    RUN CRYPTOR
```

For the interpreted version, the command is

```
RUN BASIC CRYPTOR
```

The second command engages the interpreter and then runs the program to be interpreted.

It is important to remember that the method described here is elementary, and is intended to serve as a guide. System and data security is best left to professionals and to packaged software designed for that purpose.

I feel that data security, like copy protection, is a waste of time. Both can be defeated easily when necessary. A good anecdote concerns the case of a software firm that openly challenged interested parties to break its encryption method. The company was even so foolish as to offer prize money to anyone capable of breaking the protection. The company went bankrupt in one month, with lots of prizes unpaid.

## PLUS  The PROTECT.EXE file

Ashton-Tate includes a program, PROTECT.EXE, in the dBASE III Plus package. As its name implies, this program can be used to give a certain amount of protection to the user's DBF files. The program, which obviously was designed for network use, can be used without difficulty in single-user mode. Note that, to use PROTECT.EXE's features, you need to run dBASE III Plus in DBA mode.

The program works by creating levels of password entry and R/W activity for listed users. The network manager—or whatever you call the individual in your situation—runs PROTECT when the system is first installed and whenever the system is updated. The names of individual users are entered, as well as information about who gets to go where in the database, what they can use, and how they can use it. All this information is collected and stored in a file called DBSYSTEM.DB. (At least v. 1.1 calls it that.)

Before going any farther, I want to emphasize that the people at Ashton-Tate went to a lot to trouble to develop the PROTECT.EXE file, and that it is uniquely serviceable to a dBASE III Plus environment. It allows you to create file and field protection, establish R/W privileges, define user-access levels, and create password systems—basically a darn good piece of work.

Too bad it's so darn easy to foil.

Anyone with the slightest PC experience, the ability to read a DOS manual, and no fear of the keyboard can blow your PROTECT work out the window with the ERA or DEL commands. They simply remove the DBSYSTEM.DB file from the system and—*shazam!*—your work is gone, and anybody who wants to can get into the data and ruin whatever protection you've installed.

This can happen because of DBA's loading procedure. The procedure begins with a search for the DBSYSTEM.DB file (which is really a specialized database). This database tells dBASE III Plus who gets to go where and what they get to do once they get there. What happens if DBSYSTEM.DB isn't there? dBASE III Plus says to itself, "Oh, look—DBSYSTEM.DB isn't here. I guess I'm loading and I don't have to worry about protection issues."

There are some easy ways to ensure your longevity as a developer, despite the ease of bypassing the DBSYSTEM.DB file. The first and foremost of these ways is to use the DOS ATTRIB.COM file to make DBSYSTEM.DB R/O. The second way is to make the file a hidden file. Remember that hidden files are hidden only to the DIR command; they aren't hidden to other files. DBA loads and looks for the DBSYSTEM.DB file. DBA, which doesn't care if we can't see the file, will find it.

This method works well if you are developing something for a single-user system, but what about network environments? A single computer is usually the file server for the entire system; that computer will get the DBSYSTEM.DB file. More precisely, your dBASE III Plus directories will get the DBSYSTEM.DB file. Specifically, you can include a path command that dBASE III Plus will read when it is loaded or accessed through the network; the command looks in a hidden directory for the DBSYSTEM.DB file. Not only is the file hidden and R/O, but the directory is also hidden. Supposedly, your network software makes unauthorized directory work difficult; therefore the protection factor is increased.

Still another method is to rely on some other means of file protection. This goes back to encrypting and decrypting considerations, as discussed earlier. As I said then, those who are truly interested will get what interests them.

## Protecting Your Work with DBC and DBL

Protecting your code from tampering may be more important than database protection (at least to budding capitalists). In a way, this borders on the issue of copy protection, and faithful readers know what I think of copy protection. Obviously the industry is catching up with me—what is the big feature of the latest version of dBASE? I rest my case.

You may not care whether people modify your code, but you do want it to fly. Easy enough to handle. The dBASE III Plus package includes two files called DBC and DBL (for dBASE III Plus COMPILER and dBASE III Plus LINKER, respectively).

These two files perform a pseudocompiling of your dBASE III Plus (ASCII) PRG and PRC files. Normally, these pseudocompiled files would be used by dBRUN, the dBASE III Plus Runtime module. That module, which can be purchased from Ashton-Tate, is a worthy investment that I'll discuss later.

My point in discussing DBC and DBL here is that you may find them useful for protecting your work from people who think they can code better than you. No doubt someone actually can code better than you. Feel free to find those worthies and suggest that they forfeit their existence. (I hasten to point out that I can't code better than anybody, that I'm the worst programmer around, and that all the code I've ever written comes from a guy in Tole..Los Ange . . . Phoeni . . . Quincy. Yeah, that's right, Quincy, Ma . . . Ohi . . . Alaska. Yeah, Quincy, Alaska.)

In any case, people who do know better (or at least *some*) programming may indeed help your code. I direct your attention to some of the public utilities that came from the CP/M™ world, which were the work of several authors' minor adjustments to what came before them—much like standing on the shoulders of giants.

As I was saying, DBC and DBL provide a good, inexpensive way of protecting your code yet keeping it usable with dBASE III Plus. Note that your code isn't compiled, but pseudocompiled. I discuss other benefits of DBC and DBL in the next section. Here I wish only to discuss their code-protection capabilities.

A simple routine for generating graphs based on numeric fields is shown in the next section. Feel free to tamper with that code, which is in ASCII text; you can copy it, or whatever. But what if I didn't want you to use the file? I could give you the DBC version of the file, shown below.

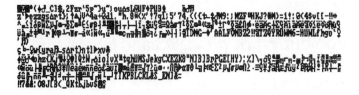

Go ahead. Tamper with it.

# III

# A Fully Developed
# dBASE III Plus System

III PLUS does some incredible things, but it can't do everything; graphics, for instance, are a real weakness. But there are packages, readily available on the market, that finish what Ashton-Tate started. Ashton-Tate did a lot with III Plus, but didn't do it all. Part III covers two areas. First, it discusses additional packages and routines that can add the final touch to your III PLUS system. Second, this part shows III PLUS code that works well and is easily transportable between the interpreters.

# 12
# dBASE III Plus
# Add-on Packages

The last section of the dBASE III Plus manual presents a somewhat confusing discussion of something called "RunTime+™" and "dBRUN™." The two are different. You can't dBRUN your dBASE III Plus PRG and PRC files until you have RunTime+d them.

## RunTime+

The RunTime+ module actually consists of two separate COM files: DBC and DBL. These files were discussed in Chapter 11 as a means of protecting code. Here they're discussed as a means of speeding up code execution.

dBASE III Plus is an interpreter. This means that you write your code in a high-level form (the ASCII text PRG and PRC files) and then DO them. DOing them tells dBASE III Plus to look at one line of the source code, translate that one line of source code into machine language, and then execute the commands in the machine language. This can be quite nice and a true time saver. For example, the one line

```
USE somefile
```

is equivalent to

1. LOAD THE WORD somefile INTO THE FIRST FILE NAME MEMORY ADDRESS AREA

2. FIND THE FILE THAT MATCHES THE WORD IN THE FIRST FILE NAME MEMORY ADDRESS AREA ON THE ACTIVE DISK

3. GOTO THE BEGINNING OF THAT FILE (IF IT'S FOUND) AND GET THE DATA THERE

4. STORE THAT DATA IN ANOTHER MEMORY AREA

5. PLACE A POINTER IN MEMORY TO REMEMBER WHERE THIS DATA IS FROM

6. PLACE A POINTER IN MEMORY TO REMEMBER WHERE THE REST OF THE DATA IS

7. GET NEXT COMMAND FROM USER

And there's more—but I didn't include it, because no one really cares. If someone did care, you would code in assemblers rather than in dBASE III Plus.

But the truth is that you do code in dBASE III Plus, and you want it to interpret your one-line command into all the machine code needed to do what you ask. Ideally, you want something done to the code that speeds up the interpretation from ASCII text to machine language. The code would still have to be interpreted to be used, but that interpretation wouldn't be as involved as direct interpretation of ASCII code. Another advantage to using such a process is that the code will be compressed, and the compressed code will take up less space on disk and in memory.

Code compression, the first step in the DBC-DBL process, is performed by DBC. DBC converts ASCII PRG and PRC files to the pseudocode that can be read by dBASE III Plus (or by DBA, in network mode). You can DBC a single source file, say a routine that draws graphs based on numeric fields in a database, or you can create a file that contains the names of several files that together comprise a system; DBC will pseudocompile each file listed in the source file. This can be done even if the separate files have nothing in common other than needing to be pseudocompiled. The reason for this is that DBL, the second program of the DBC-DBL pair, does the linking.

Linking is an operation familiar to anyone who has worked with compilers. Once a set of system programs has been translated into machine code, the separate modules of the system must be placed in one file. This single file "links" all the separate modules. The linking process does not simply place one file next to the other in the resulting file; more than that, linking involves telling one module where to look for other modules. For example, a module may make several calls to a PRC file in ASCII mode. Once compiled and linked, the module and PRC file information wind up in a single file. The linking process tells the module the address of the separate PROCedures in the linked file. This allows the finished file to JUMP to the necessary subroutines, execute those subroutines, and then (because positions are kept in stacks) RETurn to the exact location in the calling file.

Before leaving this discussion of DBC and DBL, I want to emphasize the speed advantage of DBCing a file. I mentioned earlier a graphing routine. A simple example of such a routine is

```
** GRAPHER.PRG TO GO THROUGH DBC.COM
**
CLEA
GOTO TOP
*
ACCE "What field shall we use? / " TO THISFIELD
FIELDTOP = &THISFIELD
FIELDBOT = FIELDTOP
SKIP
*
DO WHIL .NOT. EOF()
    FIELDTOP = MAX(FIELDTOP, &THISFIELD)
    FIELDBOT = MIN(FIELDBOT, &THISFIELD)
    SKIP
ENDD
*
YTICS = (FIELDTOP-FIELDBOT)/22
XTICS = IIF(RECC() > 75, RECC()/75, 1)
CLEA
@ 0,0 TO 22,0
@ 23,0 SAY "@"
@ 23,1 TO 23,75
X = 1
GOTO TOP
*
DO WHIL .NOT. EOF()
    @ 24,0 SAY "RECORD NUMBER / " + STR(RECN(),4,0) + " " +;
                "&THISFIELD VALUE / " + STR(&THISFIELD,10,2)
    Y = (&THISFIELD/YTICS) - 1
    @ 23,X SAY "A"
    @ 22-Y,X TO 22,X
    SKIP
    X = X + XTICS
ENDD
*
** EOF
```

This routine, which assumes that a database has already been placed in USE, doesn't care whether an NDX file is active or not. Figure 12.1 shows an NDX active, whereas figure 12.2 shows the same file being graphed with no NDX file active. This simple routine can be improved in many ways. Although I intend it to provide a spine and nothing more, the routine can be useful for quickly graphing database values inside dBASE III Plus.

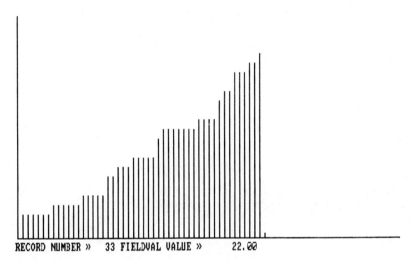

RECORD NUMBER »   33 FIELDVAL VALUE »      22.00

*Fig. 12.1. A graph generated with III Plus commands using an INDEXed file.*

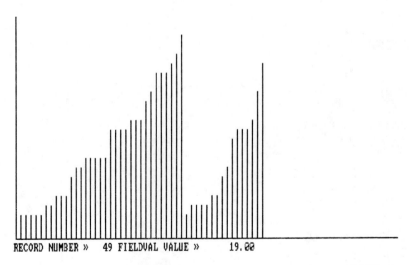

RECORD NUMBER »   49 FIELDVAL VALUE »      19.00

*Fig. 12.2. A graph generated with III Plus commands using an unINDEXed file.*

Did I say quickly? I lied. Using this routine probably is quicker than COPYing TO some file TYPE WKS, exiting dBASE III Plus, loading 1-2-3, loading the COPYed DBF to WKS file, setting axis and graphing—but not by much. (Two other methods, discussed in the next section, are eminently more practical.) But this routine does provide the ever popular "quick and dirty" graph when you need one.

GRAPHER1.PRG is slow. You can see from this directory listing,

```
E:\>dir a:

 Volume in drive A is 10555610A26
 Directory of  A:\

GRAPHER1 PRG     1024  20-10-86   3:09
GRAPHER2 PRG      630  20-10-86   3:26
```

that it is also 1K long—far too long for such a small file. You can decrease its size by almost half by running it through DBC. This not only shrinks the code to a more compact size, but also runs the program faster because it is pseudocompiled. This means that the code is almost in machine language, and therefore doesn't have to be interpreted (as much).

As a final note, the code shown below makes a few minor changes to GRAPHER that give it more flexibility. I offer the code to you because finesse is nice to have around. Using the same information that was graphed in figure 12.2, this version of GRAPHER produces figure 12.3.

```
** GRAPHER.PRG TO GO THROUGH DBC.COM
**
CLEA
GOTO TOP
*
ACCE "What field shall we use? / " TO THISFIELD
ACCE "What is the graphing character (ALT-XXX)? / " TO GRAPHCHAR
ACCE "What is the base character (ALT-XXX)? / " TO BOTTCHAR
FIELDTOP = &THISFIELD
FIELDBOT = FIELDTOP
SKIP
*
DO WHIL .NOT. EOF()
   FIELDTOP = MAX(FIELDTOP, &THISFIELD)
   FIELDBOT = MIN(FIELDBOT, &THISFIELD)
   SKIP
ENDD
```

```
*
YTICS = (FIELDTOP-FIELDBOT)/22
XTICS = IIF(RECC() > 75, RECC()/75, 1)
CLEA
@ 0,0 TO 22,0
@ 23,0 SAY "@"
@ 23,1 TO 23,75
X = 1
GOTO TOP
*
DO WHIL .NOT. EOF()
   @ 24,0 SAY "RECORD NUMBER / " + STR(RECN(),4,0) + " " +;
            "&THISFIELD VALUE / " + STR(&THISFIELD,10,2)
   Y = (&THISFIELD/YTICS) - 1
   @ 23,X SAY BOTTCHAR
   @ 22-Y,X SAY GRAPHCHAR
*
   DO WHIL ROW() # 22
      @ ROW()+1,X SAY GRAPHCHAR
   ENDD
*
   SKIP
   X = X + XTICS
ENDD
*
** EOF
```

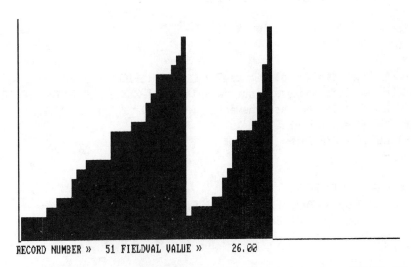

```
RECORD NUMBER »   51 FIELDVAL VALUE »      26.00
```

Fig. 12.3. A graph generated with III Plus commands using an unINDEXed file and graphics character.

# dBRUN

dBRUN is the true dBASE RunTime package, at least in the sense that a runtime package is known and understood by most programmers and developers.

Almost every language that is compiled carries with it a library of information. This information is composed of various and sundry subroutines that do most of the housekeeping and the like. The subroutines don't have much to do with your application, but your application couldn't run without them.

For example, the interpreted dBASE III Plus PRG and PRC files rely heavily on DBASE.COM and its overlay files for getting many things done. That is why you can write a 2K PRG file that does incredible things with databases and the like. It's hard to believe that 2K of code does everything.

Well, you're right to be amazed. The only reason that 2K of code can do so much is that

```
DBASE      OVL    266240   24-07-86   12:00
HELP       DBS     66560   24-07-86   12:00
CONFIG     DB        384   27-03-86   10:35
ASSIST     HLP     17642   24-07-86   12:00
DBASEINL   OVL     27648   29-07-86   12:00
DBASE      MSG     12420   13-09-86   16:56
```

is in there, too. Look at all the information necessary to get your 2K of code to do its job! Most of these files don't really have much to do with working files. dBASE III Plus, however, carries close to 300K of its own baggage when you DO a file.

Even when something has passed through DBC and DBL, all that has been compressed is the ASCII file. dBASE III Plus still carries its baggage along whenever you DO a file. The solution to this lies in the dBRUN package.

Each dBRUN package must be purchased from Ashton-Tate, just as dBASE III Plus must be purchased. Buying a dBRUN package for yourself is a good idea if you ever want to run your files faster than they run in interpreted mode.

The reason you would use a dBRUN package is to develop an application that you can market. You don't want someone who buys your program to have to purchase a complete dBASE III Plus package at whatever price is being asked. The package is costly, and the user doesn't need all that baggage. Users really need only the specific parts of the dBASE III Plus system that handle housekeeping, not all the dBASE III Plus files.

PLUS

Is there a comparable baggage gain when you use the dBRUN package? Not nearly as much. For one thing, you can fit everything you need (plus some additional work) on a single 360K floppy. Second, the complete dBRUN overlay file remains in memory when dBRUN is working. This is quite nice and speeds things up considerably.

Perhaps the biggest advantage to using the dBRUN package is that you can use PRG and PRC files exactly as they are written for interpreted dBASE III Plus. This isn't always the case when you convert interpreted files to runtime files. (One of the biggest culprits is IBM BASIC. The most massive section in the IBM BASIC manual has to do with the differences between what can be interpreted and what can be compiled.)

With dBRUN, you can put any of the files shown in Chapter 13 through DBC and DBL. You don't have to alter or rewrite the files in any way, shape, or form. This is quite an advantage, because some compilers bear next-to-no resemblance to their interpretive modes.

The one big disadvantage to using dBRUN is that you have to buy the package from Ashton-Tate whenever you want to sell your product to an interested third party. Either you have to purchase the dBRUN package (in which case you will undoubtedly pass the cost on to your client), or the client has to purchase the dBRUN package directly from Ashton-Tate. In either case, this solution may prove unsatisfactory.

# Nantucket's Clipper™ Compiler

One of the best dBASE III Plus add-on packages to hit the streets in some time is Nantucket's Clipper dBASE III Plus compiler. In the preceding section, I said that one of the nice things about Ashton-Tate's dBRUN is its ability to use dBASE III Plus code directly from the interpreted state. This isn't the case with Clipper. Although Clipper's syntax and structure is similar to that of dBASE III Plus, much of the command use, structure, and syntax is different.

The key question is, "How different is it?" You probably can run most of your dBASE III Plus code through the Clipper compiler without problems. The more advanced programming techniques, however, will run into some problems. For example, DISPLAY won't operate or accept arguments exactly as it does in dBASE III Plus. Can you code around that? Easily. Is it intuitive and obvious to the experienced dBASE III Plus programmer? Hardly.

Galen, a programmer for a national engineering firm, was a devout dBASE III Plus programmer. Clipper came along and he started using it, but he had lots of questions and not too many answers when he started compiling his dBASE III Plus code. A year later, he now won't code in anything but Clipper. But he can no longer program in dBASE III Plus.

The story illustrates the similarities and differences between the two products. You can code in dBASE II, dBASE III, and dBASE III Plus, and go back and forth between the three interpreters without experiencing tremendous difficulties. (I admit that going up the scale is easier than going down, but that is to be expected.) But going from Clipper-designed programs to dBASE III Plus-designed programs can be a bear if you're not ready for it.

Debugging is another consideration. Clipper comes with a DEBUG utility that I've used repeatedly. This powerful and extremely useful utility provides all dBASE III Plus's debugging features and more. After you have debugged your code, you can recompile the source code (without the DEBUG utility as part of the compilation) and send your package off to market.

The problem I have with the DEBUG utility is the inability to run Clipper files in interpretive mode. I can't make immediate changes to the source code and see how those changes affect my application. Rather, each change has to be recompiled and run. This puts a great deal of pressure on the programmer (as if designing a system weren't enough pressure).

Another problem is that Clipper, like most compilers, adds a great deal of baggage to each compiled source file. A file that uses 2K in ASCII format uses 118K when compiled through Clipper. That's a lot of extra information. Is it necessary? Unfortunately no, but Clipper brings it along anyway. Unlike a C compiler, Clipper brings along *everything*, not just the subroutines necessary for the application at hand.

An advantage in using Clipper is that you are the only one who has to purchase it, and you have to buy it only once. You will need the compiler to test and compile your programs, but Clipper compiles your programs completely. It doesn't create a pseudocompiled file that must be partially interpreted to run. Each Clipper file is an EXE file. The user runs the application as he or she would run a DOS-level command.

# dBASE Tools for C:
# The Programmer's Library

The Programmer's Library is the first of two packages from Jeff Cooper of J.T. Cooper & Company, located in Pittsburgh, Pennsylvania. The first thing you'll find yourself asking is "Jeff, where have you been?"

The Programmer's Library and its sibling provide an interesting link between dBASE III Plus and C. The package supports the Lattice® and Aztec C compilers. The package itself is a ready-to-use set of functions and routines, all written and compiled in C, that add power to your dBASE III Plus system. The functions cover array handling, financial functions, random number generation, trig and inverse trig functions, and statistical functions. This is quite an assortment for the dBASE III Plus programmer involved in engineering, physical science, behavioral science, and similar disciplines. But these ready-to-use functions are not the main selling point of the package, although you may not need to go beyond them.

The package is worth its price because it provides a BIN file interface between dBASE III Plus and compiled C functions. Imagine—you've been coding in dBASE III or III Plus for some time and know that it's similar to C in many aspects. Perhaps you even prototype in dBASE III Plus or C, and then convert from one to the other. You probably have some things you need to do faster than dBASE III Plus allows; you can code them in C but not in MASM, and therefore can't avail yourself of dBASE III Plus's LOAD and CALL commands, and you're up against the wall.

PLUS

Well, your troubles are over. Jeff Cooper has developed a package that LOADs into dBASE III Plus as does any other BIN file. The advantage to Jeff's package is its capacity to be a single BIN file that looks for several routines in yet another file. Normally, you would be limited to LOADing five BIN files, each of which would be limited to 32,000 bytes. Not so with this package. Slick.

The package comes with documentation written by Jeff Cooper and Jordan Bortz—not unlike using a textbook written by the professor. Cooper and Bortz know their package intimately. The documentation is clear, concise, and informative.

To those who need to extend their dBASE III Plus system beyond dBASE III Plus's ability, I strongly recommend this package. It is also a good learning tool for anyone comfortable with dBASE III Plus who wants to learn C. Yes, there are less expensive compilers than Lattice or Aztec, but these are the only two that Cooper's package supports.

# dBASE Tools for C:
# The Graphics Library

This is the sibling I mentioned. Everything I said about The Programmer's Library holds true for The Graphics Library.

Earlier in this chapter, using pure dBASE III Plus code, I demonstrated an awkward way to generate a graph. You would expect a package called The Graphics Library to generate graphs as well, and you're right. In fact, figure 12.4 shows a graph that uses the same data as those in figures 12.2 and 12.3.

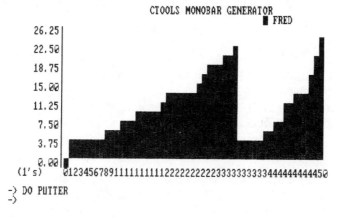

Fig. 12.4. The same graph as in figures 12.1, 12.2, and 12.3, but using a C-Tools file.

The necessary code to produce the graph shown in figure 12.4, using The Graphics Library package, is shown in the following code listing. Anyone who thinks this is no easier than the method I used previously should have his head examined.

```
USE STUDENTS
CALL GFUNC WITH 'CRARRAY FRED,'+STR(RECC(),4,0)+',N'
*
DO WHIL .NOT. EOF()
    CALL GFUNC WITH 'PUTARRAY FRED,'+STR(RECN(),4,0)+;
                    ','+STR(FIELDVAL,2,0)
    SKIP
ENDD
*
CALL GFUNC WITH 'MONOBAR FRED,'+STR(RECC(),4,0)+;
                ',CTOOLS MONOBAR GENERATOR'
```

The Graphics Library includes many of the array-handling routines found in The Programmer's Library. It also includes functions to:

- initialize and end graphics modes

- save and restore graphics screens to disk files

- print graphics screens

- produce high-level charts and graphs in both monochrome and polychrome modes

- generate pie graphs, bar graphs, line graphs, and xy plots

- generate polygons, lines, circles, and boxes

- select colors for the screen

Quite an impressive offering!

What you should know about the Tools package relates primarily to its use of memory. The package reserves 16,384 bytes for arrays alone. To give you an idea of how much memory you can lose, my 512K machine went from 45K (used by DOS and resident programs) to 186K when I loaded The Graphics Library main module. You get speed and power when you use a C Tools package, but you lop off a big chunk of memory.

This brings us to the question of whether the Tools packages are worth the price. Yes, quite so!

I have a few computers, and 512K is the least amount of memory I have on any one system. It is true that dBASE III Plus is designed to fit into a 256K machine, but look at what Ashton-Tate has to do with the CONFIG files to accomplish that. Do they still make machines with less than 512K?

## PLUS dBASE Programmer's Utilities

This is another package available through Ashton-Tate. It is written by Robert Byers, Jeb Long, and Wayne Ratliff—who obviously know what they're doing and how to do it.

The utilities package consists of 15 BIN files, their associated OBJ files, three DOS-level programs to be used with dBASE III Plus, and 17 DOS-level programs that can be used with just about anything. To be used and appreciated, this useful package for the developer-programmer does not require a knowledge of another language such as C or MASM.

Before describing the files included in the package, I want to point out that Ashton-Tate has included OBJ files that can be used with Clipper, Nantucket's dBASE III Plus compiler that I discussed earlier. This is quite nice of Ashton-Tate, as it seems to say that they know and acknowledge others with competitive (and perhaps better) add-on products.

The Programmer's Utilities include BIN files that let you increase dBASE III Plus's file-handling capacity from 15 to 20 active files (note that this doesn't increase the number of available work areas!); play music (you can determine how musical your databases are); control screen intensity, colors, and character placement; define cursors; control the parallel and serial ports; save and restore screens; and find sound-alikes.

You have to play with some of these BIN files to appreciate what they can do for you. One file allows you to create Framework II-like interfaces, similar to the dBASE III Plus ASSIST mode, for your own applications. The serial port control file gives you control to the point of writing communications routines to be executed from inside dBASE III Plus. Imagine being able to instruct dBASE III Plus to FIND, SEEK, or LOCATE someone by name in one field, look at that person's phone number in another field, dial that number, and then let you pick up the phone and talk. This is almost identical to Framework II's Point and Dial function. The SAVESCR.BIN file is one routine that you will start using immediately. You can save and restore up to five separate screen images without having to @ x, y SAY them whenever you want them on the screen. Think of the speed that can give your system, especially during menu generation.

You could include code such as

```
STOR .F. TO NEWS1, NEWS2, NEWS3, NEWS4, NEWS5
```

at the beginning of your code. Each NEWSx variable is a flag that tells dBASE III Plus whether a NEW Screen has been saved over an old one. Saving a new screen in a previously used buffer changes the corresponding NEWSx flag from .F. to .T.. When it's time to recall a screen, you can

```
IF NEWSx
   DO screen
ELSE
   CALL SAVESCR WITH 'Rx'
ENDI
```

It is assumed that this DO screen command calls a .SAY .GET combination. The CALL SAVESCR command simply brings up what's already in the buffer.

The BELL.BIN file is another nice toy. The following code shows how much fun you can have. I didn't know my students were so musically inclined.

```
LOAD BELL
USE STUDENTS
*
DO WHIL .NOT. EOF()
   CALL BELL WITH '1,'+STR(FIELDVAL*100,5,0)
   SKIP
ENDD
```

The package includes three DOS-level programs that can be used to protect databases and repair databases damaged by power surges, power failures, and the like; the package also contains a file to analyze dBASE III Plus programs. Of the three programs, the two most useful are DXREF and DREPAIR. DXREF is similar to most other dBASE III Plus PRG file-analysis tools. DREPAIR is an excellent tool for retrieving files that would otherwise be lost forever.

The last part of the package consists of various DOS-level programs that can be used in any environment. These programs are similar to Norton and other utilities.

This is a package that should be on every dBASE III Plus developer's shelf.

# Concentric Data System's dB Report Writer®

dB Report Writer is exactly what its name implies. This program lets you create reports from dBASE III Plus, dBASE III, and dBASE II DBF files. This program is simple and elegant. Its 1-2-3-like interface shouldn't dissuade anyone from using it.

You may want to know why you would purchase this program, since dBASE III Plus, dBASE III, and dBASE II come with report generators. Fair enough. First, dB Report Writer lets you work with only one DBF at a time (a drawback that is overcome in the next program discussed in this chapter). But you can do some powerful things with the one file that dB Report Writer uses.

dB Report Writer is not a utility to make designing FRM files easier. It is designed to produce different FRM files: FRM files that easily and quickly provide more information than the dBASEs REPORT FORM command can provide. With dB Report Writer, you can create any type of form for the screen and the printer—envelopes, labels, and full-page reports. That alone is beyond the capabilities of dBASE III Plus. The package, which can produce reports that remain on disk to be printed later, can be executed from the DOS prompt or from inside the dBASEs.

With db Report Writer, you can alter the shape and size of a form; change field placement, titles, headers, and page breaks; perform sample listings and printings; create headers and footers; remove and add fields; and so on—all from within the report generator and all with a minimum of keystrokes. People who are tired of dBASE III Plus's RETURN-action-RETURN methodology will appreciate this package. Furthermore, dB Report Writer gives you the freedom to sort on up to four levels of information while you're reporting. Remember that this is all done by a compiled program. You don't have to wait for interpretations to be translated into machine code for things to get done.

dB Report Writer's best feature is its capability of doing reports on MEMO fields. True, the field is limited to the first 50 characters, but that usually is enough. In medical, dental, and other service-related industries, the package's ability to report MEMO fields pays for itself.

## Concentric Data System's R&R Relational Report Writer™

R&R Relational Report Writer is another offering from the people who brought you dB Report Writer. The principal difference between the two packages is R&R's ability to use up to ten databases to generate a single report. A secondary difference is that R&R is limited to dBASE III and dBASE III Plus files.

The capacity to generate reports with up to ten databases is invaluable to me. You probably realize that I like to limit my databases to as few fields as possible, and then draw information from several databases through linked files. That can cause a lot of parent-child headaches. R&R solves that problem, and even lets you create multiple relations between files. Not only can you create parents with several children, but you can also specify bloodlines and gene pools, complete with inbreeding!

Like dB Report Writer, R&R can produce anything from labels to envelopes to complete reports. The interface, an interesting synthesis of 1-2-3 and Paradox™, makes design, modification, and all those other nasty operations a breeze.

A nice R&R feature is that all help screens direct you to specific parts of the documentation for further explanation. Asking for help with "Modes," for example, puts up a screen that suggests you look at pages 14–16 in the *User's Guide*.

It is worth noting that R&R is a memory-based package. Its LOWMEM indicator always seems to come on when you are beyond hope of return.

Even if there were no other reason to purchase R&R, the speed with which it generates reports (regardless of how many DBF files and relations have been set) would make R&R a good buy. This has nothing to do with the design phase, which is a snap in itself. R&R can generate finished reports in about one-tenth the time it takes dBASE III Plus to produce a comparable file.

Because R&R can be run either from DOS or from inside dBASE III Plus, you can include it in your applications for the price of the package. My strong recommendation: Buy it.

## Borland International's Reflex™

Some of you may wonder why I am including a 384K program as a dBASE III Plus add-on. I include Reflex because of its speed, simplicity, and graphing capabilities.

I've shown you how to create a graph with straight dBASE III Plus code. I've shown you how to generate graphs with Jeff Cooper's dBASE Tools for C: The Graphics Library. That's all fine if you're developing something for someone else and can predict fairly accurately (and hence program for unforeseen eventualities) what the user will throw into your code.

But what if you can't predict, or the user's a flake, or, more likely, you're coding for an in-house operation or for a single-user operation. The ability to analyze data quickly and easily is essential. Graphic representation is powerful. Graphic representation that can be placed side-by-side with the data in the database, and then linked and keyed through cursor movements, is the ideal. That is what Reflex offers you.

The Reflex system itself is inexpensive. It comes with good documentation that takes a light approach to teaching you the whys and wherefores of Reflex.

You should note that dBASE III Plus will not coexist comfortably in memory with Reflex. Even in a 640K machine, Reflex will take up about 384K; dBASE III Plus will reserve 192K for itself; and the DOS overhead is between 35 and 60K, depending on version and system. There's no room for any databases to load. Reflex is a memory-based package. It achieves much of its speed by loading information into memory. Analysis with Reflex obviously has to be done outside of the dBASE III Plus system. (This is not true of machines with megamemories.) Management of such packages side by side can be a downfall to the system as a whole.

# 13

# Examples of
# dBASE III Plus Code

In the first edition of this book, *dBASE III Advanced Programming*, I pointed out that good dBASE II code could be translated easily into good dBASE III code. I still believe that with a passion, and extend the statement to include dBASE III Plus.

PLUS

dBASE III Plus, however, can offer the beginning programmer a great deal more power than either dBASE II or dBASE III can. Further, to simply carry dBASE II and dBASE III code into a dBASE III Plus environment is wasteful.

In this chapter, I include the PRG files that were upgraded from dBASE II to dBASE III, and then shown the same routine coded in dBASE III Plus. In some cases the changes are minor or cosmetic. In other cases they are significant.

## A Database Access Template

The first part of this section shows a dBASE III program that is transportable to different environments. The second part shows the same code modified to make use of dBASE III Plus's features. Programmers moving their work from dBASE III to dBASE III Plus should note what I do and why.

```
1: ***MAIN.PRG CALLED FROM WRITE.PRG
2: SET PROC TO VIADEDPA
3: **
4: DO WHILE .T.
5: CLEAR
6: TEXT
```

```
 7: ==================================================================================
 8: ||                          M A I N    M E N U                                 ||
 9: ==================================================================================
10: ||                                                                             ||
11: ||                          Ø. Exit                                            ||
12: ||                          1. View                                            ||
13: ||                          2. Add                                             ||
14: ||                          3. Edit                                            ||
15: ||                          4. Pack                                            ||
16: ||                                                                             ||
17: ||                                                                             ||
18: ==================================================================================
19: ENDTEXT
20: **
21: DO CASE
22: CASE "&database"="MAGAZINE"
23: @ 10,32 SAY "5. Print Magazines by Audience"
24: selectnum=6
25: **
26: CASE "&database"="BOOKS"
27: @ 10,32 SAY "5. Print Publishers by Audience"
28: selectnum=6
29: **
30: CASE "&database"="SENDWHER"
31: @ 10,32 SAY "5. Match Manuscripts to Markets"
32: selectnum=6
33: **
34: OTHE
35: selectnum=5
36: ENDC
37: number=selectnum-1
38: **
39: DO WHILE selectnum < Ø .OR. selectnum > number
40: select=" "
41: @ 12,33 SAY " select : : "
42: @ 12,42 GET select PICTURE "#"
43: READ
44: selectnum=VAL(select)
45: ENDD
46: **
47: DO CASE
48: **
49: CASE selectnum= Ø
```

```
50: CLEA ALL
51: RETU
52: **
53: CASE selectnum= 1
54: USE &database INDEX &INDEX
55: CLEAR
56: @ 1, 0 SAY "V I E W"
57: @ 1,60 SAY "TODAY IS ->"
58: @ 1,72 SAY DTOC(DATE())
59: DO &FRAMER
60: IF (EOF() .OR. BOF())
61: select=" "
62: @ 21,0 SAY "EMPTY DATA FILE"
63: @ 22,0 SAY "Strike any key to continue..." ;
64: GET select
65: READ
66: ELSE
67: DO &GETTER
68: CLEA GETS
69: poschoice="X"
70: **
71: DO WHILE poschoice <> " "
72: DO POSITION
73: ENDD
74: ENDI
75: USE
76: **
77: CASE selectnum= 2
78: **
79: DO CASE
80: CASE "&database"="MAGAZINE"
81: USE MAGAZINE INDEX MAGAZINE,AUDIENCE
82: **
83: CASE "&database"="BOOKS"
84: USE BOOKS INDEX BOOKS,BOOKAUDS
85: **
86: OTHE
87: USE &database INDEX &INDEX
88: ENDC
89: adder="&database"+. "add"
90: COPY STRUCTURE TO &ADDER
91: SELE B
92: USE &ADDER
```

```
 93: CLEAR
 94: @ 1, 0 SAY "A D D"
 95: @ 1,60 SAY "Today is ->"
 96: @ 1,72 SAY DTOC(DATE())
 97: DO &FRAMER
 98: @ 21,0 SAY "Press <control-W> to exit"
 99: addchoice="X"
100: **
101: DO WHILE addchoice <> " "
102: APPEND BLANK
103: DO &GETTER
104: READ
105: addchoice=TRIM(&indexkey)
106: ENDD
107: DELETE
108: USE
109: SELE A
110: APPEND FROM ADDER
111: USE
112: **
113: CASE selectnum= 3
114: USE &database INDEX &INDEX
115: CLEAR
116: @ 1, 0 SAY "E D I T"
117: @ 1,60 SAY "Today is ->"
118: @ 1,72 SAY DTOC(DATE())
119: DO &FRAMER
120: IF (EOF() .OR. BOF())
121: select=" "
122: @ 21,0 SAY "Empty Data File"
123: @ 22,0 SAY "Strike any key to continue..." ;
124: GET select
125: READ
126: ELSE
127: DO &GETTER
128: CLEA GETS
129: DO EDITOR
130: ENDI
131: USE
132: **
133: CASE selectnum= 4
134: DO PACKER
135: **
```

```
136: CASE selectnum= 5
137: **
138: DO CASE
139: CASE "&database"="MAGAZINE"
140: SET CONSOLE OFF
141: USE MAGAZINE INDEX AUDIENCE
142: REPORT FORM MAGAUDS NOEJECT TO PRINT
143: SET CONSOLE ON
144: **
145: CASE "&database"="BOOKS"
146: SET CONSOLE OFF
147: USE BOOKS INDEX BOOKAUDS
148: REPORT FORM BOOKAUDS NOEJECT TO PRINT
149: SET CONSOLE ON
150: **
151: CASE "&database"="SENDWHER"
152: DO SENDWHER
153: ENDC
154: ENDC
155: ENDD
```

Line 2 SETs the PROCEDURE file to VIADEDPA, which is an acronym for VIew, ADd, EDit, PAck. I'm not requesting any information from the user, so my menu is created with TEXT . . . ENDTEXT. Because this routine accesses a database, the only options are those listed.

If special databases are passed to the program, however, some extra options must be made available. For this reason, I included the DO CASE code in lines 21 through 36. Because I always pass the names of variables from the main program, my USE and INDEX commands are no more than MACRO substitutions.

Lines 59, 97, and 119 call the subroutine, FRAMER, which is also declared in the calling program. FRAMER is simply a method of creating a workable screen. Similarly, the GETTER subroutine listed on lines 67, 103, and 127 GETs information from database to user and vice versa.

I always pack a lot of work into a little code. An example of that is in lines 81 and 84, where I activate two indexfiles for each database I open. The first indexfile is the one necessary for the job at hand. The second indexfile is there to make sure that the first is updated when the job is done.

Because dBASE III can't place new data in an existing database and make it appear when the KEYFIELDS dictate, I COPY the STRUCTURE of my database to a tank and APPEND from there, as shown in lines 89 to 111.

When I'm generating a report (lines 142 and 148), I don't need the CONSOLE on. I turn it OFF in lines 140 and 146. I'm usually very careful about the data that goes into and out of my printer, therefore I use NOEJECT in lines 142 and 149. Similarly, because I am careful about my printer, I EJECT after I'm through REPORTing in lines 143 and 150.

PLUS

How does this code change for dBASE III Plus?

```
** MAIN.PRG CALLED FROM WRITE.PRG
**
SET PROC TO VIADEDPA
**
DO WHIL .T.
CLEA
@ 1,0 TO 12,79 DOUB
@ 3,1 TO 3,78 DOUB
@ 2,19 SAY [M A I N   M E N U]
@ 5,32 SAY [0.  EXIT]
@ 6,32 SAY [1.  VIEW]
@ 7,32 SAY [2.  ADD]
@ 8,32 SAY [3.  EDIT]
@ 9,32 SAY [4.  PACK]
NUMBER = 5
**
DO CASE
CASE DATABASE = "M"
@ 10,32 SAY [5.  PRINT MAGAZINES BY AUDIENCE]
CASE DATABASE = "B"
@ 10,32 SAY [5.  PRINT PUBLISHERS BY AUDIENCE]
CASE DATABASE = "S"
@ 10,32 SAY [5.  MATCH MANUSCRIPTS TO MARKETS]
OTHE
NUMBER = 4
ENDC
**
@ 12,33 SAY [ select    ]
@ 12,42 GET SELECTNUM PICT "9" RANG 0,NUMBER
READ
**
DO CASE
CASE SELECTNUM = 0
CLEA ALL
RETU
CASE SELECTNUM = 1
```

```
USE &DATABASE INDE &INDEX
CLEA
@ 1,0 SAY [V I E W] + SPAC(53) + [Today is / ] + DTOC(DATE())
DO &FRAMER
**
IF RECC() = 0
WAIT "EMPTY DATA FILE. Press any key to continue..."
ELSE
DO &GETTER
CLEA GETS
POSCHOICE = "X"
**
DO WHIL POSCHOICE # " "
DO POSITION
ENDD
**
ENDI
**
USE
CASE SELECTNUM = 2
**
DO CASE
CASE &DATABASE = "M"
USE MAGAZINE INDE MAGAZINE,AUDIENCE
CASE &DATABASE = "B"
USE BOOKS INDE BOOKS,BOOKAUDS
OTHE
USE &DATABASE INDE &INDEX
ENDC
**
ADDER = LEFT(DBF(),AT(".",DBF()) + 1)) + ".ADD"
COPY STRU TO &ADDER
SELE B
USE &ADDER
CLEA
@ 1,0 SAY [A D D] + SPAC(55) + [Today is / ] + DTOC(DATE())
DO &FRAMER
SET MESS TO "Press <control-W> to exit"
ADDCHOICE = "X"
**
DO WHIL ADDCHOICE # " "
APPE BLAN
DO &GETTER
```

```
**
IF ERRO() # 5
    READ
ENDI
**
ADDCHOICE = TRIM(&INDEXKEY)
ENDD
**
DELE
USE
SELE A
APPE FROM &ADDER
USE
**
CASE SELECTNUM = 3
USE &DATABASE INDE &INDEX
CLEA
SET MESS TO
@ 1,0 SAY [E D I T] + SPAC(53) + [Today is / ] + DTOC(DATE())
DO &FRAMER
**
IF RECC() # 0
WAIT "EMPTY DATA FILE. Press any key to continue..."
ELSE
DO &GETTER
CLEA GETS
DO EDITOR
ENDI
**
USE
CASE SELECTNUM = 4
DO PACKER
CASE SELECTNUM = 5
**
IF &DATABASE # "S"
SET CONS OFF
SET ORDE TO 2
REPO FORM MAGAUDS NOEJECT TO PRINT
SET ORDE TO 1
SET CONS ON
ELSE
DO SENDWHER
ENDI
**
```

```
ENDC
**
ENDD
*
** EOF
```

Precious little about this code needs to be done in dBASE III Plus, but doing that little bit improves the code's speed during execution. The first consideration is the menu-drawing routine, which is now down to eight lines. The addition of the SPACE( ) function allows us to write one line instead of three for the screen name and date statement.

The next item, the RECCOUNT( ) function, makes determining an empty database much easier than before. Also note how much easier it is to construct a secondary file name with the LEFT( ) and DBF( ) functions.

PLUS

The SET MESSAGE TO command is a particularly nice item. dBASE III Plus normally displays the STATUS bar at the bottom of the screen. You can shut that bar off if you wish, but why not use it when adding or editing records? It tells you the record number, the toggle state of the NUM, CAPS, and INS keys, the active database name, and so on. Never look a gift horse in the mouth.

A secondary check is performed when you add records with the ERROR( ) function. I truthfully can't think of a time when this particular check will be needed in this way. But once the operation is loaded into memory, it doesn't take much time. And something would go wrong if it were left out.

PLUS

Another improvement has to do with designing REPORTs that handle more than one DBF file. Because the BOOKS and MAGAZINE databases share similar fields, a single REPORT FORM can be designed to handle data in those similar fields. (Remember that the REPORT FORM doesn't care which database it works with; it only cares about which fields are in the database it's working with.)

I use the dBASE III Plus SET ORDER TO command to shuffle the NDX files. Nice. Using this command saves me from having to SET INDE TO or USE database INDEX index.

PLUS

# A Label- and Envelope-Maker Template

The first part of this section shows a dBASE III program that is transportable to different environments. The second part shows the same code modified to make use of dBASE III Plus's features. Programmers moving their work from dBASE III to dBASE III Plus should note what I do and why.

```
 1: **LABEL/ENVELOPE GENERATOR,  LABEL2.PRG
 2: PON=.F.
 3: CLEA
 4: ACCEPT "Output to S(creen), P(rinter) or Q(uit)? -> " to select
 5: **
 6: DO CASE
 7: CASE UPPER(select) = "S"
 8: **
 9: CASE UPPER(select) = "P"
10: PON=.T.
11: OTHE
12: RETU
13: ENDC
14: ACCEPT "Output to L(abels) or E(nvelopes)? -> " to select
15: **
16: DO WHILE .T.
17: condition=" "
18: **
19: DO WHILE condition = " "
20: CLEA
21: @ 2, 0 SAY "A D D R E S S    G E N E R A T O R"
22: @ 2,72 SAY DTOC(DATE())
23: @ 3, 0 SAY "========================================"
24: @ 3,40 SAY "========================================"
25: DO BMFRAMES
26: DO BMGETS
27: CLEA GETS
28: @ 19,0 SAY 'EXAMPLE :STATE="CA", <RETURN> = ALL ENTRIES, "QUIT" = QUIT'
29: @ 21,0
30: @ 20,0 SAY "-"
31: ACCEPT "Enter condition " TO condition
32: @ 19,0
33: condition=TRIM(condition)
34: **
35: DO CASE
36: CASE UPPER(condition) = "QUIT"
37: RETU
38: **
39: CASE TYPE("&condition")="U"
40: CLEA GETS
```

```
41: @ 22,0
42: select=" "
43: @ 22,0 SAY "Invalid Expression: "+ ;
44: "Press <RETURN> to continue..." ;
45: GET select
46: READ
47: @ 22,0
48: condition= " "
49: ENDC
50: ENDD
51: LOCATE ALL FOR &condition
52: **
53: IF PON
54: SET PRINT ON
55: SET CONSOLE OFF
56: ELSE
57: CLEA
58: ENDI
59: **
60: DO CASE
61: CASE UPPER(SELECT)='L'
62: **
63: DO WHILE .NOT. EOF()
64: extra=0
65: **
66: IF TRIM(CONTACT) <> " "
67: ? TRIM(CONTACT)+', '+TRIM(POSITION)
68: ELSE
69: ? POSITION
70: ENDI
71: ? NAME
72: ? ADDRESS1
73: **
74: IF TRIM(ADDRESS2) <> " "
75: ? ADDRESS2
76: ELSE
77: extra=extra+1
78: ENDI
79: ? TRIM(CITY)+', '+STATE+'    '+ZIPCODE
80: **
81: IF TRIM(COUNTRY) <> " "
82: ? COUNTRY
83: ELSE
```

```
 84:  extra=extra+1
 85:  ENDI
 86:  **
 87:  DO WHILE extra > 0
 88:  ?
 89:  extra=extra-1
 90:  ENDD
 91:  CONTINUE
 92:  ENDD
 93:  **
 94:  CASE UPPER(SELECT)='E'
 95:  gap=SPACE(30)
 96:  **
 97:  DO WHILE .NOT. EOF()
 98:  extra=2
 99:  ?
100:  ?
101:  ?
102:  ?
103:  ?
104:  ? 'Joseph-David Carrabis'
105:  ? 'Northern Lights Consulting'
106:  ? 'PO Box 3861'
107:  ? 'Nashua, NH 03061'
108:  ?
109:  ?
110:  ?
111:  ?
112:  **
113:  IF TRIM(CONTACT) <> " "
114:  ? GAP+ TRIM(CONTACT)+', '+TRIM(POSITION)
115:  ELSE
116:  ? GAP+ POSITION
117:  ENDI
118:  ? GAP+ NAME
119:  ? GAP+ ADDRESS1
120:  **
121:  IF TRIM(ADDRESS2) <> " "
122:  ? GAP+ ADDRESS2
123:  ELSE
124:  extra=extra+1
125:  ENDI
126:  ? GAP+ TRIM(CITY)+', '+STATE+'   '+ZIPCODE
```

```
127: **
128: IF TRIM(COUNTRY) <> " "
129: ? GAP+ COUNTRY
130: ELSE
131: extra=extra+1
132: ENDI
133: **
134: DO WHILE extra > 0
135: ?
136: extra=extra-1
137: ENDD
138: CONTINUE
139: ENDD
140: ENDC
141: PON=.F.
142: SET PRINT OFF
143: SET CONSOLE ON
144: ENDD
```

When starting the program, I don't know whether I will need the printer. I therefore create a logical variable in line 2 to determine whether the printer should be on. Because sending output to the screen requires no special treatment, none is given in lines 7 and 8.

Line 39 is interesting: I check errors by finding out whether a requested condition exists by determining the TYPE( ) of the condition. An undefined condition TYPE() qualifies as an error condition.

After that, the program merely prints out one-up labels or envelopes. You could modify this routine for three-up, five-up, and so on. That bit of code can be modified easily with MACROs:

```
STORE name TO ALLNAME
STORE address1 TO ALLONE
STORE address2 TO ALLTWO
STORE TRIM(city)+", "+state+" "+zipcode to ALLELSE
SKIP
```

Are you getting the idea? We're creating macros with ALLNAME, ALLONE, ALLTWO, and ALLELSE. The rest of the program becomes

```
STORE ALLNAME+name TO ALLNAME
STORE ALLONE+address1 TO ALLONE
STORE ALLTWO+address2 TO ALLTWO
STORE ALLELSE+TRIM(city)+"´ "+state+"  "+zipcode TO ALLELSE
SKIP
```

```
STORE ALLNAME+name TO ALLNAME
STORE ALLONE+address1 TO ALLONE
STORE ALLTWO+address2 TO ALLTWO
STORE ALLELSE+TRIM(city)+"  "+state+"   "+zipcode TO ALLELSE
? ALLNAME
? ALLONE
? ALLTWO
? ALLELSE
?
?
```

You can enhance this method by predetermining the size of the fields or
by creating a GAP variable, such as was used in the previous example.

How does this code change for dBASE III Plus?

```
** LABEL/ENVELOPE GENERATOR, LABEL2.PRG
*
SET STAT OFF
PON = .F.
CLEA
ACCE "Output to S(creen), P(rinter) or Q(uit)? (S/P/Q) / " TO IT
**
DO CASE
CASE UPPE(IT) = 'S'
CASE UPPE(IT) = 'P'
PON = .T.
OTHE
RETU
ENDC
**
ACCE "Output to L(abels) or E(nvelopes)? (L/E) / " TO IT
**
DO WHIL .T.
CONDITION = '  '
CLEA
@ 2,0 SAY [A D D R E S S    G E N E R A T O R] + SPAC(38) +;
          DTOC(DATE())
@ 3,0 TO 3,79 DOUB
DO BMFRAMES
DO BMGETS
CLEA GETS
@ 19,0 SAY [EXAMPLE: STATE = "CA", <RETURN> = ALL ENTRIES,] +;
          [ "QUIT" = QUIT]
```

```
@ 20,0
ACCE "Enter condition / " TO CONDITION
CONDITION = TRIM(CONDITION)
**
DO CASE
CASE UPPE(CONDITION) = "QUIT"
EXIT
CASE TYPE("&CONDITION") = "U"
@ 20,0
WAIT "INVALID CONDITION. Press any key to continue..."
CONDITION = " "
ENDC
**
ENDD
**
SET FILT TO &CONDITION
**
IF PON
SET PRIN ON
SET CONS OFF
ELSE
CLEA
ENDI
**
IF UPPE(SELECT) = 'L'
LABEL FORM CONTADDR FOR (TRIM(CONTACT) # 0 .AND.;
                        TRIM(ADDRESS2) # 0)
LABEL FORM CONTADD2 FOR (TRIM(CONTACT) # 0 .AND.;
                        TRIM(ADDRESS2) = 0)
LABEL FORM NOCNOAD2 FOR (TRIM(CONTACT) = 10 .AND.;
                        TRIM(ADDRESS2) = 0)
LABEL FORM NOCADDR FOR (TRIM(CONTACT) = 0 .AND.;
                        TRIM(ADDRESS2) # 0)
ELSE
LABEL FORM ECONTADD FOR (TRIM(CONTACT) # 0 .AND.;
                        TRIM(ADDRESS2) # 0)
LABEL FORM ECONTAD2 FOR (TRIM(CONTACT) # 0 .AND.;
                        TRIM(ADDRESS2) = 0)
LABEL FORM ENOCNOA2 FOR (TRIM(CONTACT) = 0 .AND.;
                        TRIM(ADDRESS2) = 0)
LABEL FORM ENOCADDR FOR (TRIM(CONTACT) = 0 .AND.;
                        TRIM(ADDRESS2) # 0)
ENDI
```

```
**
PON = .F.
SET PRIN OFF
SET CONS OFF
SET FILT TO
ENDD
*
** EOF
```

**PLUS**

The big news about this recoding concerns the use of the increased capabilities of the LABEL generator and the SET FILTER TO command. Both have been used to cut down significantly on code in the dBASE III Plus version.

Note that I use the full "QUIT" for my EXIT test. This (I hope) prevents someone from exiting simply because the first part of the CONDITION is "Q".

**PLUS**

In the dBASE III version of the code, I described using macros to create any necessary label strings. This isn't necessary with the new label forms. Nor can the new label forms make an envelope. I kludged an envelope by using the maximum LABEL FORM length (16 lines), and then setting the Space Between Labels to 9 lines. This comes out to the 25 lines necessary to skip over a size 10 envelope. If you need more space between labels, you can mix the Lines Between Labels and Space Between Labels settings.

# A Template for a WordStar MailMerge Module

The first part of this section shows a dBASE III program that is transportable to different environments. The second part shows the same code modified to make use of dBASE III Plus's features. Programmers moving their work from dBASE III to dBASE III Plus should note what I do and why.

```
1: **MLMRGE.PRG
2: **
3: DO WHILE .T.
4: CLEAR
5: ACCEPT "Which database do you want to use?" TO database
6: STOR TRIM(UPPER(database)) TO database
7: IF database="QUIT"
8: RETU
9: ENDI
```

```
10: USE &database
11: @ 11,0 SAY ' '
12: ACCEPT "What subset do you want?" to subset
13: STOR TRIM(subset) TO subset
14: **
15: **
16: DO CASE
17: CASE AT(subset,'QUIT quit')=0
18: RETU
19: **
20: CASE TYPE(&subset)="U"
21: **
22: DO WHILE TYPE(&subset)="U"
23: @ 12,0
24: @ 12,0 SAY "INVALID EXPRESSION"
25: WAIT
26: @ 12,0
27: @ 11,0 SAY ' '
28: ACCEPT "What subset do you want?" to subset
29: IF UPPER("&subset")="QUIT"
30: RETU
31: ENDI
32: ENDD
33: **
34: OTHE
35: COPY TO A:MLMRGE.DAT SDF DELIMITED WITH , FIELD CONTACT, POSITION, ;
36: NAME, ADDRESS1, CITY, STATE, ZIPCODE, DEAR FOR &subset
37: COPY TO A:SAMNA.DAT SDF DELIMITED WITH / FIELD CONTACT, POSITION, ;
38: NAME, ADDRESS1, CITY, STATE, ZIPCODE FOR &subset
39: @ 14,0 SAY 'Done.'
40: WAIT
41: ENDC
42: ENDD
```

Because you always need to know which tools to use, I ask that right away in line 5. Line 17 demonstrates the use of a substring search in place of a logical condition.

Again, an undefined TYPE is used in lines 20 and 22 as an error check. If no errors or stops are encountered, the main body of the program is engaged in lines 35 and 37. Here files are created for two word processors, WordStar and SAMNA. These files will be used to produce mailmerge documents.

PLUS

How does this code change for dBASE III Plus?

```
** MLMRGE.PRG
**
DO WHIL .T.
SET CATA TO &CATALOG
USE ?
**
IF DBF() = ''
RETU
ENDI
**
@ 10,0 SAY [EXAMPLE: STATE = "CA", <RETURN> = ALL ENTRIES]
@ 5,0
ACCE "What subset do you want? / " TO SUBSET
**
IF TYPE("&SUBSET") = "U"
WAIT "INVALID SUBSET. Press any key to continue..."
LOOP
ENDI
**
SET FILT TO TRIM(SUBSET)
COPY TO MLMRGE.DAT DELIM WITH , FIELD CONTACT, POSITION, NAME,;
       ADDRESS1, CITY, STATE, ZIPCODE, DEAR
SET FILT TO
WAIT "DONE. Press any key to continue..."
EXIT
ENDD
*
** EOF
```

PLUS

The big news in this dBASE III Plus file is the use of the SET CATALOG TO and USE ? commands. This usage removes from the user the burden of remembering the exact name of the desired DBF files. The use of these commands also allows dBASE III Plus to load automatically any NDX files that may be associated with the chosen DBF file. I also test for an EXIT/ RETURN condition with the DBF( ) function.

PLUS

Note also that I don't use the COPY TO FOR construct in the dBASE III Plus code. Testing the differences between SETting a FILTER TO something and COPYing TO FOR has convinced me that dBASE III Plus runs faster when you SET a FILTER TO something. Some kind of beta blocking is obviously going on—whatever. Using this method, III Plus does write the DELIMITED file faster.

# A "Where Sent" Template for Tracking Manuscripts

The first part of this section shows a dBASE III program that is transportable to different environments. The second part shows the same code modified to make use of dBASE III Plus's features. Programmers moving their work from dBASE III to dBASE III Plus should note what I do and why.

This module matches manuscripts to markets (magazines that might buy the manuscripts), and shows an example of resource planning and tracking. The module takes available resources (the manuscripts), and finds places where those resources will prosper (magazine markets). Then the user can track the progress of those resources.

```
 1: **SENDWHERE.PRG FOR MATCHING MANUSCRIPTS TO MARKETS
 2: SELE A
 3: USE MAGAZINE INDEX AUDIENCE
 4: SELE B
 5: USE SENDWHER INDEX MSSNAME
 6: GOTO TOP
 7: **
 8: DO WHILE .NOT. EOF()
 9: NUMBER=1
10: AUD=AUDIENCE
11: CLEAR
12: ? MSS_NAME
13: SELECT A
14: FIND &AUD
15: **
16: DO WHILE AUDIENCE = AUD
17: **
18: IF NUMBER=21
19: SELE B
20: CARRYNAME=MSS_NAME
21: INSERT BLANK
22: REPL MORE WITH .T.
23: REPL MSS_NAME WITH CARRYNAME
24: REPL AUDIENCE WITH AUD
25: NUMBER=1
26: SELECT A
27: ENDI
28: **
```

```
29: IF NUMBER < 10
30: FIELDNAME="T"+STR(NUMBER,1,0)
31: ELSE
32: FIELDNAME="T"+STR(NUMBER,2,0)
33: ENDI
34: MAGNAME=NAME
35: SELE B
36: REPL &FIELDNAME WITH MAGNAME
37: ? MAGNAME
38: NUMBER=NUMBER+1
39: SELECT A
40: SKIP
41: ENDD
42: SELE B
43: SKIP
44: ENDD
45: CLEA
46: ACCEPT "PRINT REPORT [(A)ll/(S)ingle/(N)one)? -> " TO PRINTREPT
47: PRINTREPT=UPPER(PRINTREPT)
48: **
49: DO CASE
50: CASE PRINTREPT='A'
51: GOTO TOP
52: **
53: DO WHILE .NOT. EOF()
54: DO SENDWHER.FMT
55: SKIP
56: ENDD
57: **
58: CASE PRINTREPT='S'
59: ANOTHER=.T.
60: **
61: DO WHILE ANOTHER
62: ACCEPT "What is the manuscript's name ('Q' to QUIT)? -> " TO PMSSNAME
63: PMSSNAME=UPPER(PMSSNAME)
64: **
65: IF PMSSNAME = 'Q'
66: RETU
67: ELSE
68: FIND &PMSSNAME
69: DO SENDWHER.FMT
70: ENDI
71: ACCEPT "Do another? ->" TO ANOTHER
```

```
72: ENDD
73: ENDC
74: RETU
```

The lines of major interest are 30 and 32, the fieldname building lines. Lines 58 to 73 permit the selective viewing or printing of format files based on manuscript name. You can use these lines as a template for selective file generation.

How does this code change for dBASE III Plus?

PLUS

```
** SENDWHER.PRG FOR MATCHING MANUSCRIPTS TO MARKETS
**
SELE 2
USE MSSFILE INDE MSSFILE, SUBWHEN
**
DO WHIL .T.
CLEA
ACCE "Manuscript to match (RETURN to quit, '?' for list)? ";
     TO MSSNAME
**
DO CASE
CASE LEN(TRIM(MSSNAME)) = Ø
SELE 1
**
IF B->MSSTYPE = "B"
USE BOOKS INDE BOOK, BAUDS
ELSE
USE MAGAZINE INDE MAGAZINE, MAUDS
ENDI
**
RETU
CASE MSSNAME = "?"
CLEA
DISP ALL TRIM(B->TITLE) FOR UPPER(B->MSSTYPE) = LEFT(DBFILE, 1)
WAIT
LOOP
OTHE
FIND &MSSNAME
**
IF .NOT. FOUND()
WAIT "I can't find that manuscript. Press any key to continue"
ELSE
SELE 1
```

```
**
IF B->MSSTYPE = "B"
USE BOOKS INDE BAUDS
ELSE
USE MAGAZINE INDE MAUDS
ENDI
**
SEEK (B->AUDIENCE)
PRINTERON = .N.
@ 10,10 SAY "Do you want this printed? (Y/N) -> " GET PRINTERON
READ
**
IF PRINTERON
SET CONS OFF
TOPR = "TO PRINT"
ENDI
**
REPO FORM MATCHER1 WHIL AUDIENCE = (B->AUDIENCE) FOR ;
AT(STR(RECNO(),3,0),B->SUBMISSION) = 0 HEADING "&MSSNAME" &TOPR
SEEK (B->AUDIENCE)
REPO FORM MATCHER2 WHIL AUDIENCE = (B->AUDIENCE) FOR ;
MSSMIN < B->LENGTH .AND. MSSMAX > B->LENGTH .AND. ;
AT(STR(RECNO(),3,0),B->SUBMISSION) = 0 HEADING "&MSSNAME" &TOPR
SET CONS ON
TOPR = ""
WAIT
ENDC
*
SELE 2
ENDD
*
* END OF MATCHMSS.PRG
```

Of all the rewrites presented so far, this one has gone through the most modifications. It is still shorter than the original dBASE III code, but does a great deal more.

First, the code provides for a list of available manuscripts. Then it selects work area A's database based on the type of manuscript (book or magazine). It also includes more elaborate error checking should things go awry.

Note that I now SEEK things based on information in alias A. This information is used in the work area B databases, which are INDEXed on the items I'm SEEKing. This means I've set the record pointer to REPORT WHILE. To further limit my search pattern, I include a FOR qualifier.

An interesting feature is the line

```
AT(STR(RECNO(),3,0),B->SUBMISSION) = 0
```

The SUBMISSION field holds a list of the records that have already been matched with previous scans. The command tells dBASE III Plus not to repeat a listing if the record has already been matched.

# A Main Menu Template

The first part of this section shows a dBASE III program that is transportable to different environments. The second part shows the same code modified to make use of dBASE III Plus's features. Programmers moving their work from dBASE III to dBASE III Plus should note what I do and why.

```
 1: ***WRITE.PRG MAIN DRIVER
 2: SET EXAC ON
 3: SET TALK OFF
 4: SET BELL OFF
 5: SET DELIMITER OFF
 6: **
 7: DO WHILE .T.
 8: CLEAR
 9: TEXT
10: ==================================================================
11: ||          W R I T E !    W R I T E !    W R I T E !          ||
12: ==================================================================
13: ||                                                            ||
14: ||               0. Quit to System                           ||
15: ||               1. Quit to dBASE                            ||
16: ||               2. Quit to WordStar                         ||
17: ||               3. Magazine Menu                            ||
18: ||               4. Book Publisher Menu                      ||
19: ||               5. Get Subset for Mailmerge                 ||
20: ||               6. Make Labels/Envelopes                    ||
21: ||               7. Send What to Who                         ||
22: ||                                                            ||
23: =========================select : :============================
24: ENDT
25: selectnum=8
```

```
26: **
27: DO WHILE selectnum < 0 .OR. selectnum > 7
28: select=" "
29: @ 14,40 GET select PICTURE "#"
30: READ
31: selectnum=VAL(select)
32: ENDD
33: **
34: DO CASE
35: CASE selectnum= 0
36: QUIT
37: **
38: CASE selectnum= 1
39: CLEA ALL
40: RETU
41: **
42: CASE SELECTNUM= 2
43: RUN WS
44: **
45: CASE selectnum= 3
46: STOR "MAGAZINE" TO database, index
47: framer="BMFRAMES"
48: getter="BMGETS"
49: keyfield="NAME"
50: DO MAIN
51: **
52: CASE selectnum= 4
53: STOR "BOOKS" TO database, index
54: framer="BMFRAMES"
55: getter="BMGETS"
56: keyfield="NAME"
57: DO MAIN
58: **
59: CASE selectnum= 5
60: DO MLMRGE
61: **
62: CASE selectnum= 6
63: CLEAR
64: Accept "Which database do you want to use?" TO database
65: USE &DATABASE
66: DO LABEL2
67: **
68: CASE SELECTNUM= 7
```

```
69: database="SENDWHER"
70: index="MSSNAME"
71: framer="SEFRAME"
72: getter="SEGETS"
73: keyfield="MSS_NAME"
74: DO MAIN
75: ENDC
76: ENDD
```

This is the main program from which all others are called. Because this program starts and stops each session for the client, I SET many conditions at the beginning (lines 2 to 5).

Because we request no messages from the user, the menu is created with TEXT . . . ENDTEXT lines (9 to 24) instead of with a series of @@ SAY . . . GETs.

The DO CASE . . . ENDCASE construction that runs the length of the program (lines 27 to 76) uses the PUBLIC command without specifying it. The key is that variables become PUBLIC to all called programs. Because I don't want the variables to be changed, I declare them without the use of the PUBLIC command.

How does this code change for dBASE III Plus?

PLUS

```
** WRITE.PRG MAIN DRIVER
**
SET EXAC ON
SET TALK OFF
SET BELL OFF
SET DELI OFF
SET SCOR OFF
SET STAT OFF
**
REST FROM WRITE
**
DO WHIL .T.
CLEA
@ 1,0 TO 14,79 DOUB
@ 2,11 SAY [W R I T E !    W R I T E !    W R I T E !]
@ 3,1 TO 3,78 DOUB
@ 4,32 SAY [0. QUIT TO SYSTEM]
@ 5,32 SAY [1. QUIT TO III PLUS]
@ 6,32 SAY [2. QUIT TO WORD PROCESSOR]
@ 7,32 SAY [3. MAGAZINE MENU]
```

```
@ 8,32 SAY [4.  BOOK PUBLISHER MENU]
@ 9,32 SAY [5.  GET SUBSET FOR MAILMERGE]
@ 10,32 SAY [6.  MAKE LABELS/ENVELOPES]
@ 11,32 SAY [7.  SEND WHAT TO WHO]
@ 14,36 SAY [ select / . ]
SELECTNUM = 0
@ 14,40 GET SELECTNUM PICT "9" RANG 0,7
READ
**
DO CASE
CASE SELECTNUM = 0
SAVE TO WRITE
QUIT
CASE SELECTNUM = 1
CLEA ALL
RETU
CASE SELECTNUM = 2
! &WP
CASE SELECTNUM = 3
STOR "MAGAZINE" TO DATABASE, INDEX
FRAMER = "BMFRAMES"
GETTER = "BMGETS"
KEYFIELD = "NAME"
DO MAIN
CASE SELECTNUM = 4
STOR "BOOKS" TO DATABASE, INDEX
FRAMER = "BMFRAMES"
GETTER = "BMGETS"
KEYFIELD = "NAME"
DO MAIN
CASE SELECTNUM = 5
DO MLMERGE
CASE SELECTNUM = 6
CLEA
SET CATA TO MASTER
USE ?
DO LABEL2
SET CATA TO
CASE SELECTNUM = 7
DATABASE = "SENDWHER"
INDEX = "MSSNAME"
FRAMER = "SEFRAME"
GETTER = "SEGETS"
```

```
KEYFIELD = "MSS_NAME"
DO MAIN
ENDC
**
ENDD
*.
** EOF
```

Many of the differences are minor and cosmetic, but they do speed up processing.

Note that I've included more SET statements. The two new ones handle the SCOREBOARD and STATUS lines on the dBASE III Plus screen. Other modules activate and deactivate these system lines as the application dictates. Another new addition is the line

```
  REST FROM WRITE
```

dBASE III Plus makes much better use of memory than either dBASE II or III did, so why not use that power with a MEM file? This MEM file contains all the necessary default information for the WRITE programs.

The menu has been rewritten to make use of dBASE III Plus's line-drawing capabilities. Note that I've substituted RANGE qualifiers for specific error checks. I believe that users have become much more sophisticated, and that they won't go into conniptions if things don't behave as anticipated. This is something you'll have to decide for yourself when you're writing application- and environment-specific code.

I've also made use of dBASE III Plus's SET CATALOG TO and USE ? commands to get database information from the user in option 6. I have already noted that this allows dBASE III Plus to offer databases in case the user can't think of the correct file name, and also lets dBASE III Plus handle NDX file opening when necessary.

PLUS

PLUS

# Epilogue

Well, how was it? Did you learn anything? Were you at least entertained?

I frequently was asked what this book was about while I was writing it. My standard reply was "It's a mystery: the programmer did it, and the computer dies in the end."

I hope nothing like that happens to you, and I do hope that you have benefited from this book. And I hope that you prosper when you go on your next programming gig.

# ASCII Character Set

The table lists the ASCII characters and their codes in decimal notation. Characters can be displayed with

   ? CHR(n)

where *n* is the ASCII value. Characters not appearing on the keyboard can be entered by holding down the Alt key while you enter the ASCII value, using the numeric keypad. The standard interpretations of ASCII codes 0 to 31 are presented in the Control Character column.

| ASCII Value | Character | Control Character | ASCII Value | Character | Control Character |
|---|---|---|---|---|---|
| 000 | (null) | NUL | 016 | ► | DLE |
| 001 | ☺ | SOH | 017 | ◄ | DC1 |
| 002 | ● | STX | 018 | ↕ | DC2 |
| 003 | ♥ | ETX | 019 | !! | DC3 |
| 004 | ♦ | EOT | 020 | ¶ | DC4 |
| 005 | ♣ | ENQ | 021 | § | NAK |
| 006 | ♠ | ACK | 022 | ▬ | SYN |
| 007 | (beep) | BEL | 023 | ↨ | ETB |
| 008 | ■ | BS | 024 | ↑ | CAN |
| 009 | (tab) | HT | 025 | ↓ | EM |
| 010 | (line feed) | LF | 026 | → | SUB |
| 011 | (home) | VT | 027 | ← | ESC |
| 012 | (form feed) | FF | 028 | (cursor right) | FS |
| 013 | (carriage return) | CR | 029 | (cursor left) | GS |
| 014 | ♫ | SO | 030 | (cursor up) | RS |
| 015 | ☼ | SI | 031 | (cursor down) | US |

| ASCII Value | Character | ASCII Value | Character |
|---|---|---|---|
| 032 | (space) | 069 | E |
| 033 | ! | 070 | F |
| 034 | '' | 071 | G |
| 035 | # | 072 | H |
| 036 | $ | 073 | I |
| 037 | % | 074 | J |
| 038 | & | 075 | K |
| 039 | ' | 076 | L |
| 040 | ( | 077 | M |
| 041 | ) | 078 | N |
| 042 | * | 079 | O |
| 043 | + | 080 | P |
| 044 | , | 081 | Q |
| 045 | - | 082 | R |
| 046 | . | 083 | S |
| 047 | / | 084 | T |
| 048 | 0 | 085 | U |
| 049 | 1 | 086 | V |
| 050 | 2 | 087 | W |
| 051 | 3 | 088 | X |
| 052 | 4 | 089 | Y |
| 053 | 5 | 090 | Z |
| 054 | 6 | 091 | [ |
| 055 | 7 | 092 | \ |
| 056 | 8 | 093 | ] |
| 057 | 9 | 094 | ∧ |
| 058 | : | 095 | — |
| 059 | ; | 096 | ` |
| 060 | < | 097 | a |
| 061 | = | 098 | b |
| 062 | > | 099 | c |
| 063 | ? | 100 | d |
| 064 | @ | 101 | e |
| 065 | A | 102 | f |
| 066 | B | 103 | g |
| 067 | C | 104 | h |
| 068 | D | 105 | i |

| ASCII Value | Character | ASCII Value | Character |
|---|---|---|---|
| 106 | j | 143 | Å |
| 107 | k | 144 | É |
| 108 | l | 145 | æ |
| 109 | m | 146 | Æ |
| 110 | n | 147 | ô |
| 111 | o | 148 | ö |
| 112 | p | 149 | ò |
| 113 | q | 150 | û |
| 114 | r | 151 | ù |
| 115 | s | 152 | ÿ |
| 116 | t | 153 | Ö |
| 117 | u | 154 | Ü |
| 118 | v | 155 | ¢ |
| 119 | w | 156 | £ |
| 120 | x | 157 | ¥ |
| 121 | y | 158 | Pt |
| 122 | z | 159 | ƒ |
| 123 | { | 160 | á |
| 124 | \| | 161 | í |
| 125 | } | 162 | ó |
| 126 | ~ | 163 | ú |
| 127 | ⌂ | 164 | ñ |
| 128 | Ç | 165 | Ñ |
| 129 | ü | 166 | ª |
| 130 | é | 167 | º |
| 131 | â | 168 | ¿ |
| 132 | ä | 169 | ⌐ |
| 133 | à | 170 | ¬ |
| 134 | å | 171 | ½ |
| 135 | ç | 172 | ¼ |
| 136 | ê | 173 | ¡ |
| 137 | ë | 174 | « |
| 138 | è | 175 | » |
| 139 | ï | 176 | |
| 140 | î | 177 | ▒ |
| 141 | ì | 178 | ▓ |
| 142 | Ä | 179 | │ |

| ASCII Value | Character | ASCII Value | Character |
|---|---|---|---|
| 180 | ⊣ | 218 | ⌐ |
| 181 | ╡ | 219 | ■ |
| 182 | ╢ | 220 | ▬ |
| 183 | ╖ | 221 | ▮ |
| 184 | ╕ | 222 | ▮ |
| 185 | ╣ | 223 | ▬ |
| 186 | ‖ | 224 | $\alpha$ |
| 187 | ╗ | 225 | $\beta$ |
| 188 | ╝ | 226 | $\Gamma$ |
| 189 | ╜ | 227 | $\pi$ |
| 190 | ╛ | 228 | $\Sigma$ |
| 191 | ┐ | 229 | $\sigma$ |
| 192 | └ | 230 | $\mu$ |
| 193 | ┴ | 231 | $\tau$ |
| 194 | ┬ | 232 | $\Phi$ |
| 195 | ├ | 233 | $\Theta$ |
| 196 | ─ | 234 | $\Omega$ |
| 197 | ┼ | 235 | $\delta$ |
| 198 | ╞ | 236 | $\infty$ |
| 199 | ╟ | 237 | $\emptyset$ |
| 200 | ╚ | 238 | $\epsilon$ |
| 201 | ╔ | 239 | $\cap$ |
| 202 | ╩ | 240 | $\equiv$ |
| 203 | ╦ | 241 | $\pm$ |
| 204 | ╠ | 242 | $\geq$ |
| 205 | ═ | 243 | $\leq$ |
| 206 | ╬ | 244 | $\lceil$ |
| 207 | ╧ | 245 | $\rfloor$ |
| 208 | ╨ | 246 | $\div$ |
| 209 | ╤ | 247 | $\approx$ |
| 210 | ╥ | 248 | ° |
| 211 | ╙ | 249 | • |
| 212 | ╘ | 250 | · |
| 213 | ╒ | 251 | $\sqrt{}$ |
| 214 | ╓ | 252 | n |
| 215 | ╫ | 253 | 2 |
| 216 | ╪ | 254 | ■ |
| 217 | ┘ | 255 | (blank 'FF') |

# B
# Summary of dBASE III Plus Commands

The commands used in interactive-processing and batch-processing modes are summarized in this appendix. Many of these commands have been discussed in this book, but you will find some commands that have not been used. In many cases, several different commands can be used to perform the same task. Feel free to explore any unfamiliar commands, using the information in this appendix.

## I. Definition of Terms

The following special terms are used in this appendix. When entering the commands, enter only the file name or other element; do not enter the angle brackets (<>).

### <file name>

A string of up to 8 characters, including the underscore, with a file extension (for example, .DBF, .DBT, .FMT, .FRM, .LBL, .MEM, .NDX, .PRG, and .TXT). A sample file name is EMPLOYEE.DBF.

### <data field name>

A string of up to 8 characters, including the underscore, such as

    LAST_NAME

## <data field list>

A series of data field names separated by commas, such as

LAST_NAME, FIRST_NAME, AREA_CODE, PHONE_NO

## <variable name>

A string of up to 10 characters, including underscores, such as

TOTALPRICE

## <variable list>

A series of variable names separated by commas, such as

HOURS, PAYRATE, GROSSWAGE, TOTALSALE

## <expression>

An alphanumeric or numeric expression.

## <alphanumeric expression>

A collection of alphanumeric data joined with plus signs, such as

"Employee's Name: "+TRIM(LAST_NAME)+FIRST_NAME+MIDDLENAME

## <numeric expression>

A collection of numeric data joined with arithmetic operators (+, −, *,
/, ^), such as

40*PAYRATE+(HOURS−40)*PAYRATE*1.5

## <expression list>

A series of expressions separated by commas, such as

<expression 1>, <expression 2>, <expression 3>, . . .

## <qualifier>

A clause that begins with FOR, followed by one or more conditions.

FOR AREA_CODE="206"
FOR ANNUAL_PAY>=25000
FOR LAST_NAME="Smith" .AND. FIRST_NAME="James C."

## II. A Listing of dBASE III Commands by Function

### *To Create, Modify, and Manipulate Files*

APPEND FROM
CLOSE ALTERNATE
CLOSE DATABASES
CLOSE FORMAT
CLOSE INDEX
CLOSE PROCEDURE
COPY TO
COPY FILE
COPY STRUCTURE TO
CREATE
CREATE LABEL
CREATE QUERY
CREATE REPORT
CREATE SCREEN
CREATE VIEW
EXPORT
IMPORT
INDEX ON
JOIN
MODIFY COMMAND
MODIFY LABEL
MODIFY QUERY
MODIFY REPORT
MODIFY SCREEN
MODIFY STRUCTURE
MODIFY VIEW
REINDEX
RENAME
SAVE TO
SELECT
SORT
TOTAL
USE

### *To Add Data Records to a Database File*

APPEND
BROWSE
INSERT

### To Edit Data in a Database File

BROWSE
CHANGE
DELETE
EDIT
PACK
READ
RECALL
REPLACE
UPDATE

### To Display Data

@ . . . SAY
?
??
AVERAGE
BROWSE
COUNT
DISPLAY
LIST
REPORT
SUM
TEXT

### To Control the Record Pointer

CONTINUE
FIND
GO BOTTOM
GOTO
GO TOP
LOCATE
SEEK
SKIP

## To Use Memory Variables

ACCEPT
AVERAGE
CLEAR ALL
CLEAR MEMORY
COUNT
DISPLAY MEMORY
INPUT
READ
RELEASE
RESTORE FROM
SAVE TO
STORE
SUM
WAIT

## To Program

ACCEPT TO
CANCEL
CASE
DO
DO WHILE . . . ENDDO
DO CASE . . . ENDCASE
EXIT
IF . . . ENDIF
IF . . . ELSE . . . ENDIF
INPUT
LOOP
MODIFY COMMAND
PARAMETERS
PRIVATE
PROCEDURE
PUBLIC
QUIT
RETRY
RETURN
TEXT
WAIT TO

## To Control Media Display*

CLEAR
EJECT
SET COLOR TO
SET CONFIRM on/OFF
SET CONSOLE ON/off
SET INTENSITY ON/off
SET PRINT ON/off
SET DEVICE TO PRINT
SET DEVICE TO SCREEN
SET MARGIN TO

*Uppercase indicates default settings.

## To Specify Control Parameters*

SET ALTERNATE TO
SET ALTERNATE on/OFF
SET BELL ON/off
SET CARRY on/OFF
SET CATALOG ON/off
SET CATALOG TO
SET DATE
SET DEBUG
SET DECIMALS TO
SET DEFAULT TO
SET DELETED on/OFF
SET DELIMITERS on/OFF
SET DOHISTORY on/OFF
SET DOHISTORY TO
SET ECHO on/OFF
SET ESCAPE ON/off
SET EXACT on/OFF
SET FIELDS on/OFF
SET FIELDS TO
SET FILTER TO
SET FIXED on/OFF
SET FORMAT TO
SET FUNCTION TO
SET HEADING ON/off
SET HELP ON/off

SET HISTORY ON/off
SET INDEX TO
SET MARGIN TO
SET MENUS ON/off
SET MESSAGE TO
SET ORDER TO
SET PATH TO
SET PROCEDURE TO
SET RELATION TO
SET SAFETY ON/off
SET SCOREBOARD ON/off
SET STATUS ON/off
SET STEP on/OFF
SET TALK ON/off
SET TITLE ON/off
SET TYPEAHEAD TO
SET UNIQUE on/OFF

∗Uppercase indicates default settings.

## III. Summary of Commands

### ?

Displays the contents of an alphanumeric or numeric expression on a new display line, such as

    ? "Employee's name . . . "+FIRST_NAME+LAST_NAME
    ? HOURS∗PAYRATE
    ? "Gross Pay . . . "+STR(GROSSPAY,7,2)

### ??

Displays output on the same display line, such as

    ?? "Invoice number: "+INVNO

### @<row,column> GET

Displays user-formatted data at the screen location specified by
<row,column>, as in

    @5,10 GET LAST_NAME
    @8,10 GET SC_NO PICTURE "###-##-####"

## @<row,column> SAY

Displays user-formatted data on the screen or printer at the location specified by <row,column>, as in

    @5,10 SAY LAST_NAME
    @5,10 SAY "Last name . . . " LAST_NAME
    @10,5 SAY "Annual salary:" ANNUAL_PAY PICTURE "$##,###.##"

## @<row,column> SAY. . . GET

Displays user-formatted data on screen at the location specified by <row,column>; used for appending or editing a data field.

    @5,10 SAY "Last name : " GET LAST_NAME

## ACCEPT

Assigns an alphanumeric string to a memory variable, with or without a prompt.

    ACCEPT "Enter your last name . . . " TO LASTNAME
    ACCEPT TO LASTNAME

## APPEND

Adds a data record to the end of the active database file. The data fields are the field labels on the entry form.

    USE EMPLOYEE
    APPEND

## APPEND BLANK

Same as APPEND, but does not use a label to display the field on the entry form.

    USE EMPLOYEE
    APPEND BLANK

## APPEND FROM

Adds data records from one database file (FILE1.DBF) to another database file (FILE2.DBF), with or without a qualifier.

    USE FILE2
    APPEND FROM FILE1

    USE FILE2
    APPEND FROM FILE1 FOR ACCT_NO<="10123"

## ASSIST

Activates The Assistant.

## AVERAGE

Computes the average of a numeric expression and assigns the value to a memory variable, with or without a condition.

    AVERAGE ANNUAL_PAY TO AVERAGEPAY
    AVERAGE QTY_SOLD TO AVERAGESALE FOR MODEL_NO="XYZ"
    AVERAGE HOURS*PAYRATE TO AVERAGEPAY FOR .NOT. MALE

## BROWSE

Displays for review or modification up to 17 records from the active database file.

    USE EMPLOYEE
    GO TOP
    BROWSE

## BROWSE FIELDS

Browses selected data fields in the current database file.

    USE EMPLOYEE
    GO TOP
    BROWSE FIELDS FIRST_NAME, LAST_NAME, PHONE_NO

## CANCEL

Terminates the processing of a program file and returns the program to the dot prompt.

```
IF EOF( )
   CANCEL
ENDIF
```

## CHANGE

Displays the data records in an active database file sequentially, with or without a qualifier.

```
USE EMPLOYEE
CHANGE
```

```
USE EMPLOYEE
CHANGE FOR AREA_CODE="206"
```

## CHANGE FIELDS

Displays selected data fields sequentially, with or without a qualifier.

```
USE EMPLOYEE
CHANGE FIELDS ANNUAL_PAY
```

```
USE EMPLOYEE
CHANGE FIELDS AREA_CODE,PHONE_NO FOR AREA_CODE="206"
```

## CLEAR

Clears the screen.

## CLEAR ALL

Closes all open database files (including .DBF, .NDX, .FMT, and .DBT files) and releases all memory variables.

## CLEAR FIELDS

Releases the data fields that have been created by the SET FIELDS TO command.

## CLEAR GETS

Causes the subsequent READ command to be ignored for the
@ . . . SAY . . . GET commands issued before the command, such as

@5,10 SAY "Account number : " GET ACCT_NO
CLEAR GETS
@7,10 SAY "Account name : " GET ACCT_NAME
READ

## CLEAR MEMORY

Releases or erases all memory variables.

## CLEAR TYPEAHEAD

Empties the type-ahead buffer.

## CLOSE

Closes various types of files:

CLOSE ALL
CLOSE ALTERNATIVE
CLOSE DATABASES
CLOSE FORMAT
CLOSE INDEX
CLOSE PROCEDURE

## CONTINUE

Resumes the search started with the LOCATE command.

USE EMPLOYEE
LOCATE FOR AREA_CODE="206"
DISPLAY
CONTINUE
DISPLAY

## COPY TO

Copies the contents of a source database file to a destination file, with or without a qualifier.

```
USE SALE
COPY TO NEWSALE.DBF
COPY TO OLDSALE.DBF FOR ACCT_NO<="100123"
```

## COPY TO

Copies selected fields of a source database file to a new file, with or without a qualifier.

```
USE EMPLOYEE
COPY TO ROSTER.DBF FIELDS FIRST_NAME, LAST_NAME
COPY TO SALARY.DBF FIELDS LAST_NAME, ANNUAL_PAY FOR MALE
```

## COPY FILE

Duplicates an existing dBASE III file of any type.

```
COPY FILE MAINPROG.PRG TO MAIN.PRG
COPY FILE COST.FMT TO NEWCOST.FMT
COPY FILE ROSTER.FRM TO NAMELIST.FRM
```

## COPY STRUCTURE

Copies the data structure to another database file.

```
USE COST
COPY STRUCTURE TO NEWCOST.DBF
```

## COUNT

Counts the number of records in the active database file and assigns the number to a memory variable.

```
USE EMPLOYEE
COUNT TO NRECORDS
COUNT FOR ANNUAL_PAY>="50000" .AND. MALE TO
RICHMEN
```

### CREATE

Sets up a new file structure and adds data records, if desired.

CREATE EMPLOYEE

### CREATE LABEL

Displays a design form to set up a label file (.LBL).

CREATE LABEL MAILLIST

### CREATE QUERY

Creates a new query file (.QRY).

PLUS

USE EMPLOYEE
CREATE QUERY FINDEMPL.QRY

### CREATE REPORT

Displays a design form to set up a report-form file (.FRM).

CREATE REPORT WEEKLY

### CREATE SCREEN

Creates a new screen file (.SCR).

PLUS

USE EMPLOYEE
CREATE SCREEN SHOWEMPL.SCR

### CREATE VIEW

Creates a new view file (.VUE).

PLUS

USE EMPLOYEE
CREATE VIEW SAMPLE.VUE

## DELETE

Marks the records in the active database file with a deletion symbol (\*).

```
USE EMPLOYEE
DELETE
DELETE RECORD 5
DELETE NEXT 3
DELETE FOR AREA_CODE="503"
```

## DIR

Displays the file directory:

| | |
|---|---|
| DIR | *(Displays .DBF files)* |
| DIR *.* | *(Displays all files)* |
| DIR *.PRG | *(Displays program files)* |
| DIR *.NDX | *(Displays index files)* |
| DIR X*.DBF | *(Displays .DBF file names beginning with X)* |
| DIR ??X???.PRG | *(Displays .PRG file names having six letters and X as the third character)* |
| DIR ???.* | *(Displays all file names that are three characters long)* |

## DISPLAY

Shows the contents of the data records.

```
USE EMPLOYEE
DISPLAY
DISPLAY RECORD 3
DISPLAY NEXT 2
DISPLAY LAST_NAME,FIRST_NAME
DISPLAY AREA_CODE,PHONE_NO FOR AREA_CODE="206"
```

## DISPLAY MEMORY

Shows the contents of active memory variables.

## DISPLAY STATUS

Shows the current processing situation, including the names of active files, the work area number, etc.

## DISPLAY STRUCTURE

Shows the data structure of an active database file.

    USE EMPLOYEE
    DISPLAY STRUCTURE

## DO

Executes a program file.

    DO MAINPROG

## DO CASE . . . ENDCASE

A multiple-avenue branching command, such as

    DO CASE
        CASE  ANSWER="Y"
            . . .
        CASE  ANSWER="N"
            . . .
        OTHERWISE
            RETURN
    ENDCASE

## DO WHILE . . . ENDDO

A program loop command, such as

    DO  WHILE  .NOT.  EOF( )
        . . .
        . . .
    ENDDO

## EDIT

Displays a data record for editing, such as

```
USE EMPLOYEE
GOTO 5
EDIT

USE EMPLOYEE
EDIT RECORD 5
```

## EJECT

Advances the printer paper to the top of the next page.

## ERASE

Removes a file from the directory. The file to be erased must be closed.

```
ERASE SALE.DBF
ERASE SAMPLE.PRG
```

## EXIT

Exits from a program loop, such as one created with DO WHILE . . .
ENDDO.

```
DO  WHILE .T.
    . . .
    . . .
    IF EOF( )
        EXIT
    ENDIF
    . . .
ENDDO
```

## EXPORT TO

Converts a dBASE III Plus file to a PFS file.

```
EXPORT TO <name of the dBASE III Plus file> TYPE PFS
```

## FIND

Searches for the first data record in an indexed file with a specified search key, such as

```
USE EMPLOYEE
INDEX ON AREA_CODE TO AREAS
FIND "206"
DISPLAY
```

## GO BOTTOM

Positions the record pointer at the last record in the database file.

```
USE EMPLOYEE
GO BOTTOM
```

## GO TOP

Positions the record pointer at the first record in the database file.

```
USE EMPLOYEE
GO TOP
```

## GOTO

Positions the record pointer at a specified record.

```
USE EMPLOYEE
GOTO 4
```

## HELP

Calls up the help screens. Can be used with a key word to specify the subject, such as

```
HELP
HELP CREATE
HELP STR
```

## IF

A conditional branching command, such as

```
WAIT "Enter your choice ([Q] to quit) " TO CHOICE
IF CHOICE="Q"
    RETURN
ELSE
    . . .
    . . .
ENDIF
```

PLUS

## IMPORT FROM

Converts a PFS file to a dBASE III Plus file.

```
IMPORT FROM <name of the PFS file> TYPE PFS
```

## INDEX

Creates a key file in which all records are ordered according to the contents of the specified keyfield. The records can be arranged in alphabetical, chronological, or numerical order.

```
INDEX ON AREA_CODE TO AREACODE
INDEX ON AREA_CODE+PHONE_NO TO PHONES
```

## INPUT

Assigns a data element to a memory variable, using information entered from the keyboard.

```
INPUT PAYRATE
INPUT "Enter units sold :" TO UNITSSOLD
```

## INSERT

Adds a new record to the database file at the current record location.

```
USE EMPLOYEE
GOTO 4
INSERT
GOTO 6
INSERT BEFORE
GOTO 5
INSERT BLANK
```

## JOIN

Creates a new database file by merging specified data records from two open database files.

```
SELECT A
USE NEWSTOCKS
SELECT B
USE STOCKS
JOIN WITH NEWSTOCKS TO ALLSTOCK FOR STOCK_NO=A—>STOCK_NO
JOIN WITH NEWSTOCKS TO ALLSTOCK FOR STOCK_NO=A—>STOCK_NO;
FIELDS MODEL_NO, ON_HAND, ON_ORDER
```

## LABEL FORM

Displays data records with labels specified in a label file.

```
USE EMPLOYEE
LABEL FORM ROSTER
LABEL FORM ROSTER TO PRINT
LABEL FORM ROSTER TO AFILE.TXT
LABEL FORM ROSTER FOR AREA_CODE="206" .AND. MALE
```

## LIST

Shows the contents of selected data records in the active database file.

```
USE EMPLOYEE
LIST
LIST RECORD 5
LIST LAST_NAME,FIRST_NAME
LIST LAST_NAME,FIRST_NAME FOR AREA_CODE="206" .OR. MALE
```

## LIST MEMORY

Shows name, type, and size of each active memory variable.

## LIST STATUS

Lists current processing situation, including the names of active files, work area number, etc.

```
LIST STATUS
LIST STATUS TO PRINT
```

## LIST STRUCTURE

Displays the data structure of the active database file, such as

```
USE EMPLOYEE
LIST STRUCTURE
LIST STRUCTURE TO PRINT
```

## LOCATE

Sequentially searches data records of the active database file for a record that satisfies a specified condition, such as

```
USE EMPLOYEE
LOCATE FOR LAST_NAME="Smith"
LOCATE FOR UPPER(FIRST_NAME)="JAMES"
LOCATE FOR FIRST_NAME="J" .AND. LAST_NAME="S"
```

## LOOP

Transfers execution from the middle of a program loop to the beginning of the loop:

```
DO  WHILE .T.
    . . .
    . . .
    IF . . .
          LOOP
    ENDIF
    . . .
ENDDO
```

## MODIFY COMMAND

Invokes the text editor to create or edit a program file (.PRG), a format file (.FMT), or a text file (.TXT). The default file extension is .PRG.

```
MODIFY COMMAND MAINPROG
MODIFY COMMAND BILLING.PRG
MODIFY COMMAND EMPLOYEE.FMT
MODIFY COMMAND TEXTFILE.TXT
```

## MODIFY LABEL

Creates or edits a label file (.LBL) for the active database file.

    USE EMPLOYEE
    MODIFY LABEL MAILLIST

## MODIFY QUERY

PLUS

Creates or edits a query file (.QRY).

    USE EMPLOYEE
    MODIFY QUERY FINDEMPL.QRY

## MODIFY REPORT

Creates or edits a report file (.FRM) for the active database file.

    USE QTYSOLD
    MODIFY REPORT WEEKLY

## MODIFY SCREEN

PLUS

Creates or edits a screen file (.SCR).

    USE EMPLOYEE
    MODIFY SCREEN SHOWEMPL.SCR

## MODIFY STRUCTURE

Displays for modification the structure of the active database file.

    USE EMPLOYEE
    MODIFY STRUCTURE

## MODIFY VIEW

PLUS

Creates or edits a view file (.VUE).

    USE EMPLOYEE
    MODIFY VIEW SAMPLE.VUE

## NOTE

Marks the beginning of a remark line in a program.

```
SET TALK OFF*
SET ECHO OFF
NOTE Enter hours worked and payrate from the keyboard
INPUT "Enter hours worked . . . " TO HOURS
INPUT "hourly rate . . . " TO PAYRATE
. . .
. . .
```

*This is a simplified payroll program.*

## PACK

Removes data records marked for deletion by the DELETE command.

```
USE EMPLOYEE
DELETE RECORD 5
PACK
```

## PARAMETERS

Assigns local variable names to data items that are to be passed from a calling program module.

```
***** Program: MULTIPLY.PRG *****
* A program to multiply variable A by variable B
PARAMETERS A,B,C
C=A*B
RETURN
```

The preceding program is called from the main program:

```
* The main program
HOURS=38
PAYRATE=8.5
DO MULTIPLY WITH HOURS,PAYRATE,GROSSPAY
?"Gross Wage =",GROSSPAY
RETURN
```

## PRIVATE

Declares private variables in a program module, for example

```
PRIVATE VARIABLEA, VARIABLEB, VARIABLEC
```

## PROCEDURE

Identifies the beginning of each procedure in a procedure file.

## PUBLIC

Declares public variables to be shared by all program modules.

PUBLIC VARIABLEA, VARIABLEB, VARIABLEC

## QUIT

Closes all open files, terminates dBASE III processing, and exits to DOS.

## READ

Activates all the @ . . . SAY . . . GET commands issued since the last CLEAR GET was issued.

USE EMPLOYEE
@5,10 SAY "Last name : " GET LAST_NAME
@6,10 SAY "First name : " GET FIRST_NAME
READ

## RECALL

Recovers all data records marked for deletion.

RECALL
RECALL ALL
RECALL RECORD 5

## REINDEX

Rebuilds all active index (.NDX) files.

USE EMPLOYEE
SET INDEX TO AREACODE
REINDEX

## RELEASE

Deletes all or selected memory variables, such as

    RELEASE ALL
    RELEASE ALL LIKE NET*
    RELEASE ALL EXCEPT ???COST

## RENAME

Changes the name of a disk file, such as

    RENAME FILE XYZ.DBF TO ABC.DBF
    RENAME MAINPROG.PRG TO MAIN.PRG
    RENAME MAILIST.LBL TO MAILLIST.LBL

## REPLACE

Changes the contents of specified data fields in an active database file.

    USE EMPLOYEE
    REPLACE ALL ANNUAL_PAY WITH ANNUAL_PAY*1.05
    REPLACE FIRST_NAME WITH "James K." FOR FIRST_NAME="James C."
    REPLACE ALL AREA_CODE WITH "206" FOR AREA_CODE="216"

## REPORT FORM

Displays information from the active database file with the custom form specified in the report form (.FRM) file.

    USE QTYSOLD
    REPORT FORM WEEKLY                         *(Sends output to screen)*
    REPORT FORM WEEKLY TO PRINT                *(Sends output to printer)*
    REPORT FORM WEEKLY TO TEXTFILE.TXT         *(Sends output to text file)*

## RESTORE FROM

Retrieves memory variables from a memory (.MEM) file.

    RESTORE FROM MEMLIST.MEM
    RESTORE FROM MEMLIST ADDITIVE

## RESUME

Resumes execution of a program or procedure after it has been stopped by the SUSPEND command.

## RETURN

Terminates a program and either returns to the dot prompt or transfers execution to the calling program module.

## RUN

Executes an .EXE or .COM DOS disk file from within dBASE III Plus.

RUN B:XYZ                          *(Where XYZ.EXE or XYZ.COM is an executable disk file in a DOS directory)*

## SAVE TO

Stores all or selected memory variables to a memory (.MEM) file.

SAVE TO ALLVARS
SAVE TO VARLIST ALL EXCEPT NET*
SAVE TO VARLIST ALL LIKE COST????

## SEEK

Searches an indexed database file for the first data record containing the specified key expression.

USE EMPLOYEE
INDEX ON AREA_CODE TO AREACODE
SEEK "206"

## SELECT

Places a database file in a specified work area.

SELECT 1
USE EMPLOYEE
SELECT A
USE COSTS

## SET

Sets control parameters for processing. The default settings (indicated by uppercase letters) are appropriate for most purposes.

## SET ALTERNATE ON/off

Creates a text file, as designated by the SET ALTERNATE TO command, to record the processing activities.

## SET BELL ON/off

Turns on/off the warning bell.

## SET CATALOG ON/off

Adds files to open catalog.

## SET CATALOG TO

Creates, opens, and closes a catalog file.

## SET CENTURY off/ON

Shows the century in date displays.

## SET COLOR ON/OFF

Sets output display to color/monochrome monitor. The default is the mode from which dBASE III Plus is started.

## SET COLOR TO

Sets color screen attributes. Available colors and their letter codes are

| Color | Letter |
|---------|--------|
| black | N |
| blue | B |
| green | G |
| cyan | BG |
| blank | X |
| red | R |
| magenta | RB |
| brown | GR |
| white | W |

An asterisk indicates blinking characters, and a plus sign (+) indicates high intensity. Format of the command is

SET COLOR TO <standard>,<enhanced>,<border>,<background>

For example,

SET COLOR TO GR+/R,W/R,GR

sets standard video to yellow characters on a red background and enhanced video to white letters on a red background, with a yellow screen border.

## SET CONFIRM on/OFF

Controls the cursor movement from one variable to the next when the first variable is filled.

## SET CONSOLE ON/off

Turns the video display on/off.

## SET DATE

Specifies the format for date expressions.

| | |
|---|---|
| SET DATE AMERICAN | (mm/dd/yy) |
| SET DATE ANSI | (yy.mm.dd) |
| SET DATE BRITISH | (dd/mm/yy) |
| SET DATE ITALIAN | (dd-mm-yy) |
| SET DATE FRENCH | (dd/mm/yy) |
| SET DATE GERMAN | (dd.mm.yy) |

PLUS

## SET DEBUG off/ON

Traces the command errors during processing. When DEBUG is ON, messages from SET ECHO ON are routed to the printer.

## SET DECIMALS TO

Sets the number of decimal places for values, such as

SET DECIMALS TO 4

## SET DEFAULT TO

Designates the default disk drive, such as

    SET DEFAULT TO B:

## SET DELETED on/OFF

Determines whether data records marked for deletion are to be ignored.

## SET DELIMITERS on/OFF

Marks field widths with the delimiter defined by means of the SET DELIMITERS TO command.

## SET DELIMITERS TO

Specifies the characters for marking a field.

    SET DELIMITERS TO '[ ]'
    SET DELIMITERS ON

## SET DEVICE TO SCREEN/printer

Selects a display medium.

## SET ECHO on/OFF

Displays instructions during execution.

## SET ESCAPE ON/off

Controls the capability of aborting execution with the Esc key. When ESCAPE is ON, pressing Esc aborts execution of a program.

## SET EXACT on/OFF

Determines how two alphanumeric strings are compared.

## SET FIELDS on/OFF

Activates the selection of data fields named with the SET FIELDS TO command.

## SET FIELDS TO

PLUS

Selects a set of data fields to be used in one or more files.

    USE EMPLOYEE
    SET FIELDS TO LAST_NAME, FIRST_NAME
    SET FIELDS ON

## SET FILTER TO

Defines the filter conditions.

    USE EMPLOYEE
    SET FILTER TO AREA_CODE="216"

## SET FIXED on/OFF

Sets all numeric output to the fixed number of decimal places defined by SET DECIMALS TO.

## SET FORMAT

Selects custom format defined in a format (.FMT) file.

## SET FUNCTION

Redefines a function key for a specific command, such as

    SET FUNCTION 10 TO "QUIT"

## SET HEADING ON/off

Uses field names as column titles for display of data records with the DISPLAY, LIST, SUM, and AVERAGE commands.

## SET HELP ON/off

Determines whether Help screen is displayed.

## SET HISTORY ON/off

PLUS

Turns on the history feature.

## SET HISTORY TO

Specifies the number of executed commands to be saved in the HISTORY.

    SET HISTORY TO 10

## SET INDEX

Opens the specified index files.

## SET INTENSITY ON/off

Displays data fields in reverse video with EDIT and APPEND commands.

## SET MARGIN

Adjusts the left margin for all printed output, such as

    SET MARGIN TO 10

## SET MEMOWIDTH TO

Defines the width of memo field output (default width is 50).

    SET MEMOWIDTH TO 30

## SET MENUS ON/off

Displays a cursor-movement key menu.

## SET MESSAGE TO

Displays an alphanumeric string in the message window.

    SET MESSAGE TO "Hello!"

## SET ORDER TO

Sets up an open index file as the controlling index file. The format is

SET ORDER TO <n>

where <n> is the number of the file within the series of index files named with the INDEX command. The following commands cause AREACODE.NDX to be used:

USE EMPLOYEE INDEX LASTNAME.NDX, PAYRANK.NDX, AREACODE.NDX
SET ORDER TO 3

## SET PATH TO

Defines the search directory path.

SET PATH TO C:\DBDATE\SALES

## SET PRINT on/OFF

Directs output generated with @ . . . SAY commands to the printer and the screen.

## SET PROCEDURE

Opens a specified procedure file.

## SET RELATION TO

Links two open database files according to a common key expression.

## SET SAFETY ON/off

Displays a warning message when overwriting an existing file.

## SET STATUS ON/off

Displays or hides the status bar at the bottom of the screen.

## SET STEP on/OFF

Causes execution to pause after each command.

### SET TALK ON/off

Displays interactive messages during processing.

### SET TITLE ON/off

Displays the catalog file title prompt.

### SET TYPEAHEAD TO

Specifies the size of the type-ahead buffer (possible values are 0 to 32,000 characters; default is 20 characters).

    SET TYPEAHEAD TO 30

### SET UNIQUE on/OFF

Prepares an ordered list with the INDEX command.

### SET VIEW TO

Selects the view file.

    SET VIEW TO EMPLOYEE.VUE

### *SKIP*

Moves the record pointer forward or backward through the records in the database file, such as

    USE EMPLOYEE
    GOTO 3
    DISPLAY
    SKIP 3
    DISPLAY
    SKIP –1
    DISPLAY

## SORT

Rearranges data records on one or more keyfields in ascending or descending order. The default setting is ascending order.

    USE EMPLOYEE
    SORT ON AREA_CODE TO AREACODE
    SORT ON ANNUAL_PAY/D TO RANKED
    SORT ON AREA_CODE, LAST_NAME TO PHONLIST FOR AREA_CODE="206"

## STORE

Assigns a data element to a memory variable.

    STORE 1 TO COUNTER
    STORE "James" TO FIRSTNAME

## SUM

Totals the value of a numeric expression and stores the total in a memory variable, such as

    USE EMPLOYEE
    SUM ANNUAL_PAY TO TOTALPAY
    SUM ANNUAL_PAY*0.1 TO DEDUCTIONS

## SUSPEND

Suspends the execution of a program or procedure.

PLUS

## TEXT

Displays a block of text on the screen or printer; used in a program.

    *****  Program: BULLETIN.PRG  *****
    SET PRINT ON
    TEXT
    This is a sample message to be displayed on the printer when this
    program is executed.
    ENDTEXT

## TOTAL

Sums the numeric values of the active database file on a keyfield and stores the results to another file.

```
USE STOCKS
TOTAL ON MODEL_NO TO BYMODEL
TOTAL ON STOCK_NO TO BYSTOCNO FOR ON_HAND>="2"
```

## TYPE

Displays the contents of a disk file to the screen or printer.

```
TYPE MAINPROG.PRG
TYPE EMPLOYEE.FMT TO PRINT
```

## UPDATE

Uses records in one database file to update records in another file, such as

```
SELECT A

USE RECEIVED

SELECT B

USE STOCKS

UPDATE ON STOCK_NO FROM RECEIVED REPLACE ON_HAND WITH;
ON_HAND+A—>ON_HAND
```

## USE

Opens an existing database file.

```
USE EMPLOYEE
```

## WAIT

Causes execution to pause until a key is pressed, as in

WAIT
WAIT TO CHOICE
WAIT "Enter your answer (Y/N)? " TO ANSWER

## ZAP

Removes all data records from the database file without deleting the data structure, such as

USE EMPLOYEE
ZAP

# C
# Built-in Functions

## I. Built-in Functions Listed by Purpose

To manipulate time and date data:

CDOW( )
CMONTH( )
DATE( )
DAY( )
DOW( )
MONTH( )
TIME( )
YEAR( )

To convert contents of data fields or memory variables:

CTOD( )
DTOC( )
STR( )
VAL( )

To convert alphanumeric strings:

ASC( )
CHR( )
LOWER( )
UPPER( )

To manipulate alphanumeric strings:

  AT( )
  LEFT( )
  LEN( )
  LTRIM( )
  REPLICATE( )
  RIGHT( )
  RTRIM( )
  SPACE( )
  STUFF( )
  SUBSTR( )
  TRANSFORM( )
  TRIM( )

To perform mathematical operations:

  ABS( )
  EXP( )
  INT( )
  LOG( )
  MAX( )
  MIN( )
  MOD( )
  ROUND( )
  SQRT( )

To track the record pointer:

  RECNO( )
  RECCOUNT( )
  RECSIZE( )

To identify location of the cursor and the print head:

  COL( )
  PCOL( )
  ROW( )
  PROW( )

To check file attributes, error conditions, and data-element types:

  BOF( )
  DELETED( )
  DISKSPACE( )
  EOF( )

```
ERROR( )
FILE( )
FOUND( )
IFF( )
ISALPHA( )
ISCOLOR( )
ISLOWER( )
ISUPPER( )
LUPDATE( )
MESSAGE( )
TYPE( )
```

To use the macro function:

&

To check keyboard input:

```
INKEY( )
READKEY( )
```

To identify attributes of database and DOS files:

```
DBF( )
FIELD( )
FKLABEL( )
FKMAX( )
GETENV( )
NDX( )
OS( )
VERSION( )
```

# II. A Summary of Built-in Functions

## &

Causes the contents of an alphanumeric memory variable to be substituted for the variable name.

```
STORE "ACCOUNTS.DBF" TO FILENAME
STORE "ACCT_NO" TO FIELDNAME
USE &FILENAME
LOCATE FOR &FIELDNAME="10005"
```

**PLUS**

### ABS()

Returns the absolute value of a numeric argument.

```
A=10
B=20
?ABS(A−B)
        10
```

### ASC()

Returns the ASCII code for the leftmost character of the alphanumeric argument.

```
?ASC("Smith")
83
```

### AT()

Returns the starting position of the first alphanumeric argument within the second alphanumeric argument.

```
?AT("ABC","XYZABC")
3
```

### BOF()

Returns the logical value .T. if the record pointer is at the beginning of the file.

### CDOW()

Returns the name of the day of the week from the date memory variable supplied as an argument. If today is Saturday, 6/01/85, the function returns results as follows:

```
?CDOW(DATE( ))
Saturday
```

### CHR()

Returns the ASCII character corresponding to the numeric value supplied as an argument.

```
?CHR(85)
S
```

## CMONTH()

Returns the name of the month from the date memory variable supplied as an argument. For example, if today is 6/01/85, the function returns results as follows:

?CMONTH(DATE( ))
June

## COL()

Returns the current column location of the cursor.

?COL( )
5

## CTOD()

Converts an alphanumeric string to a date.

STORE CTOD("12/25/85") TO CHRISTMAS

## DATE()

Returns the system date. Assuming that the system date is 6/01/85, the function returns results as follows:

?DATE( )
06/01/85

## DAY()

Returns the numeric value of the day of the month from a date memory variable supplied as an argument. For example, assume that the memory variable CHRISTMAS contains the date 12/25/85:

?DAY(CHRISTMAS)
25

## DBF()

Returns the name of the current database file.

USE EMPLOYEE
?DBF( )
B:EMPLOYEE.dbf

PLUS

## DELETED()

Returns the logical value .T. if the current data record has been marked for deletion. Assuming that the current data record has been marked for deletion, the function returns the following result:

```
?DELETED( )
.T.
```

## DISKSPACE()

Returns an integer representing the number of bytes available on the default disk drive.

```
? DISKSPACE( )
309248
```

## DOW()

Returns the numeric code for the day of week from the date memory variable supplied as an argument. If the date is Saturday, June 6, the function returns

```
?DOW(DATE( ))
6
```

## DTOC()

Converts a date to an alphanumeric string. If today's date is 6/25/85, the function returns results as follows:

```
?"Today's date is "+DTOC(DATE( ))
Today's date is 6/25/85
```

## EOF()

Returns the logical value .T. if the record pointer is at the end of the file.

## ERROR()

Used with the ON ERROR command for trapping errors in programming. When an error occurs in the program, this function returns the error number. The number can be used with a conditional command (such as IF or CASE) so that corrective action can be taken if recovery from the error is possible.

## EXP()

Returns the exponential value of the numeric argument.

　?EXP(1.00000000)
　2.71828183

## FIELD()

Returns name of the field whose position in the database file structure corresponds to the numeric argument. Assuming that LAST_NAME is the second field defined in EMPLOYEE.DBF, the function returns results as follows:

　USE EMPLOYEE
　?FIELD(2)
　LAST_NAME

## FILE()

Returns the logical value .T. if a file in the current directory has the name specified in the alphanumeric argument.

　?FILE("EMPLOYEE.dbf")
　.T.

## FKLABEL()

Returns the name of the function key whose number correponds to the numeric argument.

　?FKLABEL(3)
　F4

## FKMAX()

Returns an integer representing the maximum number of programmable function keys available.

　?FKMAX( )
　9

PLUS

## FOUND()

Returns the logical value .T. if the previous FIND, SEEK, or CONTINUE command was successful. Otherwise, a logical .F. is returned.

```
USE EMPLOYEE
LOCATE FOR LAST_NAME="Smith"
Record = 1
?FOUND( )
.T.
```

PLUS

## GETENV()

Returns a character string describing the contents of a specific DOS environmental variable.

PLUS

## IIF()

Evaluates the condition specified in the first argument, and returns the second argument if the condition is true. Otherwise, the third argument is returned.

```
TITLE = IIF(MALE=.T., "Mr. ", "Ms. ") + LAST_NAME
```

## INKEY()

Returns the numeric code of the key most recently pressed. Consult the dBASE III PLUS manual for these key codes.

## INT()

Converts a numeric value to an integer.

```
?INT(3.568)
3
```

PLUS

## ISALPHA()

Returns a logical .T. if the specified character expression begins with an alpha character. Otherwise, returns a logical .F.

```
?ISALPHA("ABC–123")
.T.
?ISALPHA("123–abc")
.F.
```

## ISCOLOR()

Returns the logical value .T. if the program is running in color mode. Otherwise, returns a logical .F.

    ?ISCOLOR( )
    .T.

## ISLOWER()

Returns a logical .T. if the leftmost character of the alphanumeric argument is a lowercase letter. Otherwise, returns a logical .F.

    ?ISLOWER("aBC–234")
    .T.
    ?ISLOWER("Abc–234")
    .F.

## ISUPPER()

Returns a logical .T. if the leftmost character of the alphanumeric argument is an uppercase. Otherwise, returns a logical .F.

    ?ISUPPER("aBC–234")
    .F.
    ?ISLUPPR("Abc–234")
    .T.

## LEFT()

Returns the specified number of characters from the left of the alphanumeric argument.

    ?LEFT("John J. Smith", 6)
    John J.
    ?"Dear "+LEFT("John J. Smith",4)+":"
    Dear John:

## LEN()

Returns the number of characters in the alphanumeric argument.

    ?LEN("James Smith")
    11

## LOG()

Returns the natural logarithm of the numeric argument.

```
?LOG(2.71828183)
1.00000000
```

## LOWER()

Converts to lowercase characters any uppercase characters in the alphanumeric argument.

```
?LOWER("James Smith")
james smith
```

 ## LTRIM()

Trims leading blanks from the alphanumeric argument. This function is useful for trimming a character string created with the STR function.

```
. ?STR(3.145,10,2)
      3.15
. ?LTRIM(STR(3.145,10,2))
3.15
```

 ## LUPDATE()

Returns the date of the last update of the current database file.

```
?LUPDATE( )
06/27/86
```

## MAX()

Returns the larger value of the two numeric arguments.

```
A=3.45
B=6.78
?MAX(A,B)
6.78
```

## MESSAGE()

Returns error-message character strings. See the dBASE III Plus manual for error messages.

## MIN()

Returns the smaller value of the two numeric arguments.

```
A=3.45
B=6.78
?MIN(A,B)
3.45
```

## MOD()

Returns the remainder that results from dividing the first numeric argument by the second numeric argument.

```
A=10
B=3
?MOD(A,B)
        1
```

## MONTH()

Returns the numeric code for the month from the date memory variable supplied as an argument. Assuming that the memory variable CHRISTMAS contains 12/25/85, the function returns results as follows:

```
?MONTH(CHRISTMAS)
12
```

## NDX()

Returns the name of the current active index file in the selected work area.

```
USE EMPLOYEE
INDEX ON LAST_NAME TO LASTNAME.NDX
. . . .
?NDX(1)
B:LASTNAME.NDX
```

## OS()

Returns the name of the version of DOS under which the program is running.

```
?OS( )
DOS 2.00
```

## PCOL()

Determines the current column position of the print head.

```
?PCOL( )
10
```

## PROW()

Determines the current row position of the print head.

```
?PROW( )
5
```

## READKEY()

Returns the numeric key code for the key pressed in order to exit from a full-screen command.

```
?READKEY( )
271
```

PLUS
## RECCOUNT()

Returns the number of records in the current database file.

```
USE EMPLOYEE
?RECCOUNT( )
        10
```

## RECNO()

Returns the number of the active data record.

```
?RECNO( )
5
```

PLUS
## RECSIZE()

Returns the number of records in the active database file.

```
USE EMPLOYEE
?RECSIZE( )
        51
```

## REPLICATE( )

Repeats the first argument the number of times specified in the second argument.

    ?REPLICATE("Hello! ",3)
    Hello! Hello! Hello!

## RIGHT( )

PLUS

Returns the number of characters specified in the second argument from the right of the first argument.

    ?RIGHT("John J. Smith", 5)
    Smith
    ?"Dear Mr. "+RIGHT("John J. Smith",5)+":"
    Dear Mr. Smith:

## ROUND( )

Rounds the first numeric argument to the given number of decimal places specified in the second numeric argument.

    ?ROUND(3.71689,2)
    3.72

## ROW( )

Returns the current row location of the cursor.

    ?ROW( )
    5

## RTRIM( )

PLUS

Trims the trailing blanks from a character expression. The effect of this function is identical to that of the TRIM function.

    ?RTRIM(FIRST_NAME)+" "+RTRIM(LAST_NAME)

## SPACE( )

Creates an alphanumeric string of blanks.

    ?SPACE(10)+LAST_NAME+SPACE(5)+AREA_CODE+PHONE_NO

## SQRT()

Returns the square root of the numeric argument.

```
?SQRT(9)
3
```

## STR()

Converts the numeric argument to an alphanumeric string.

```
ANNUALPAY=25950.50
?"Annual salary = "+STR(ANNUALPAY,8,2)
```

PLUS ## STUFF()

Replaces a portion of the first alphanumeric argument with the second alphanumeric argument, beginning at the character position specified in the second argument and continuing for the number of characters specified in the third argument.

```
STUFF(<1st string>,<beginning position>, <number of
characters>,<2nd string>)
```

```
?STUFF("Mary Jane Smith",6,4,"Kay")
Mary Kay Smith
```

## SUBSTR()

Returns characters from the first alphanumeric argument. The second argument specifies the starting position, and the third argument specifies the number of characters to be returned.

```
?SUBSTR("ABCDEFG",4,3)
DEF
```

## TIME()

Returns the system time. Assuming that the system time is 22:15:35, the results are as follows:

```
?TIME( )
22:15:35
```

## TRANSFORM()

Used with ?, ??, DISPLAY, LABEL, LIST, and REPORT to display a character expression with the specified picture format.

```
. USE EMPLOYEE
. GOTO 5
. DISPLAY TRANSFORM(LAST_NAME, "@R X X X X X X X X X X X X"
Record# TRANSFORM(LAST_NAME, "@R X X X X X X X X X X X X"
     5   B a k e r
```

## TRIM()

Removes trailing blanks from an alphanumeric string.

```
?TRIM(FIRST_NAME)+" "+TRIM(LAST_NAME)
James Smith
```

## TYPE()

Returns a single character representing the type of the specified expression:

```
?TYPE(BIRTH_DATE)
D
?TYPE(ASTRING)
C
```

## UPPER()

Converts to uppercase letters any lowercase letters in the alphanumeric argument.

```
?UPPER("James Smith")
JAMES SMITH
IF UPPER(ANSWER)="Y"

. . .
ENDIF
```

## VAL()

Converts an alphanumeric string to an integer value.

```
?VAL("34.567")
34
?VAL("34.567")*1000
34567
```

PLUS

## VERSION()

Returns the version number of the dBASE III PLUS program.

    ?VERSION( )
    dBASE III PLUS version 1.0

## YEAR()

Returns the numeric code of the year from a date memory variable supplied as an argument. Assuming that the system date is 06/01/85, the function returns results as follows:

    ?YEAR(DATE( ))
    1985

# D
# Examples of FRAMER and GETTER routines

## A Typical FRAMER routine

```
*** BMFRAMES.PRG
@  4,  0 SAY "Name:"
@  5,  0 SAY "Address1:"
@  6,  0 SAY "Address2:"
@  7,  0 SAY "City:"
@  7,40 SAY "State:"
@  7,54 SAY "Zip:"
@  8,  0 SAY "Country:"
@  8,40 SAY "Phone:"
@ 10,  0 SAY "Contact:"
@ 10,50 SAY "Dear:"
@ 11,  0 SAY "Position:"
@ 12,  0 SAY "Audience:"
@ 12,40 SAY "Mss Length:"
@ 14,  0 SAY "Qry:"
@ 14,10 SAY "Mss:"
@ 14,20 SAY "SmS:"
@ 14,30 SAY "DMP:"
@ 14,40 SAY "Gdl:"
@ 14,52 SAY "Source:"
@ 16,  0 SAY "Comment:"
RETURN
```

## A Typical GETTER Routine

```
*** BMGETS.PRG
IF DELETE()
@ 1,30 SAY "DELETED"
ELSE
@ 1,30 SAY "         "
ENDIF
*
@  4, 7 GET name
@  5,10 GET address1
@  6,10 GET address2
@  7, 6 GET city
@  7,47 GET state
@  7,59 GET zipcode
@  8, 9 GET country
@  8,47 GET phone
@ 10, 9 GET contact
@ 10,55 GET dear
@ 11,10 GET position
@ 12,10 GET audience
@ 12,52 GET msslength
@ 14, 5 GET qry
@ 14,15 GET mss
@ 14,25 GET sms
@ 14,35 GET dmp
@ 14,45 GET gdl
@ 14,60 GET source
@ 16, 9 GET comment
RETURN
```

# E

# MAGAZINE.DBF and SENDWHER.DBF for Chapter 13 and Appendix D

```
Structure for database : A:MAGAZINE.DBF
Number of data records :        0
Date of last update    : 00/00/00
Field  Field name  Type         Width    Dec
1   NAME        Character       50
2   ADDRESS1    Character       50
3   ADDRESS2    Character       50
4   CITY        Character       30
5   STATE       Character        2
6   COUNTRY     Character       20
7   ZIPCODE     Character       10
8   CONTACT     Character       30
9   DEAR        Character       20
10  AUDIENCE    Character       30
11  PHONE       Character       15
12  GDL         Character        1
13  POSITION    Character       20
14  QRY         Character        1
15  MSS         Character        1
16  SMS         Character        1
17  DMP         Character        1
```

```
18  MSSLENGTH   Character    20
19  SOURCE      Character    20
20  COMMENT     Character    151
** Total **                  524

Structure for database : A:SENDWHER.DBF
Number of data records :       0
Date of last update    : 00/00/00
Field  Field name  Type       Width    Dec
1   MSS_NAME    Character     30
2   AUDIENCE    Character     30
3   MORE        Logical        1
4   T1          Character     30
5   T2          Character     30
6   T3          Character     30
7   T4          Character     30
8   T5          Character     30
9   T6          Character     30
10  T7          Character     30
11  T8          Character     30
12  T9          Character     30
13  T10         Character     30
14  T11         Character     30
15  T12         Character     30
16  T13         Character     30
Press any key to continue...
17  T14         Character     30
18  T15         Character     30
19  T16         Character     30
20  T17         Character     30
21  T18         Character     30
22  T19         Character     30
23  T20         Character     30
24  M           Numeric       10
25  C1          Character     75
26  C2          Character     75
27  C3          Character     75
28  C4          Character     75
** Total **                  972
```

# F
# Function Keys and
# Their ASCII Values

Wouldn't it be nice to be able to use the Fn, ALT-Fn, SHIFT-Fn, and CTL-Fn keys in your code? You can, thanks to III Plus's WAIT TO variable command and the INKEY( ) function. The following are the values as they are passed to III Plus from the keyboard buffer.

| Function Key | INKEY() | WAIT TO | ALT (BOTH) | SHIFT (BOTH) | CTL (BOTH) |
|---|---|---|---|---|---|
| F1 | 28 | 0 | 104 | 84 | 94 |
| F2 | −1 | 255 | 105 | 85 | 95 |
| F3 | −2 | 254 | 106 | 86 | 96 |
| F4 | −3 | 253 | 107 | 87 | 97 |
| F5 | −4 | 252 | 108 | 88 | 98 |
| F6 | −5 | 251 | 109 | 89 | 99 |
| F7 | −6 | 250 | 110 | 90 | 100 |
| F8 | −7 | 249 | 111 | 91 | 101 |
| F9 | −8 | 248 | 112 | 92 | 102 |
| F0 | −9 | 247 | 113 | 93 | 103 |

# Glossary

Words set in **boldface** are defined elsewhere in the Glossary

---

**Application.** A logical idea for which a program is designed. Each block in a **flowchart** is an **application**.

**Background programming.** Code, unseen by the user, that performs about 90 percent of the **database** manipulations. The user may see only the data-input and interrogation screens (the **foreground programming**), which are a small part of the overall **working code**.

**Database.** A set of information with a common link among individual members of the set.

**Environment.** The physical setting in which a **database** system is to be used.

**Flowchart.** A graphic representation of a program's logic.

**Foreground programming.** The part of the **working code** with which the user interacts; includes input and interrogation screens, **menu systems**, etc.

**Indexkey.** The value to be searched for in an INDEXed **database**.

**Job.** The object of a program, or the function performed by a **task** or group of **tasks**.

**Keyfield.** The **database** field that is INDEXed ON.

**Masterbase.** A large **database** that contains detailed information on each member of a group of **databases**. A **database** fits a unique need, but a masterbase is a storage tank for several **databases**.

**Menu system.** A set of linked foreground **tasks** that provides the user with some control over the **database** system.

**Module.** The code that is generated to perform a **task.**

**Primary key.** The **keyfield** the computer uses to keep track of a record. dBASE III uses RECNO( ) as a primary key.

**Qualifier.** A restrictor in a command line that directs the command to perform its operation on a subset of the whole **database**. When you use these words with a condition, they qualify the information to be processed. For example,

```
REPLACE ALL LASTNAME WITH "Kramden" FOR FIRSTNAME="Ralph"
```

**Random access.** A method of organizing a **database** in which the user controls the order and organization of records.

**Secondary key.** The **keyfield** humans use to keep track of records. Usually our **keyfields** are randomly oriented: We keep track of things by name (or address, value, etc.), not by the position in a **database**.

**Sequential access.** The computer's method of organizing and ordering a **database**. The computer and dBASE III Plus use a FIFO (first in, first out) ordering system.

**Subroutine.** A program specifically designed or modified for one **application** or **environment**.

**Task.** A general program that can be easily adapted as a **subroutine** or a **job.**

**Working code.** The final, debugged version of a program.

# Index

# More Computer Knowledge from Que

# BOOKS TO HELP YOU MASTER SOFTWARE AND OPERATING SYSTEMS

## Using 1-2-3, 2nd Edition
### by Geoffrey LeBlond and Douglas Cobb

Nationally acclaimed, *Using 1-2-3* is "the book" for every 1-2-3 user. Whether you are using Release 1A or 2, you will find *Using 1-2-3*, 2nd Edition, your most valuable source of information. Spreadsheet, database, graphics, and macro capabilities common to both Releases 1A and 2 or new to Release 2 are all covered in depth. Notations in the text and a tear-out command chart help you locate quickly the differences between Releases 1A and 2. Like thousands of other 1-2-3 users, you will consider this book indispensable.

> This title must surely be one of the greats when it comes to good books on 1-2-3.
> —*Computer Shopper*

## Using PC DOS
### by Chris DeVoney

In the lucid, easy-to-understand style that made him a best-selling author, Chris DeVoney describes both the common and not-so-common operations of PC DOS. DeVoney guides users—both novice and intermediate—through basic and advanced DOS commands. A Command Reference defines every DOS command, gives examples, and tells how to handle common problems. *Using PC DOS* is two books in one—a concise tutorial and a valuable reference you will refer to over and over again.

> This is the best DOS book I know of. It covers everything and has lots of examples.
> —*Jerry Pournelle, BYTE Magazine*

## dBASE III Plus Handbook, 2nd Edition
### by George T. Chou, Ph.D.

A complete, easy-to-understand guide to dBASE III Plus commands and features. The *Handbook* provides full discussion of basic and advanced operations for displaying and editing data. Numerous examples of databases show the options for handling, sorting, summarizing, and indexing data. The book explains error messages in detail and offers tips on how to avoid errors when you create files and enter data. For both newcomers to dBASE III and former dBASE III users, the *dBASE III Plus Handbook*, 2nd Edition, will help you manage your office or business more efficiently.

## dBASE III Plus Applications Library
### by Thomas W. Carlton

Tap the built-in potential of dBASE III Plus for building complex, highly efficient applications. The *dBASE III Plus Applications Library* contains five complete business applications—Personnel System, Sales Tracking System, Fixed Asset Manager, Accounts Receivable Manager, and General Ledger and Financial Reporting System. Containing complete code listings and step-by-step directions, these applications can be used "as is" or adapted to individual needs. Practical and timesaving, this book provides a wealth of dBASE III Plus code, suggestions on how to extend each application, and sound advice on applications development. A companion disk is available.

**Mail to: Que Corporation • P. O. Box 50507 • Indianapolis, IN 46250**

| Item | Title | Price | Quantity | Extension |
|------|-------|-------|----------|-----------|
| 130 | Using 1-2-3, 2nd Edition | $21.95 | | |
| 180 | Using PC DOS | $21.95 | | |
| 68 | dBASE III Plus Handbook, 2nd Edition | $19.95 | | |
| 192 | dBASE III Plus Applications Library | $19.95 | | |

| | |
|---|---|
| **Book Subtotal** | |
| Shipping & Handling ($2.50 per item) | |
| Indiana Residents Add 5% Sales Tax | |
| **GRAND TOTAL** | |

**Method of Payment:**

☐ Check    ☐ VISA    ☐ MasterCard    ☐ American Express

Card Number _____ Exp. Date _____

Cardholder's Name _____

Ship to _____

Address _____

City _____ State _____ ZIP _____

If you can't wait, call **1-800-428-5331** and order TODAY.

All prices subject to change without notice.

DB3PAL-871

# REGISTER YOUR COPY OF
# *dBASE III PLUS ADVANCED PROGRAMMING,*
## 2nd Edition

Register your copy of *dBASE III Plus Advanced Programming*, 2nd Edition, and receive information about Que's newest products. Complete this registration card and return it to Que Corporation, P.O. Box 50507, Indianapolis, IN 46250.

Name _____

Address _____

City _____ State _____ ZIP _____

Phone _____

Where did you buy your copy of *dBASE III Plus Advanced Programming,* 2nd Edition?

_____

How do you plan to use the programs in this book?

_____

_____

_____

What other kinds of publications about *dBASE* would you be interested in?

_____

_____

_____

_____

Which computer do you use? _____

THANK YOU!